Last of the Whalers

Last of the Whalers
Charlie Heberley's Story

by

Heather Heberley

CAPE CATLEY LTD

First published August 2002

CAPE CATLEY LTD
Ngataringa Road, P O Box 32 622, Devonport, Auckland
New Zealand
Email: cape.catley@xtra.co.nz
Visit our website: www.capecatleybooks.co.nz

Typeset by P K Publications, Picton
Designed by Bill Wieben and Christine Cathie Design
Cover photo: Charlie Heberley at his harpoon gun
Printed in Malaysia

ISBN 0-908561-90-3

When you've had the experiences with whales that we had recently, you know – they're seemingly intelligent, they stick together as families, as groups, they communicate, they travel long distances, yet there are some people who are not just killing them for ethnic reasons, but they're mass slaughtering them... in the face of world pressure, they don't care. I'm not so sure that I want my kids to only be able to see a large whale in a book. I think that's not acceptable any more. I think everyone really needs to understand that we are a part of the environment, not apart from it.

July 2001
Sir Peter Blake, 1948-2001

Author's Note and Acknowledgements

"LOOK AFTER the photos. You're doing a good job."

This is what my father-in-law, Charlie Heberley said to me shortly before he died in 2000. I felt it was his blessing for me to write his biography.

The year before he died I had spent many hours with him, taping his earliest memories. He enjoyed re-living those times. Over the years I had frequently run the tape recorder when he had been reminiscing, and I also had many of his stories on video, captured when I'd used the video camera at family parties. So often I'd caught him on tape as he held those around him enthralled, first with one story, and then laughing with the next. He was a kaumatua and a born story-teller.

One of the precious whaling photos Charlie was referring to is used on the cover of this book.

Because of his colourful past, many people made recordings of Charlie. In particular I am grateful for being able to obtain the raw tapes of a Spectrum documentary, *The Last of the Whale-Hunters*, produced by National Radio in 1996.

Charlie spoke to many groups in the last few years of his life. His last talk was to the Nelson Historical Society, on 14 February 2000. The president, Athol Blair, gave me a copy of the tapes they had recorded for their archives. They were invaluable.

This is a book I could never have written without the help of so many people.

Rita Powick from Picton helped me with Maori translations and tried hard to make my Pakeha mind think Maori so I could speak the language correctly.

The Maori proverbs at the beginning of each chapter are from *Maori Proverbs*, Reed Books 1992.

Dr Graham Smart and nurse Jan Webb helped me with medical information.

Ian Garrod from Happy Snappa in Picton gave me advice when I was selecting photos, especially those from Charlie's collection.

Charlie kept many newspaper and magazine articles from the years he whaled, particularly while he was at Great Barrier. He also kept notes and tallies of whales caught, material which I have used extensively. Many I have been able to check against the figures recorded in *The Perano Whalers* by Don Grady, published by Reed in 1982. It is always satisfying when double-checked figures agree. Between 1959 and 1962 the two daily papers, the *Auckland Star* and *New Zealand Herald,* gave wide coverage to the whaling from Whangaparapara. Also two pictorials, *The Weekly News* and *Free Lance,* regularly ran articles, while in Marlborough the *Marlborough Express* was a source I used in the years of the whales' decline.

Most especially I would like to thank three of Charlie's special friends whose input gave me another side of Charlie. Reg Jackson, who'd been Charlie's friend since they were young boys, had mustered and hunted with him around the hills in Tory Channel, and both had whaled in Cook Strait. Tom Norton had also whaled with Charlie in Cook Strait, and went up to Great Barrier with him. Bill Gibbs lived on Great Barrier and was the full-time spotter on Cape Barrier lookout. After Charlie died, Bill, Tom and Reg visited our home in the Marlborough Sounds and they caught many whales around our kitchen table as they and Joe pored over whaling photos and remembered.

Photos are precious memories. I was overwhelmed by the generosity of those ex-whalers who willingly lent me their photos. Two I'd like to thank especially were Dave Medland who still lives on Great Barrier, and Basil Jones from Picton.

Even with the wonderful material I had, this book wouldn't have been written without the support and encouragement my publisher Chris Cole Catley gave me. I began writing this book eight months after Charlie died. Writing the words while I still heard his voice clearly in my mind made the book more authentic. At times when I felt I couldn't continue, Chris became the wind beneath my sails and persuaded me to carry on.

My final thanks go to Charlie's son Joe, my husband. Without him I could not have written this book. He worked with his father all his life. As Charlie said, "We were a good team". Joe has brought the whaling stories to life. They are not stories woven in bright colours, written gently for readers to enjoy. They are stark, often cruel stories of a savage occupation not followed now by any New Zealander, but they are true and a significant part of our history.

Heather Heberley
April 2002

Contents

Haere mai ra e te taonga, e te tauheke

Ki roto i te aroha o to whanau whanui

E tangi hotuhotu ana

E noho mokemoke ana

I to wehenga atu I a matou

Welcome, treasure of all treasures, respected elder

Into the love of your extended family

Who mourn unceasingly

Who remain bereft

Because you have left us.

Karanga given by Rita Powick at Charles Thomas Heberley's funeral as he was carried into Picton's Holy Trinity Church, 4 July 2000.

Chapter One

IN THE BEGINNING

Mahia nga mahi kei tamariki ana.
Make the most of your time while you are young.

"KAUA e patu i a ia!"

The Maori warrior stood in the bow of Te Rauparaha's canoe, his patiti – axe – poised ready to crash down on the white man's head. In that split second Te Rauparaha recognised the white man. He leapt across the stretch of water between the two canoes, threw a mat over the man, and screamed out not to kill him.

Before jumping back into his own canoe to return to Kapiti Island, the chief demanded all the tobacco which the white man had, and issued a warning.

"Hoki ki to kainga." "Go home."

James Heberley, better known as Worser, took that advice. He paddled the short distance back to Waikanae to pick up Maata Te Naihi, also named Te Wai, the woman who was to become his wife. Earlier he'd brought her and their daughter Margaret, six months old, to safety within her own tribe until the fighting settled down between the Maori tribes in the North and South Islands.

Then Worser paddled his canoe back across Cook Strait, to Te Awaiti, their home in Tory Channel in the Marlborough Sounds. The year was 1833.

Those words of the great fighting chief Te Rauparaha, which he screamed out across the water, and a man's pouch of tobacco, made it possible for this story to evolve. Otherwise there would have been no Heberley family, and a small part of New Zealand's history would never have come about.

My father-in-law Charles Heberley, great-grandson of Worser, knew his whakapapa – family history – by heart, and I always enjoyed listening to it. It was easy to close my eyes and believe I was sitting near a fire, shadowed faces all around me. The imagined flames warmed my face. Whenever I listened to his whakapapa, those family members, whom I knew only through listening to his words time and time again, grew closer.

This is what he told us:

My name is Charles Thomas Heberley although I am always called Charlie. I am a kaumatua of the Ngati Awa people living in the top of the South Island of New Zealand. This is a brief history of our whanau – family – our hapu which was Ngati Tauho, and our tribe, Ngati Awa, as told to me by my tupuna – ancestors.

My whakapapa, supplied by our mother tribe, the Ngati Awa of the Bay of Plenty, confirms that our people first came to Aotearoa New Zealand with Kupe in 950AD, the second migration with Toi in 1100AD, and with the third main migration in 1350AD. They landed in the Bay of Plenty, and over several generations took possession of large areas in the North Island. Taranaki and Wellington were their main tribal areas.

In the early 1800s they joined forces with Ngati Toa under Te Rauparaha and succeeded in driving out small nomadic-type holdings of other tribes in Tory Channel and Queen Charlotte Sound, including Arapawa and other islands in the Sounds. Ngati Toa returned to the north, leaving Ngati Awa in sole possession of the areas taken.

My great-grandfather, Captain James (Worser) Heberley, first came to New Zealand in 1826 in the whaler *Caroline*. After whaling around New Zealand and as far north as Japan for four years, he joined Captain John Guard in 1830, setting up the first shore-based whaling station in New Zealand at Te Awaiti. It was here that Worser met, and later married, Te Wai. Worser gave Te Wai's relatives a blanket for his wife. They were married on 13 December 1841 when the Reverend Samuel Ironside came to Te Awaiti. Their three children were baptised on the same day.

I watched Charlie's face as he related his story once again and I saw the fierce pride of a Maori warrior etched deeply into his age-lined face. It was weatherbeaten from his years spent whaling and then commercial fishing, and also farming Oyster Bay on the southern side of Tory Channel and later Okukari Bay on the northern side of Tory Channel in the Marlborough Sounds.

Te Wai was of high rank in the Ngati Awa tribe. She was a niece of Ropoama Te One, the paramount chief of the Ngati Awa people in Picton. He signed the Treaty of Waitangi in Port Underwood, and was involved in the negotiations in the land sales of the Marlborough Sounds and the relocation of the Waitohi people in Picton to Waikawa.

Over the past 170 years the Heberley family have owned and farmed Oyster Bay and Okukari Bay in Tory Channel at the edge of Cook Strait.

My wife Ruby was a direct descendant of Captain 'Jacky' Guard, father of John Guard, the first white child born in the South Island. Ruby and I raised a family at Okukari. Today our son Joe, with his wife Heather and their two sons and families, farm and run a fishing company at Okukari, the place where my tupuna first set foot in the South Island.

According to Maori lore our whanau has kept 'ahi kaa roa' – kept the fires burning for Ngati Awa – a proud and strong tribe who have fought for hundreds of years to preserve the name and mana of their tribe.

Charlie's birth certificate says that he was born at Oyster Bay, Tory Channel, Picton, on 11 December 1918 to Arthur, Worser's grandson, and Ada Heberley. He was the youngest of four boys. Joe, Charlie's oldest brother, was born in 1909, Herbert in 1911 and Jim in 1913. In 1911 one of Arthur's cousins died in childbirth and they adopted the child, Mona Agnes. Their home was at the head of Oyster Bay and the 3000-acre farm became Charlie's playground, and, later, his workplace.

I first met Charlie, my father-in-law, in 1961 when he was managing the whaling station at Great Barrier. He was 43 years old. Up until four months before he died he never grew old to me. His quick humour and wonderful capacity for embracing everything he did with enthusiasm kept him young. He could argue with the best, and usually win, but he'd be the first to

11

apologise if he discovered he was wrong. He played hard, worked harder, and loved forever.

It was easy to visualise the little boy in Charlie as he sat in our lounge at Okukari, reminiscing. From our window his eyes followed the ever-changing waters of Tory Channel until they disappeared from sight around Wirikarapa Point. Opposite this is Clay Point, the entrance to Oyster Bay. The sharp cone shape of Pukeatua reaches up behind Clay Point. Its slopes disappear into lower hills and gullies. Their tops, crinkly with rows of pine trees, stand out in sharp relief against the sky.

Charlie's grandfather and his brothers cleared that land by what they called a drive. First they'd cut out all the undergrowth, then climb up the steep faces, scarfing the trees as they went. At the top each brother would take a tree and cut it right through, but it had to be done at the same time, to create the domino effect. The top tree fell against the next one and that fell against the next and so on. The trees all fell and lay in the same direction, so that when they were set alight a better fire would sweep over the land. The Kennys owned Okukari at the time, and they could hear the noise of the felling from there.

Charlie's mind swept back to the present time. "The land's gone the full circle. It's hard to believe 3000 sheep grazed those hills 40 or 50 years ago."

These memories, and the vista in front of him, opened the floodgates. I sat back in my chair to listen to a story of a life that would leave me spellbound.

"My mother worked damned hard. In fact she was always working. I never saw her in anything but dresses and shoes and stockings. Her hair was long and always tied up in some way. Even in the woolshed when she was fleece-picking and classing the wool she'd have on a dress and shoes. I don't know how she kept up with three shearers. All the food was prepared the night before, and at morning and afternoon tea time she'd race over to the house which was quite close to the shed and bring back jellies and trifles in glasses, and scones. When she returned, the wool would be stacked to one side waiting for her. She'd think nothing of going down to the woolshed after a day's work to kill a sheep for the house."

Because he was the youngest, with a five-year gap between John, his next sibling, and himself, Charlie spent a lot of time with his mother while she worked. At the end of the pantry was an area for the separator and the cream from 10 or 12 cows which were milked twice daily. The cream was stored in four-gallon kerosene tins, and every two or three days Ada, Charlie's mother, made up the butter. Then it was packed into Heberleys' own butter papers and kept in the kerosene fridge until it was sent into Picton on the once-weekly mail boat. Berry's, the local grocery shop, took it, and the proceeds paid for the Heberleys' groceries.

"While Mum worked she'd make me practise my counting. Rows of bottled fruit and jam were in lines on the pantry walls. I'd slide my elbow along the bench, rest my head on the palm of my hand and between the rhythmic slap slap slap of the butter churn I'd count the jars of golden queen peaches, apples and pears, then the wild cherries, my favourites. As everything came into season, Mum bottled it or made it into jam. I loved the way those jars glistened, and as I counted along the rows I wished the winter would hurry and we could start eating what was in the jars."

Charlie's three brothers and adopted sister began their schooling with a governess. I couldn't understand the laughter in Charlie's voice when he told me they never wore shoes. My thoughts of bare feet running across frozen grass made me curl up my toes with imagined pain but his next words soon had us both laughing.

"Mum baked bread every day. My pet penguin loved the raw dough and I'd often sneak inside and pinch a piece of dough while Mum had it proving – rising – somewhere warm. This day as I walked along the verandah past the open French doors of the schoolroom, I noticed the governess busy at the back of the room. I crept into the room with my penguin, crawled under the desks, and poked little balls of dough between the boys' bare toes. I hurried out."

A memory long forgotten, but now as vivid as if it were yesterday, caused tears of laughter to slide down Charlie's face.

"The penguin pecked frantically at their toes, trying to get at the pieces of dough. They kicked and rubbed their feet together as they tried to escape the pecking."

Charlie shook his head in disbelief as he spoke through his laughter.

"Those boys didn't say a word. They were too scared of their teacher.

"Can you imagine today's kids like that?"

This penguin was often joined by others that Charlie had reared from chicks he'd found beneath the gratings in the woolshed. It was easy to picture a young boy running barefooted down a flat stony beach, carefully selecting the smoothest flattest stones to skim across the water's surface while the penguins swam around the bay, catching herrings.

Many of the animals on the farm became pets – even the old sow. Whenever she had piglets the younger boys took some of them to rear. After their mother had finished the washing, the piglets were scrubbed in the warm soapy water. At night the boys tucked up squeaky-clean piglets in their father's socks, and took them to bed.

"But in lots of ways," Charlie continued, "we grew into men before we'd finished being boys."

Arthur Heberley was away whaling when the family's old draughthorse died, and Ada told her sons to bury it. It was far too large for the boys to take it anywhere so they dug the hole beside the horse and when it was deep enough they tied ropes on its legs and pulled the horse into the grave. But rigor mortis had set in and its legs stuck straight up in the air. They couldn't lift it out to make the hole deeper, so they took their father's saw, sawed off its legs and laid them in beside the horse. Then they filled in the grave.

Each story opened to another in Charlie's memory. His brothers outgrew their teacher, and as a five-year-old he watched them setting off from Oyster Bay, in all weathers, to row the eight kilometres to Te Weka to take lessons from Mr Baxter, a retired school teacher.

"Mum decided I wasn't old enough to go in the dinghy so I was taught for a short time by our governess. The Correspondence School had opened in 1922, but there was only one teacher, Miss Janet Mackenzie, running it from Wellington. She hand-wrote all the lessons for a hundred isolated primary school pupils, but I wasn't one of them."

When he was about six a school started up in School House Bay or Te Weu Weu as it is known today. Harry Heberley, Charlie's uncle, ran a guesthouse in Te Pangu Bay, south of Oyster Bay, and Charlie stayed with him from Monday to Friday. Every Monday morning Charlie walked five kilometres over the hills to Te Pangu and from there he'd walk to school over the hill or around the rocks to the next bay.

The McManaway children from Eerie Bay walked over the hill, and the Wilsons from the opposite side of the Channel brought their children by boat. Charlie enjoyed those days but most especially he loved Fridays, knowing he had two whole days to spend at home.

No television, no lying about inside reading books, no staying in bed until late. With a father and brothers working at the whaling station in Tipi Bay in the winter months, and running a farm the rest of the year, there were always jobs lined up for Charlie.

One of these was getting wood for his mother's copper. It had to be a certain size, and good and dry. In a story reminiscent of Huckleberry Finn, I heard how he'd persuaded a visiting cousin to help.

"If you get a load, I'll let you have a ride on the woodwire."

The two boys climbed the hill to the woodstack from where Arthur would send bundles of firewood down a wire which was about 300 metres long, and coming from a height of 60 metres. This day the two cousins had gathered enough wood for the copper and had it tied up ready to bring home.

"The only trouble was I forgot to tell him to let the wire go before he reached the edge of the steep drop. It's funny now, but hell, I was too scared to look. I peered through the cracks in my fingers, imagining the splatter when he fell. He went right to the bottom, hit the ground at an angle and rolled along the ground, just missing Dad's huge pile of wood. He lived, and came back for more."

Arthur dreamed of having electricity in Oyster Bay. He designed a waterwheel 12 feet in diameter and sent the plans over to a Mr Walker, the manager of the Ford Motor Company in Wellington. There the waterwheel was made up in sections. This made it easier to ship across Cook Strait to Picton, and for Arthur to bring it up to Oyster Bay in his own boat.

A creek, from a large catchment area, ran down the flat in Oyster Bay to the sea. A dam was built across the creek and Arthur set a 15-inch diameter steel pipe, which he'd acquired from the old Mahakipawa goldmine near Picton, into the dam. There was no governor to control the power being generated so the water that flowed through the steel pipe onto the water wheel had to be controlled. Arthur did this by making a wooden slide that could be lifted up and down over the end of the pipe to adjust the flow, and there was a spillway at one end of the dam that could be opened in a flood.

"This time I persuaded my cousin to squeeze his way through the pipe. I told him I'd often done it. But I didn't tell him I'd done it when there wasn't any water flowing through. When he was in the pipe I lifted the slide and let some water run down. He slid through the pipe so fast it skinned his face and he had such a look of horror when he burst out into the creek bed. All I could do was laugh."

Instead of the 230-volt system we are familiar with today, the power produced was 110 volts. This meant all the appliances in the house had to be changed to 110 volt, and only 110 volt light bulbs could be used. This power source lasted for years until a massive flood washed the end of the dam away, and it collapsed. After that Arthur brought one of the first diesel motors to generate electricity into the Sounds. It was a semi-diesel which had a little round bulb that had to be heated with a blow lamp to start it.

Unlike the modern diesel engine, the compression ratio of a semi-diesel wasn't high enough to produce enough heat to explode the diesel and fire the engine – hence the heating of the bulb. When the diesel squirted onto the heated bulb, the engine started.

Whenever Arthur took Ada into Picton to do her shopping the boys stayed home and managed to do many things that they normally weren't allowed to do when their mother was around. One of their favourite games was with eggs – not a hit or miss competition with rotten eggs, but rather more refined.

Jim and Charlie would hard-boil a pot of eggs and have a competition to see who'd eat the most. I could detect the pride in my father-in-law's voice when he told me he'd eaten 14 one day.

"I don't know why we did it," Charlie said. "We were always well fed."

As his brothers finished their schooling they joined their father at the Tipi Bay whaling station in the winter months and worked on the farm the rest of the year. Joe was a whale gunner with Tommy Norton senior, and Charlie still remembered the fear on the night the two men didn't return from a whale chase.

"They'd had a few lean days and this day they'd shot and got fast to a humpback off Tokori, that small rock near the

Brothers Islands in Cook Strait. A southerly buster came in and all the other boats were making a run for Tory Channel. Dad, on one of the other boats, ordered them to cut the whale loose and get the hell out of it. It wasn't worth their lives.

"They'd refused. They tied the dead whale alongside the chaser and, running with the seas, steamed around the top end of Arapawa Island in through the northern entrance of Queen Charlotte where they sheltered for the night. They arrived at the station next morning with their whale."

There are few remains at Tipi Bay now and I'd always found it hard to picture the whaling station there without something tangible. Now as I listened to Charlie I realised I was at last being given something real. Tipi Bay was no longer another beach in Tory Channel, but a place where real men had worked in one of the most dangerous occupations in the world.

Whaling had begun in Tipi Bay in 1912. Joe Perano Snr and his brother Charlie, Arthur Heberley, Billy Gillice and Sid and Billy Thoms all had shares. It operated for 16 years. In its early days not enough steam was produced to haul a 50-tonne whale up the ramp, so it was cut up in the sea.

The men used a whale spade to remove the blubber. It was like a paint-stripping knife, but on a larger scale. The flat face was kept razor-sharp. Until he died, Arthur carried a legacy of the bitterly cold conditions he worked in – especially on a cold southerly day. He didn't know he'd cut his foot with a whale spade until he kicked off his boots that night and two toes fell out.

"I've watched my dad, after they'd pulled the blubber off the whale, dive down to cut underneath its ribcage, come up for a breath and then dive down again to get inside the chest cavity. There he'd fix a chain onto the heart of the whale before cutting the heart adrift. Then he'd go back down again to pull the heart out. The fat around the heart produced a terrific amount of oil, and it was the only way they could get it out."

In 1923 Joe Perano established the Fishing Bay whaling station in Tory Channel immediately opposite Tipi Bay, and an intense rivalry between the two stations developed. Competition between the stations to catch each whale that was spotted became a serious race until a collision in 1927. A court case ensued and the Tipi Bay partnership lost. Legal costs and diminishing returns forced the closure of their station in 1929. Arthur Heberley took over two of the chasers. The *Oria* was used as a farm boat, and the *Crescent II* was converted to a fishing boat with Charlie's brother Joe fishing on it out of Wellington.

During the late '20s the number of children attending the school at Te Weu Weu dropped when many, all of a similar age, left, and the school finally closed. Arthur and Ada Heberley made the decision to send Charlie to school in Wellington. He was eight years old.

Unhappy memories spanning over 70 years brought a flatness to my father-in-law's voice. It almost sounded like a tape recorded on fast speed and played back on slow.

"I hated leaving Oyster Bay. That very first time, knowing I was leaving home, all I could do was howl. The wet grubby hanky in my pocket would become useless well before I left the house. It never got any easier, 'specially when I knew I wouldn't be home all term. Mum and Dad couldn't afford my fare.

"I travelled on the *Tamahine* and after a few trips became friendly with an old steward, Jimmy Hull. He'd look out for me and always gave me animal biscuits with coloured icing. In later years, when Ruby and I used to take our kids to Wellington, Jimmy was still on the *Tam* and he'd give them the same sort of biscuits."

For the first two years Charlie stayed with an aunt and uncle in Upper Hutt and attended a primary school in the Hutt Valley. This was followed by three more years at Miramar Primary School, when he stayed with one of Arthur's sisters, Edith Maddock.

On 30 September 1930 the door on Charlie's childhood closed forever. That is when his brother Joe drowned.

That day Joe, with his crew of three, had left Island Bay at 6am. A southerly buster came in later in the day. When the boat was running for home the engine stopped because the dry batteries ran down – not like the wet-cell batteries we have today. A sea anchor failed to stop the boat being carried towards the rocks off Owhiro Bay. Nobody saw their rockets. When these were all gone, Joe doused his jersey in petrol, lit it and used that as a distress signal.

People living in Island Bay then watched the tragedy unfold. They signalled to an earlier *Arahura*, not the Interislander, to see if she could help. She came within 37 metres but the horrendous seas prevented her from coming any closer. As darkness fell, cars were parked on the shore, shining their head-lights out over the sea. Local fishermen made a vain attempt to send a rescue party from the shore, and many of the Italian fishermen jumped into the seas in brave attempts to reach the men.

The light from the cars lit up the boat and as they watched she was swept broadside on to the waves. About 11pm she capsized. The four fishermen were thrown into the sea. There was one survivor, Arthur Hodgman.

Charlie knew nothing about it until the next day. It was early in the morning and he was in class when a teacher came in and told him his mother was here to see him. When he went out-side Ada told him there'd been a dreadful accident and Joe had drowned. Charlie left school and went with her to Island Bay.

The whole family stayed in a friend's bach close to the place where the boat was wrecked, hoping Joe's body would be found. Charlie stayed away from school. He helped his family patrol the rocks.

When the boat broke up the engine dropped amongst the rocks. It was only about 18 metres offshore at low tide. In a low voice, Charlie told how he'd climb up the bank and stare down at the place where it lay, easily visible by the rings of oil that kept seeping out. The 11-year-old could not believe that his big brother could drown so close to shore.

Ada Heberley had become friendly with an elderly woman in Petone who told fortunes. She told Ada not to go home be-cause his body would be found, on the 13th day, by a plump fisherman who walked with a waddle. He'd be on a boat that was pointed at both ends.

On 13 October 1930, 13 days after the accident, Joe's body was found floating near Karori light by Tommy Isbistor, a Shetland Islander fishing out of Island Bay in a double-ended boat. He was described by his friends as being plump and bald-headed, and like so many fishermen had a rolling gait.

A tangi for Joe was held in Petone at the same time that Joe's funeral was held in Picton. Several lorries were needed to carry the wreaths to the graveside. Joe was a very popular young man and only recently had been picked to train with the rowing squad for the 1932 Olympics. Because of the circum-stances, his death seemed all the more tragic.

An article in the *Auckland Weekly* on 8 October 1930 reads, "Had Joseph Heberley, the skipper of the launch which was wrecked in a heavy sea, endeavoured to swim straight in when the boat capsized, he would have probably reached the rocks and been rescued. Instead he stayed in a vain attempt to help one of his comrades, Magnus Hunter, who could not swim, and so sacrificed his own life."

Arthur and Ada commissioned Tom Heberley, Arthur's cousin and the government carver, to carve a shield which they donated to the Marlborough Amateur Rowing Association in 1932, for inter-club welter-weight "eight" competitions between Wairau, Picton, Blenheim and Nelson. The ornate shield is carved in a full Maori design. Joe's life on the sea was depicted by a large Maori fishhook in the centre of the shield with whales and crayfish set among the more traditional carvings. The sides were left plain for the silver shields with the winning club name engraved. There is a silver inscribed scroll at its base with the words, 'The Heberley Memorial Shield'.

As government carver Thomas had been commissioned by the government to carve presents for every member of the Royal family who visited New Zealand, or on their marriages. He carved a casket for the ashes of Sir Maui Pomare, and a chair which was presented to Lord Bledisloe at Picton for the treaty house at Waitangi, as well as restoring many Maori carvings at the Dominion Museum, including war canoes. Charlie was proud of the whaka huia box in his possession which he believed had been also carved by Thomas Heberley. Thirty centimetres long, shaped like a Maori canoe or whaka and hollowed out, it had a carved lid inlaid with paua. It was used to store the prized huia feathers.

Carving was in the Heberley blood and Charlie was also proud of the work his father did. He carved many trays and breadboards inlaid with paua, and in his spare time had begun to carve the panels for the doors of a dresser he intended to make one day, but a different use was found for them.

Shearing was in full swing when a leg on the wool table snapped. With four stands in the shed, three or four fleeces pass over the table every two minutes to be skirted and cleaned so the table had to be fixed in a hurry with a piece of timber found lying in the shed. Soon another leg broke, and when Arthur couldn't find anything to fix it with he grabbed one of his carved panels and used that.

"No other shed in the Sounds had a wool table with carved legs," Charlie told me, "but Dad never did finish that dresser."

That year Charlie was one of the two youngest boys in Wellington to gain his Proficiency Certificate. It gave him entry into the first grade class of electrical engineering at Wellington Technical High School. Besides art and French, he took mechanical engineering which covered blacksmith's skills.

"The art and French weren't a lot of use to me," he grinned, "but later on being able to work with metals and lathes stood me in good stead."

While Charlie was at Wellington Tech he stayed in Island Bay with Jack Tait, a fisherman, and biked to the school which was situated behind the carillon. Days of biking up Berhampore hill into a stiff northerly wind were vivid in his mind as were his school uniform, his enjoyment of sports, his love of mathematics, and the occasional strapping.

Now there was a distinct shift in Charlie's story. Although he still maintained he hated leaving home, his college memories flowed easily. "I don't know what I should tell you next," he said. "I was always in trouble because I stood up for myself."

It soon became apparent that it was the college uniform and talking to a girl in class that got him into the most trouble. His words brought pictures into my mind of a teenager chatting up the girl sitting next to him in class and the teacher telling him that just because he was wearing long trousers it didn't mean he was a man. Charlie's reply, "Well, you've got to be over five foot four to be a man," to the teacher who was only about five foot two, earned him a fast removal from class by the lobe of his ear, a quick march to the headmaster's office and six of the best.

Other teachers favoured the strap, but it wasn't given across the hand. The offender had to hold his hand out in front while the teacher cracked the piece of leather over the fingers and palm, up to the wrist. Too many of these strappings had Charlie sneaking back into the classroom on the last day of a term, removing the coiled strap from the corner of the drawer of the teacher's desk and bringing it home. When the new term began, no amount of questioning located that strap – which now hung on Charlie's bedroom wall in Oyster Bay.

"It was my trophy head."

But sport and mathematics far outweighed the strappings and canings. Charlie played rugby and cricket. He played for the Miramar Rugby Club as well as halfback in the college first fifteen, and cricket in the second eleven. He remembered the day he made his first century and was presented with a cricket bat. Class memories of being well ahead in mathematics were even more pleasant when he was allowed to read while waiting for the rest of the class to catch up.

In Charlie's last year of college, quite a bit of 'horse trading' was done. During the last couple of days of his holidays Charlie caught blue cod. They'd be split and then salted overnight in a brine "stiff enough to float a potato". For the first few days of term, favourite teachers would have smoked blue cod on their menu.

Charlie left school at the end of 1933, a few days before his fifteenth birthday. It wasn't until he grew older that he appreciated what his parents had given him and what sacrifices they must have made for him to go away to school.

Throughout New Zealand the depression of the 1930s had lowered wool and stock prices, while in the cities there was unrestrained rioting and looting as growing numbers of workers, including public servants, protested against wage cuts and unemployment. With Charlie home to work alongside his two brothers, Herbert and Jim, Arthur knew the time had come to bring about the idea that had been forming in his mind since the demise of the Tipi Bay whaling station.

The verandah around the homestead at Oyster Bay was collapsing. Rather than spend the money to bring it back to its original state, Arthur decided to build a concrete wall right around it, glass it in, divide it into partitions and make them into rooms.

One side of the verandah opened onto the existing dining room, and when it was glassed in and the inside wall removed the huge room became not only the dining room for guests but the social room. Eight other rooms became bedrooms. From the door at the front of the house a passage ran right down the middle, at the end of which was the kitchen, bathroom, and toilet. Somehow they ended up with a room in the middle of the house with no windows, so this was utilised as a storage room where anything that wasn't used or needed was stored, from vases to suitcases, old pictures and furniture. It was aptly called 'the dungeon'. When the building was completed and the rooms furnished, Arthur's dream became a reality and the Oyster Bay Guesthouse opened its doors – a business which was to grow and flourish for the next 25 years. As it grew, annexes were built around the perimeter of the house section, bringing the total number of beds to 40.

The ex-whale chaser *Oria,* which had been in use as the farm boat, was altered and used to take holiday-makers out on picnics and fishing trips as well as picking up guests from Picton, or, if there were quite a few guests aboard the *Tamahine,* she'd slow down as she steamed past the mouth of Oyster Bay, and wait for the *Oria* to come up alongside. Without either boat stopping, a ladder was dropped over the side of the *Tamahine,* letting the more adventurous guests off.

As Charlie talked on, I was thinking of the times I've travelled to Wellington, and how marvellous it would be if today's Cook Strait ferries still did that. Instead, we have to travel all the way from Okukari to Picton, and then pass our place again on our way to Wellington. Charlie's laughter brought me back to reality.

"Once I ended up going across to Wellington when I was helping guests up onto the ferry. There was a crowd of them, and I'd helped shift their luggage away off the deck of the *Tamahine.* We were nearly at the entrance of Tory Channel when I realised that our boat had left without me. And a return trip to Wellington without getting off isn't much fun," he added wryly.

While the income from the guesthouse kept the family together during the Depression, it was the farm and the sea that Charlie loved. While at school he'd counted the years, then the months, weeks, and finally the days until he'd be home to the Sounds he loved. Whether it was scrubcutting, fencing, mustering or shearing, or days out on the boat fishing for crayfish or groper, this was what he'd come back for. In those years Charlie never forgot that it was the guesthouse that allowed him to come home, and he helped out with that when he wasn't busy on the farm.

Oyster Bay had been in the Heberley name since 1 March 1888 when John Heberley, Worser's and Te Wai's oldest son, was granted a lease in perpetuity for 1048 acres. The rent was 20 pounds 19 shillings and 2 pence which was paid twice yearly in advance. He farmed it in conjunction with the Yellaton Run of 1156 acres which adjoined Oyster Bay, and which had been given to Worser and Te Wai by Ropoamo Te One and his wife Haneta Torea, (Toea), Te Wai's uncle and aunt.

John Heberley not only farmed. He had his Master's Certificate of Service which was granted on 21 May 1885. He was a master in the British merchant service in the home trade. Like his father, Worser Heberley, he whaled from the rowing boats based at Te Awaiti, alongside the Nortons, Jacksons and Thoms, until the early 1900s. Then he set up a whaling factory at the head of Yellaton. They used a Cornish boiler and digesters which were about five feet high and four feet in diameter.

While the men got the fire going in the boiler to raise the steam, the cut-up blubber was pushed into the digesters and the steam was then piped in. The only way the water could be replenished was to draw the fire out, and then let the manhole go to let off the pressure. Water was bucketed back in, the fire re-lit, and the process started again. The inefficiency of the boiler plus the seven kilometres to the entrance of Cook Strait, together closed John Heberley's station down.

By the time John died in 1909, Arthur had fulfilled his dream when he bought the farm. This was the same dream that stirred in Charlie as he'd worked alongside his father, mustering the hills and working in the woolshed.

"I knew every square inch of that land, and I didn't get to know it from a four-wheeled motor bike. I walked."

Chapter Two

HOME TO OYSTER BAY

Kia mau koe ki te kupu a tou matua.
Hold fast to the words your father gives you.

ARTHUR HEBERLEY added to the size of the farm when he bought another block of land taking in Glasgow Bay and as far south as Rerunder Point. This block was called the Far End. It had never been farmed and was covered in native bush and scrub. Rather than walk seven kilometres each day to reach the block so they could begin clearing the land, the brothers decided it would be a good idea to build a bach out there. Charlie spent many of his school holidays carrying timber and corrugated iron out to the Far End, and helping build the bach. They used some of the iron to make a fireplace where they cooked their meals. A hearth was made from stones and mud. Bunks were built against the walls, and covered with wire netting. Every time they came out to stay they gathered fresh bracken to use as a mattress.

"It was like sleeping on the warm ground."

When they finished it they lived there for three months each year until the land was cleared. I thought of the times at Okukari when I've watched my boys swinging the petrol-driven scrub cutters from side to side, slicing through thick scrub, and I tried to imagine the hours and hard work involved when the men had only slashers.

Once Charlie was living at home the trip out to the Far End became a regular event. All the stores were brought from the homestead, and when stocks became low someone walked back to Oyster Bay to replenish their cupboard.

Most times they were able to catch a wild nanny goat. It was tied up, assuring them of fresh milk whenever it was needed. For a change in the diet a walk down to the rocks in Glasgow Bay would guarantee a meal of fish caught on a hand line, paua prised off the rocks, one or two kina pulled ashore on a lump of bull kelp and, if they were lucky, a crayfish plucked from under a rocky ledge.

"It was hard work, very hard work," Charlie emphasised, "but Dad never asked us to do anything he wouldn't do himself."

Years later Charlie was mustering that block when he came across the old bach, leaning from the prevailing nor'westerly wind, but still recognisable. Paua, that 20 years ago had been left strung up on the wire clothes line to dry, were still there. They were so dehydrated they looked like the snout of a pig. He cautiously pushed open the door with the toe of his boot. Dust particles danced in the shafts of sunlight coming from holes in the roof where the nails had let go. Rats had obviously moved in, and he resisted the urge to brush some of their droppings off the flat surfaces. A few pieces of charred wood still lay in the blackened fireplace, and an old aluminium pot on the hearth brought back the anticipation of the roast dinner they knew their mother would have ready on their return. Everything else looked the same, but glimpses of shadowed faces, now only memories, drove him outside to whistle up his dogs and continue the day's muster.

Mustering Oyster Bay was a family affair. Arthur, Charlie, Herbert and Jim got up before daylight, and had breakfast in time to be on the hill at first light. By 10am they'd be back at the woolshed with a mob big enough to keep them busy shearing for the rest of the day. Days when there was a big mob to shear they'd get up in time to have a cup of tea and toast and begin shearing at 5.30am to do a run before breakfast at 6.30am.

"Mind you, we could only do that in the summer because we didn't have electricity in the woolshed. The Lister diesel only ran the four-stand shearing plant, and we pressed the wool at night by candlelight."

The bales of wool were shipped out of Oyster Bay by barge. Charlie Tarrant, an old Picton identity, ran the essential Sounds transport into the early 1960s and lived a hermit's life on the boat he used to tow the barge. Shipping out the wool from Oyster Bay had to be timed with the high tide in the morning so Charlie Tarrant could drive the barge aground and then anchor his boat out in the bay. At low tide, when the barge was high and dry, wooden fence gates were laid across the wet sand from the woolshed to the barge and the bales of wool were rolled over these and up onto the barge. At the next high tide the barge floated, and Charlie towed it to Picton.

When the boys were young, Arthur Heberley took out an insurance policy for each of them, to mature when they turned 21. During the Depression years, instead of paying wages, Arthur paid the premiums. Charlie had never had wages from the farm until he married. Then he paid his own premiums.

One year more than 2000 sheep were shorn, and the wool cheque was 150 pounds. Charlie knew his father paid out 130 pounds of that towards the insurance policies. The family lived on the income from the sales of the sheep and lambs, a bit of fishing, the guesthouse, and the balance of the wool cheque.

"People today don't realise what it was like," Charlie said.

With New Zealand still in the grip of the Depression, Herbert and Jim Heberley decided to leave Oyster Bay to try to find work in Wellington. Jim stayed in Wellington but Herbert headed across the Tasman and worked around Australia as a labourer. Charlie chose to stay at Oyster Bay and help his father and mother with the farm and guesthouse.

Ada and Arthur had taken in a young boy, Alfie Nimmo, as a foster child, and now the young man worked alongside Charlie on the farm. Some days Arthur, with Charlie and Alfie, left the farm and headed up Tory Channel out into Cook Strait to fish. Blue cod, which were later smoked, were caught on handlines and then they'd steam to their 'special' rocks and drop a heavy line with five hooks to target groper. I thought of the times I've heard Charlie describing some of those rocks when you 'open up one peak behind the other', or 'line that low scrubby hill in front of that high peak', and it made me realise how fishing has developed in today's electronic age when the fishermen rely on the Global Positioning System or GPS. With the automatic pilot running through the GPS, the longitude and latitude of the fishing spots can be plotted in, and the GPS will navigate the boat to the exact position.

Arguments among other fishermen often flared, and Charlie still remembered the day his father and a fisherman of Italian descent had a heated argument when their gear became entangled.

Arthur called the Italian "a bloody spaghetti-eating bastard". The Italian retorted that he was a naturalised New Zealander. Arthur's waspish answer was, "Just because the cat had kittens in the chookhouse they weren't called chickens."

They caught crayfish using ring pots. These had a steel ring which was about one metre in diameter with a netting bag attached to it. Paua, fish frames or fish heads were tied in the bag for bait before they dropped the pot over the side of the boat to the bottom. After half an hour they hauled up the pot, took out the crayfish and repeated the process. It was no trouble to fill 10 or 12 chaff sacks with the crays each night. They were sold for threepence a pound. Even as Charlie was still telling me how they were caught, I could see laughter in his eyes as his mind raced on to the events of one particular night.

"We were wet and cold and had just re-set the pots. I asked Alfie to light the primus and make a cuppa while we waited. A yell came out of the cabin and the next thing this ball of flames, which I recognised as the primus, flew through the air and over the side. He hadn't left the burning methylated spirits long enough, to warm up the burner," Charlie explained, "and when he turned the primus on, it flared up. That was the end of our hot drink."

Throughout the summer and other holidays, the guesthouse was always full. People returned to Oyster Bay year after year, especially for the fishing. Every fine day the *Oria* left Oyster Bay and headed into Tory Channel with a boatload of would-be fishermen from the city. Arthur usually took them out but occasionally Charlie found himself in charge, although he maintained he didn't like it.

"I was too impatient. Untangling lines, dealing with blind eels when they twisted up the lines, making excuses for the lack of fish – it wasn't me."

Guests often spoke of their wonderful days out on the boat: picnics on the beach with billy tea, fish wrapped in leaves and cooked to perfection over an open fire, and children being schooled in the art of catching fresh water cockabullies, using spider webs wrapped around the stems of rushes.

On the way home they weighed up the catches to find the heaviest fish. After dinner, amidst much ceremony, the winner from the previous day handed over the trophy, a medallion on a chain, to the new champion. This was worn until the next day's winner was announced.

Some days they held horse races with child jockeys riding on the backs of adults. Some evenings they would push back the tables and chairs in the dining room, exposing a huge expanse of black and white checked linoleum. Twenty-four salt and pepper shakers taken off the tables became the draught pieces, and many serious competitions took place on the polished floor.

On New Year's Eve the tables and chairs were once again pushed back, and they held a dance with everyone getting dressed up in fancy dress, usually with a theme.

One family who returned every year had two boys. Charlie remembers the two young brothers as being totally different. One loved to be around the shed when a sheep was being killed for meat. "He'd pull out the guts to see what it had been eating, and cut out the organs and pull them to pieces, much to his mother's disgust. He became a doctor."

The other brother related well to people and could make conversation with anyone.

"He became a lawyer and later our governor-general, and," Charlie added almost surreptitiously, "I'm probably the only New Zealander able to say I've kicked a governor-general up the backside."

I heard the story, of a young man sitting on a box in the cow bale, away from everyone, his head pressed against the side of the cow and watching the rhythmic squirts of warm frothy milk filling up the bucket. The day was hot and the late afternoon sun streamed down on to Charlie's back. In the distance he could hear the muted crack of a tennis ball coming from the tennis court, and he dreamily followed the game in his mind.

Suddenly a great clatter of stones on the cowshed roof shook Charlie out of his reverie. The cow jumped and knocked over both the bucket and Charlie's stool, leaving him flat on his back.

"Hell, I was wild. I jumped up and tore outside. There was Sir Michael Hardie Boys, all eight years of him, with another handful of stones ready to throw. He felt the toe of my boot all the way down the paddock."

On 16 July 1934 at the Island Bay Methodist church, Mona, Charlie's adopted sister, married a Shetland Islander, Thomas Tait, who was fishing out of Wellington's Island Bay. They lived in Napier where Mona nursed. Two years later she developed tuberculosis of the spine and died in Napier's public hospital on 7 February 1938. She was 26 years old. Mona is buried at the Park Island Cemetery in Napier.

Talking about Mona, Charlie remembered a time when Mona was sick, and Ada had gone to spend a few days with her. Arthur and Charlie had a longing for a sponge cake with lashings of cream. The Edmonds cookery book came out, and Charlie followed the recipe exactly. When it was cooked and turned out on the cake cooler it looked so perfect he put it outside on an old macrocarpa stump, which was used as a chopping block, to cool – and where it would be noticed.

"It was noticed all right. The damned dogs ate it and the birds finished off the crumbs."

I asked Charlie why he never continued with his cooking. He maintained he could cook if he had to, but he'd never had to. I grinned to myself when he told me weetbix or porridge was his breakfast speciality. I thought of the time when Charlie had made a pot of porridge, really thick porridge, and had ended up with three pots full as he added more and more water to thin the porridge down enough to be able to pour it from the pot. And the times he'd greeted my mother-in-law when she'd arrived home from Picton with the words, "What's to eat?"

During the Depression, Hugo and Leila Terrill bought land in Tauranga Bay, now called Eerie Bay and two kilometres south of Oyster Bay, where they ran a very successful guesthouse. When their guests were arriving or departing they shared the transport for their guests with the Heberleys', and when either guesthouse was having a special function everyone joined in. Hugo Terrill loved ballroom dancing and laid a sprung floor in the 40x20ft boatshed. The Terrills held two or three dances a year, but the grandest was the Spinsters' Ball. Anyone who could play a musical instrument brought it along and people danced the valeta, maxina, quickstep and foxtrot to the sound of piano accordions, button accordions, violins and a piano that was carried down from the house for the night. It was at one of these dances that Charlie met the young girl who later became his wife.

Ruby Guard was Hugo and Leila Terrill's granddaughter. She lived in Blenheim and often stayed with her grandparents during school holidays, playing when she was young, and helping in the guesthouse as she grew older. Ruby's ties with the Sounds went back as far as Charlie's.

In 1827 the young woman who was to become her great-grandmother, 13-year-old Betty Parker, first came out to New Zealand from Sydney aboard the schooner *Waterloo*. It was captained by John Guard, who later called himself Jackie, a man described as a huge, black-bearded character, afraid of neither God nor man. While he was sailing through Cook Strait, a storm drove his ship towards the cliffs on the eastern coast of Arapawa Island. All on board believed the ship was going to sink in the huge seas breaking on the shore – when suddenly an opening appeared, and the strong flood tide carried the *Waterloo* into Tory Channel.

Three kilometres from the entrance of Cook Strait, Jackie Guard laid anchor in a small bay. Its close proximity to Cook Strait, its sheltered waters, the beach where a good-sized stream poured over it into the sea, a large area of flat land, plus the numerous sightings of humpback whales in the Strait – all these made the whaler realise that Te Awaiti would be a perfect site for a whaling station.

Betty Parker sailed back to Sydney with Captain Jackie Guard and on his return to Te Awaiti he set up the first shore-based whaling station in New Zealand.

On 14 April 1830 Charlie's great-grandfather, James 'Worser' Heberley, arrived at Te Awaiti on board the *Waterloo* to begin whaling with Jackie Guard. That same year Betty came back to Te Awaiti as Jackie's wife, and, in 1831, 16-year-old Betty gave birth to John, the first white child born in the South Island of New Zealand. John Guard was Ruby's great-grandfather. He lived to be 87 and died in Kakapo Bay, Port Underwood, in 1918, the place where Jackie Guard had later whaled from.

The Guard men were men of the sea and land. They whaled, farmed and fished. Ruby's father, Maurice Ivanhoe, was a commercial fisherman. He fished from Mondays through to Fridays, steaming down Blenheim's Opawa River and over the Wairau Bar where he trawled for flounder in Cloudy Bay. He was contracted to deliver mail into Port Underwood as there was no road into the area, and every Saturday he loaded his boat, *Midlothian*, with mail and boxes of groceries, or anything else the isolated residents had ordered, steamed down the river to Cloudy Bay and up into Port Underwood. Some of Ruby's happiest memories were going with her father on that Saturday mail run.

Now Charlie didn't mind taking the guests on the boat. Especially if he thought he'd see Ruby.

"Mind you, I didn't dance. But I kept an eye on the talent."

Even as Charlie spoke I caught a glance he exchanged across the room with Ruby.

People came by boat from Picton, Endeavour Inlet and Resolution Bay to these dances, he said. The Floods walked from their farm, at the head of Port Underwood, over the hill into Maraetai Bay where they were picked up by boat. The Baldicks and Derbyshires all arrived by boat while Colin Mackenzie with a piano accordion on his back walked 10 kilometres over the hill from Otanerau to Okukari where he caught a boat owned by one of the locals.

Young girls, more accustomed to leaping on and off boats in work clothes and gumboots, climbed out of boats and stepped onto the wharf in ball gowns and party shoes. As Charlie described the scene I shut my eyes and pictured Cinderella arriving at the ball after her transformation by her fairy godmother. For one night these women too could be Cinderella with the anticipation of maybe finding their Prince Charming. In a boatshed decorated with tree ferns, old lifebuoys and streamers, the Cinderellas, on the arms of their princes, swirled around to music made popular by Richard Rogers, Hoagy Carmichael and Jerome Kern, on a floor that had been polished earlier in the day by sprinkling it with French chalk and polished with sacks. The princes drank their beer taken from barrels outside the shed, while the Cinderellas had cups of tea served inside.

When midnight struck the Cinderellas never lost their glass slippers and their boats never changed into pumpkins, and the dancing carried on into the early hours of the morning. Boats pulled away from the wharf in the grey light, goodbyes and promises to meet again soon being made over the noise of boat engines as they steamed out the bay. At home, cows waited to be milked, chooks had to be fed, fences needed to be mended, or sheep that had been shedded up all night waited to be shorn. The night before soon became a memory to enjoy while the land was worked and the stock attended.

Visitors passing through Tory Channel today have no idea of how it was then. Instead they see mostly native bush, pine plantations and scrub, with holiday homes perched on hillsides or half-hidden in the bush. Power lines, strung across gullies, hang from red and white striped poles bringing electricity to both sides of Tory Channel since the area was reticulated in 1982. But in the 1930s and '40s all the land on both sides of Tory Channel was clear, and ran 35,000 sheep. In those days all the farmers helped one another out, mustering and shearing, giving 'day for day' instead of wages.

These were the days before the Bowen style of shearing. In the Sounds, shearing Romneys, 100-120 sheep was a good tally. Charlie admitted to feeling proud when he reached a tally of 200. Occasionally he went out shearing to Seddon, and was paid 18 shillings per 100 sheep. In 1940 the price increased to two pounds per 100. That year Charlie shore 13,000 sheep and earned 260 pounds.

This decided Charlie to ask for wages instead of giving 'day for day', as he realised that he'd often be working more days that those he was getting in return. After speaking with the other farmers in the area, they agreed on a fixed wage. Whether it was a day shearing or a day mustering, – the flat rate per day was one pound. Sometimes the most mundane muster turned into an exciting pig hunt.

On this particular occasion Charlie was helping Reg and Tom Jackson muster Te Iro on the south-western end of Arapawa Island. Heat and fatigue were forgotten when the dogs chased and caught a wild pig. Reg and Charlie could taste wild pork as they fought to hold it.

"All I had in my pockets were a few four-inch nails, which I couldn't do a lot with, and a jar of Vicks Vaporub. I broke the jar and cut, or more likely hacked, the pig's throat, and lugged it back to the yards."

When he was a child, regular colds often developed into flu, leaving Charlie with a bronchial cough. Ada often brought him into Picton to see Dr J L Gregg.

"He'd always listen to my chest and tell Mum I had had a cloud on my lung. She always worried about TB."

Throughout Charlie's teenage years his condition worsened, and came to a head when he was 19. Once again he was mustering for Reg and Tom Jackson. Before dawn the men had steamed the boats to the head of Ngaruru, a bay on Arapawa Island immediately opposite Te Weu Weu where Charlie had gone to school. There they anchored. At the end of the muster someone brought the men back to Ngaruru to collect their boats and go home.

The sheep from the area of land that wasn't native reserve in Ngaruru were mustered in semi-darkness and driven up and over the top of the hill overlooking Umuwheke Bay on the western side of Arapawa Island. The whole of this western side of the island, from Umuwheke Bay as far south as a bay at the back of Te Iro, was mustered. There, a fence ran from the beach up to a height of 387 metres, then down into Te Iro Bay, cutting off the sou'western end of the island. The mob was driven up this fenceline and down to Jacksons' sheepyards in their bay.

"This was the longest muster on the farm and we always tried to be on top of the hill by daybreak. It was one of those stinking hot days you get before a southerly buster. It ripped in about 11am. Tom left Reg and me to finish the muster while he went back to the boats in case they dragged. It was dark when we got in with the sheep. We'd been wet and cold all day."

That night Charlie went home to Oyster Bay. He was already beginning to feel ill with severe pains in his chest. By morning he felt worse but got up because the sheep they'd brought in the day before had to be crutched.

"I collapsed." Remembered pain made Charlie rub his chest as he tried to describe the intense agony. "I didn't know if it was the pain or what, but I couldn't stop vomiting. All I was bringing up was water."

Charlie was taken by boat into Picton and Mrs Tom Jackson drove him through to the Lister Hospital in Blenheim. The speeding car was noticed by a traffic cop who chased it from Grovetown but the driver was too worried about Charlie to stop. At the hospital they were met by a Miss Bush who ran the small hospital, and when the traffic cop pulled in behind the car Miss Bush soon had him organised to help carry Charlie inside. There he was put to bed to wait for Dr Hogg to arrive. As Mrs Jackson left she glanced back at the man in the bed and silently said what she believed would be her final goodbye.

Chapter Three

FARMING AND WHALING

Tena ko te toa mahi kai e kore e paheke.
A warrior who works hard at growing food will not fail.

PNEUMONIA was diagnosed. There were no drugs or the pain relief that one can expect today. Instead Charlie had regular mustard plasters slapped on his chest, so hot they burnt his nipples. His temperature was so high he came out in water blisters. To bring it down they put him on a cold water bed similar to the water beds of today, except it was very cold. His pain relief was laudanum.

"I was either in a delirious stupor or intense pain."

Fluid was drained off the pleural cavity, a space between lung and chest wall, so often that Charlie maintained he knew what it was like to be stabbed. Every few hours he would be sat up in bed and then had to lean forward on a pillow placed on a bed-table. An aspirating needle was inserted between his ribs below the base of his shoulder blade. Once the needle was inserted into the pleural cavity the fluid was drawn into the syringe, the tap turned over and the fluid ejected into a bottle. The tap was then turned on again and the syringe re-filled. This process was repeated until sufficient fluid was withdrawn.

"I felt that needle go in. The pain was terrible. The fluid that came out was a dirty grey colour with pinky flecks of blood."

Charlie was in hospital for three months, and when he was well enough Ruby Guard visited him, bringing baking from her mother. When he had sufficiently recovered, he stayed with Ruby's family until he was fit enough to go home to Oyster Bay.

It was November, 1938. Although Charlie was home he wasn't well. His doctor had warned him his convalescence would take time because he had been extremely ill with pneumonia. Mustering and shearing had taken place and he could do little to help. The walk to the woolshed left him feeling hot and shaky, the milk bucket felt heavy, and some mornings the thought of climbing out of bed and getting dressed kept him there.

"It wasn't me."

The guesthouse was full for Christmas, and Ada had employed someone to help out in the kitchen. Charlie was sitting on a couch when he overheard this woman telling people that she didn't waste her time making 'real' gravy like Ada. Instead she used gravy mix.

"I told her my mum wouldn't waste money like that. She always made her gravy the old-fashioned way. That woman up and kicked me fair in the chest. It lowered me."

Charlie remembered the waves of nausea that kept passing over him and the relief when they stopped. That night after he'd gone to bed he had a dreadful coughing fit and coughed up a lump almost the size of a tennis ball. It nearly choked him. He described it as 'raggy edged'. Ada kept it and took it into the doctor who took one look and said it was hydatids. He sent it away for analysis. It was indeed hydatids. The results showed it was the main or mother cyst. It had been lodged on the inside of Charlie's lung, most probably causing his illness throughout the years. His latest illness presented the symptoms of pneumonia and so he had been treated for it, and the thump he'd received on his chest caused it to tear away.

An X-ray showed his lungs were clear of pneumonia but where the cyst had torn away there was a five-inch scar which blocked a portion of Charlie's lung. It left him susceptible to colds which often developed into bronchitis and sometimes pneumonia.

Today, hydatids in New Zealand has almost been eradicated. This has been achieved by public awareness, co-operation of dog owners, complete dog registration, movement control in some areas, and regular worm-destroying medication for dogs which do have contact with raw offal.

The mature worm inhabits the intestines of dogs which can become infected by eating contaminated raw offal of sheep, goats, cattle, pigs or deer. The body of the worm is made up of three segments while the head has four suckers and a double row of hooklets which attach to the intestinal wall of the dog. It matures in six to eight weeks and during its two-year life span sheds in the dog's faeces, one segment every 10 to 14 days. Each segment contains up to 800 eggs. Grazing animals continue the cycle.

When these eggs are swallowed by man, the embryo is liberated, and burrows through the intestinal wall, into the blood stream. The blood carries it to the liver, lungs, kidneys or the brain where the embryo develops into a small cyst with two definite layers. As it increases in size, buds form from the inner layer. These become daughter cysts, which later produce granddaughter cysts all growing within the original cyst.

"All those years when I had pleurisy or bronchitis it was probably caused by the hydatid cyst growing in my lung.

"That woman did me a favour when she kicked me," he grinned.

My mind slipped back to the many times when he'd roared at my children for letting the farm dogs lick their faces, or perhaps they'd been playing around the dog kennels, or drinking water from a creek. I'd often felt like telling him to get off my kids' backs – but at last I understood.

Arthur and Ada felt a change of climate would help Charlie recover so they made plans to send him to Australia to meet up with his older brother Herbert. He was working for a construction gang, building a freezing works in the Snowy Mountains, at a small place called Nimitabel. There were only about 30 houses there, and Herbert lived in one of them.

The trip across the Tasman Sea took two days by ship and Charlie arrived in Australia early in 1939. A life of leisure combined with hunting foxes and kangaroos soon palled. I felt his frustration even as he described the excitement of the hunt followed by the skinning and curing of any well-marked fox skins which he kept, with the idea of having a fur stole made for Ruby. All the men in the village worked at the freezing works. Charlie hated having no one to talk to during the day, the coldness of the snow that covered the ground from April added to his misery, and he missed Ruby.

"Mum and Dad expected me to stay for two or three years."

In the evenings the men working on the freezing works always gathered at the hotel to talk about their day over a few beers. Charlie soon got to know the workers, many of whom had come from New Zealand's West Coast. Two had actually stayed at the guesthouse in Oyster Bay. Although Charlie was not supposed to work, when the boss of the construction gang told him he needed a second plumber and he'd pay four pounds ten shillings a week, he jumped at it.

"After all, you don't live in the Sounds and run a guesthouse without being able to unblock toilets and drains or fix spouting that's blown away. I reckoned if I couldn't braize a couple of pieces of pipe together, or use a soldering iron, there was something wrong with me."

On 3 September 1939 the British Prime Minister, Neville Chamberlain, announced that a state of war existed between Britain and Germany. New Zealand's Prime Minister, Michael Joseph Savage, replied:

"Both with gratitude for the past, and with confidence in the future, we range ourselves without fear beside Britain. Where she goes we go; where she stands we stand. We are only a small and a young nation, but we are, one and all, a band of brothers, and we march forward with a union of hearts and wills to a common destiny."

Herbert decided to stay in Australia, but Charlie was adamant. "If we were at war I didn't want to be stuck on Australia's side of the Tasman."

Before Charlie left Australia he made plans. He turned 21 on 11 December 1939, so he wrote to Ruby telling her he was arriving in Lyttelton about that time, and asking if she could meet him. Ruby's parents had separated in 1938 and her mother was now living in Christchurch, so when Charlie was due home Ruby headed for Christchurch to visit her mother and meet Charlie.

They were married in the Registry Office in Christchurch on 14 December 1939. They arrived back in Blenheim where Ruby decided to stay with her father for a few days while her husband went home to tell his parents that he was married.

It was a part of Charlie's life I didn't know, and the thought of him having to explain his marriage to his parents shocked me until he explained that although he didn't understand at the time, he did now.

"I was the youngest. Mum and Dad had lost both Joe and Mona, and they'd sacrificed a lot to send me away to school. I think they thought I wasn't old enough to get married, and Ruby had only just turned 18. They probably would've *always* thought I was too young."

Ruby arrived on the weekly mail boat a few days before Christmas, and although Charlie admitted it must have been hard for her, Ruby's memories of stepping off the boat at Oyster Bay were extremely vivid. Her nervousness was made worse when she realised Charlie wasn't among the crowd of guests down meeting the mail boat. It was only later that she found out he was working in the woolshed and didn't know she'd arrived. Lonely among the crowd, and feeling the bay was closing in on her, Ruby walked up to the house. It had a high corrugated iron fence built right round it. A stand of macrocarpas growing behind the house leaned out over the roof and somehow added to the feeling of isolation that was now creating a prickling in her eyes. Reaching the gate, her dragging footsteps took her to the door where she was met by only a blast of heat and the smell of cooking mutton that emanated from the coal range somewhere within the dark interior. She never forgot her arrival.

Ruby waited on tables, made beds, cleaned rooms and helped her mother-in-law in the kitchen, and between them Charlie and Ruby earned two pounds fourteen shillings per week, or $5.80 in dollars and cents, although of course it was worth much more then. On their days off they'd row out into Tory Channel and fish for blue cod from daylight to dark. When they arrived home Ruby prepared dinner while Charlie first cleaned then split the fish before putting them in tubs of brine to soak overnight. Next morning, before the sun was on the line to bring blowflies, the salted fish had wire hooks driven through their eyes and were hung up to dry. While they dried, Charlie lit the smokehouse fire, using manuka. Once the fire had burnt down and manuka sawdust was piled over the smouldering wood, the fish were hung up and smoked. The smoked fish was sent up to Picton and sold to a local grocer, Mr Peek, for eleven pence per pound. It helped cover the cost of their groceries.

One trip had been particularly successful and Charlie went to bed that night exhausted but on a high as he pictured the fifteen dozen blue cod – a month's groceries – in the tubs of brine he'd prepared, standing in the boatshed at the end of the wharf. During the night, the pet pig, nameless except for the names Charlie then called it, cleaned up or spoiled the lot.

Oyster Bay was named because of its abundance of oysters. On a calm day at low tide it was easy to wade around the bay and pick them up. When the fire-breaks were bulldozed for the pine trees being planted in the 1980s, clay washing down the hillsides into the sea smothered most of the shellfish. The last few years have seen their numbers increasing, but Charlie believed they will never be as thick as they used to be.

Arthur was a ranger with the right to inspect any boat that came in the bay if he thought they had more than the legal number of oysters on board. Over the years he confiscated many oysters, even from his own family, and liberated them back in the bay – but not from where they'd originally come.

"He built an oyster bed out of stones below low water mark and he'd throw the confiscated oysters into his own bed.

"Days when Mum and Dad weren't in the bay, Ruby and I rushed through our chores and when we'd finished we'd go and get oysters from Dad's supply and have a real feed. Other days, if all the guests were out, we'd borrow a couple of racquets and have a game of tennis."

I heard story after story, all told with candour. It was of a life filled with more hardships than I'd ever experienced or imagined, but it was the only life he knew, and he accepted it.

For the first three years of their married life Ruby and Charlie lived in the main house, but when their room was needed for extra guests they had to sleep outside in a tent. Any romantic thoughts I had of sleeping under canvas on beautiful balmy summer nights were soon dispelled when Charlie told me the wind was such that he'd seen chooks pinned against a wire netting fence, and cows kneeling into the wind. He was adamant that no other place in the Sounds has winds as strong as in Oyster Bay.

With a toddler, Donna, and their second child, Jocelyn, due in June, Charlie knew he had to earn more, so when the 1941 whaling season opened and the Peranos offered him a job at the whaling station at Fishing Bay, he jumped at it. During the Second World War this was one of the few remaining whaling stations still operating. All the British factory ships and many of the Norwegian ships were lost while the threat of U-boats around the west coast of Australia, Africa and South Georgia closed these stations. Whale oil was needed as it was used in the hardening of gun metals, and frozen edible whale meat was sent to Britain.

During his first season Charlie shared a hut in Fishing Bay with Barney (no one knew his other name) Wilson, who was the fifth foreman employed by the Peranos at the factory. Charlie came home to Oyster Bay only on odd occasions. For every whale caught, 12 pounds was shared among the 12 factory workers, with the foreman – who also tended the boiler – getting an extra pound. The hours were long and at the end of the season – which had seen the first whale caught in mid-May and the last in mid-August – Charlie had earned 150 pounds.

But when he tallied up the hours he had worked he discovered he had earned nine pence an hour – less than 10 cents.

"That year 86 humpbacks were caught."

The first time I saw the whaling station was in 1963. It was a station the locals were proud of. But, coming from Auckland city, I saw only blood and guts, rusted corrugated iron buildings and huts perched on the hillside, the smoke pouring from their chimneys. Muddy tracks from the whaling station to their doors were the only other sign that people actually lived in them. My Auckland nose hated the smell.

But when Charlie began working at the station it was still as it was when its founder, Joe Perano Sr, literally carved a chunk out of the hillside with a pick and shovel in 1923. The 12 factory workers either lived in nearby bays, shared a hut in Fishing Bay, or built one of their own. Now, as I listened to Charlie, I was swept into a period of our history I found hard to believe happened only some 80 years ago.

"The conditions were appalling. No safety guards on any machinery or belts – nothing was guarded at all. There were no toilets, showers, dressing rooms or a smoko room. We never escaped the smell but I guess we got used to it. One of the men, Stan Derbyshire, lived further down the channel at Onapua Bay where he worked on his father's farm during the off-season. He always smoked a pipe but when he was working at the station he left his pipe on a rail near the coal stack. I'd arrived before Stan this day. I took his pipe, dug out the tobacco, pushed some shavings of whalemeat down into the bowl then covered them up with the tobacco I'd removed.

"Stan arrived for smoko, reached for his pipe and lit up. We could all hear the bubbling in the bowl, but what with the smell around us – and no doubt in us – Stan didn't notice a thing.

"To make a cuppa we boiled the water in the furnace in a cut-down four-gallon benzene tin. When she boiled we chucked in a couple of handfuls of tea leaves. We plonked ourselves on the coalheap. It was warm. There was only one problem," Charlie told me. "The one who drank the most tea, ate the most cinders."

Charlie never took his job for granted. The conditions were rough but he came back, season after season. Men clamoured to work at the station. Hard men worked in hard conditions. Friendships lasted a lifetime. His memory of Fishing Bay at the height of the season was etched in his mind as sharply as if it were yesterday, and I felt privileged that he shared with me a part of our history that has gone forever.

"No matter how dark it is, it's never dark on the water. If a whale'd been caught late the previous afternoon I could make out its outline shackled to the mooring in the bay. It was hard to pick out the factory until I was closer when I'd catch a glimmer of light coming from the building. Everything was run off steam, and as I got closer the noise of coal being shovelled into the furnace blotted out any other sound.

"A blast of heat came from the opened door of the furnace. There the boilerman was shovelling coal off the huge stack into the fire, and the roaring of the flames greeted me. Gumboots and clothes wet from the last shift sat around the edge of the boiler, drying. The steam from the boiler drove everything, from the winches to the cooking in the digester. Once we had steam the factory came alive. Winches clanged and their steam exhausts roared. It sounded like a steam train.

"Now it was time for the whale lying in the bay to make its final journey. A stationhand rowed out to it with a wire rope which was attached to a winch in the factory. He unshackled the whale from the mooring and fastened the winch wire to the wire strop the chaser crews had put through the fluke of the tail after it was caught.

"A whale nearly always died on its side because the weight of the flukes, hanging down on the bottom side, tipped it over, leaving the top point of the fluke sticking out of the water. As a means of controlling it, one of the chaser crew, usually the gunner, threw a lasso over the fluke and drew the whale up to the boat. Then he leaned on his stomach over the side of the boat and cut a hole through the fluke and passed a wire strop about three metres long through it. A piece of rope placed through this was then passed to the crew on the mother ship. The crew used the wire strop to winch its tail up the side of the ship, high enough to put a towing chain around the small of the tail – where it joined the body. Once fast alongside the ship, the whale was towed tail first back to the factory mooring.

"The winch pulled the whale to the bottom edge of the ramp, still tail first, where it was pulled up high enough on the ramp for another large wire strop to be placed round the small of the tail. The main hauling out wire was shackled to it, and the largest steam winch in the factory, capable of pulling over

50 tonnes, hauled the whale up the ramp onto the flensing deck.

"Here the blubber was marked out in large strips the length of the whale. Someone cut a hole in one end of the blubber, a chain strop was put through, and, as the winch slowly peeled it off, a flenser cut between the blubber and the layer of fatty meat that lay beneath. The blubber came off in three or four strips.

"Just like skinning a sheep," I was told.

Charlie had been so engrossed he'd talked non-stop.

"After the blubber had been stripped off, the body fat and meat were removed, exposing the ribs which could now be pulled off by the steam winch. At this stage the whale's intestines as well as its liver, heart, lungs, and stomach were taken out. Once the head was cut off, the remains of the whale were rolled over and the remaining blubber taken off.

"The backbone and head were then pulled aside, to where they were cut up into smaller pieces with chainsaws before being fed into the digester.

"In those days everything went into the digester," he summed up.

Charlie's words brought back the remembered smell of the station when it was operating. I shuddered.

"That's money," he laughed.

When the season ended, the family still headed out into Tory Channel whenever they had a day off to fish for blue cod to smoke and sell, but with their two girls, Donna, and one-year-old Jocelyn, days had to be chosen more carefully. Jocelyn sat in a wooden apple box that was jammed between the seats while Donna sat in the bow. Whenever an octopus was caught Charlie chopped off its legs and the girls spent their days sticking them to the wooden planks of the dinghy and on to themselves – "better than any toy".

The first whale of the 1942 season was caught on 14 May and once again Charlie spent the next three months working at the station. Seventy-three humpback whales were caught – the worst season since 1937 when the tally was 55, although in that year a blue whale, which yields an average of 25.4 tonnes of oil, was caught. In comparison, about 4.5-5 tonnes could be expected from the humpback. [Ref. *The Perano Whalers,* Don Grady p 221. Reed 1982.]

Only five blue whales were caught in the 53 years of Perano whaling in Cook Strait. The biggest, which measured 98 feet – 27 metres – was caught in 1938 and holds the record as being the biggest whale ever caught in New Zealand waters. The story of its chase has been recorded as being the most thrilling ever. It is a story that is still told, and one that I now listened to in awe.

"The blue whale is one of the fastest swimming fish in the sea – particularly in short bursts. The only way the three chasers could get onto the whale was to get it going in a circle and then one of the chasers would cut across the diameter of the imagined circle, travelling in a shorter distance than the whale which was swimming around its circumference.

"Seven harpoons were fired into that whale. It kept breaking the ropes and was travelling so hard the harpoons pulled out. When it was finally killed and brought into the factory, it was too big to haul up on the slipway so it was pulled tail first, part way out, cut in half, and processed in two lots.

"It was a cow whale and when the men cut her open they discovered she was pregnant and they removed the foetus, which was only nine inches long, and placed it in a pyrex bowl. Later, Gilbert took it home and preserved it in formalin."

Charlie recalled the wonder at seeing something so small from such a massive creature, and told me it was more like the formation of a bird than a fish.

At the end of the 1942 season Charlie came back to a wife who had lost her mother suddenly, and who had just been told she was pregnant with their third child. With the children, it was becoming more difficult living with Arthur and Ada, so Ruby and Charlie decided to shift into one of the two-bedroomed self-contained annexes. Charlie vividly remembered Ruby's excitement – more than his own – as they set up their first home together, and her horrified shame when she confessed she'd spent a whole five pounds to stock up her cooking cupboard – nearly twice as much as Charlie's weekly wage on the farm.

The youngest child, Joe, named after Charlie's brother who drowned, and who later became my husband, was born on 3 January 1943. I know Charlie loved all his children but he lived in a time when great importance was placed upon carrying on the family name and he was proud that his son would carry the Heberley name into the next generation. With his brother Joe dead, and neither Jim nor Herbert having a son, he felt he was giving something back to his parents.

Just before the 1943 whaling season began, Charlie's oldest brother Herbert arrived home from Australia and took over the running of the farm in Oyster Bay. Charlie's dream of its being his farm, a dream nurtured for as long as he could remember, was shattered.

When he was offered a two-roomed bach to live in at Te Awaiti, one bay further down Tory Channel from Fishing Bay, Charlie with Ruby packed up their belongings and left Oyster Bay. It didn't matter that the stars shone through the roof, and that when it rained Ruby ran out of containers to catch the water – the family was together, and although Charlie was whaling again he was home most nights.

The beauty of the stars shining through the roof of the bach palled when heavy winter rains set in. Gilbert Perano, the managing director and co-owner of the whaling station, suggested to Charlie he might like to live in an army recreation hall that had been built on their Whekenui farm property earlier in the war, and was no longer used.

In the two years while the concrete gun emplacement and the observation post above it were being built on the headland between Whekenui Bay and Fishing Bay by the Public Works Department, the population at Whekenui Bay grew to 60. Gilbert Perano often used to bring in supplies for the men on one of the whale chasers. Before he left Whekenui for Picton, this particular day, one of the men asked Gilbert if he'd mind bringing back a few bottles of beer if they got them delivered to the boat in Picton. "Not a problem," Gilbert said but he told the men to make sure it was put into the back hold. He preferred not to be seen carrying alcohol because he didn't encourage his men to have a lot of it when they were working.

Charlie was on the boat this day and he told me when they left Picton neither Gilbert nor he could understand why the boat was dragging her stern so much and he quickly lifted the back hatch to check they hadn't sprung a leak and were making water. The hold, which was approximately one-third of the boat's length, and where 200 fathoms of rope were stored when they were whaling, was crammed with bottles of beer.

"It must have been hellishly thirsty work building that emplacement and lookout."

At the same time Gilbert offered Charlie the recreation hall to live in, he offered Charlie work on his farm in the off-season. So the family moved once again and in the evenings, when he wasn't working, Charlie and Ruby converted the hall into a four-roomed house.

In the 53 years of Perano whaling with the power-boats there were four fatalities. The first occurred in the first year the station was operating out of Fishing Bay, when Sam Herangi fell into an open digester which was full of cooked whale meat and oil. A second factory death occurred in similar circumstances, when Gilbert Jones died. Charlie knew this man and, as he related the gruesome details I didn't really want to hear, I could tell it was an event that would stay with him forever.

Charlie explained how the bones of a whale were cooked in a large digester which was really just like a big pressure cooker. It was a big vessel standing on its end and filled from the top, with a door at the bottom. When it was full of meat and bone, it was shut up and a measured quantity of water was added. The contents were cooked by steam pressure. After they had been cooking about four hours, salt water pressure was turned into the bottom of the digester. This floated the oil to the top, and it was drained off. Then the top lid was opened, followed by the bottom door, and the remains – which were still boiling – spewed out into a big square cavity where the bones were picked out and sent up north, where they were made into blood and bone as a farm fertiliser.

This particular day Gilbert Jones was working in the bone department. When he opened the bottom door, a knuckle bone of the fin was jammed in it. He put a hook in the bone to try to pull it out, and as he was jerking on it the hook ripped out and he fell backwards into the residue.

"I was on the boat taking him to town, and when I pulled off his gumboots his whole foot came away from the bone. It was a godsend when he died."

Billy Gillice, master of the mother ship, *Tuatea,* was killed when dust from blasting powder he had been drying landed on the hot stove in his cabin, causing an explosion. The fourth of these fatalities was the only one that occurred while the men were actively hunting a whale.

In June 1943, Johnny Huntley, gunner aboard the *Awatea,* was in the process of shooting a whale when the locking device of the barrel – which had crystallised over the years – suddenly snapped. Instead of the charge firing the harpoon out, the gun broke open and the cartridge came back. Naturally he was sighting along the barrel, and he was hit in the face. He died shortly afterwards. To prevent further such fatalities the Peranos had the Public Works design a new locking device which made the guns much safer.

The day following this accident, Charlie was behind the gun for the first time. It was a day he never forgot.

"It was a howling sou'easterly in Cook Strait with the wind gusting 40-50 knots in Tory Channel, when two whales were spotted swimming through the channel. I'd never been on a chaser in a hunt, or used the gun, but I had a fair idea. I worried how I'd perform, but – whaling being in my blood – I slipped gradually into it. We managed to kill them fairly quickly. I learnt by experience."

The sea was in Charlie's blood. His great-grandfather, James Heberley (Worser), was the eldest child of John Jacob Heberley, a German, whose name is thought to have originally been Heberlein. About 1790 John Jacob was captured at sea by James Curtis, an English privateer, and taken to Weymouth where he later worked for Curtis, and on 2 January 1809 married his oldest daughter, Elizabeth. In 1817 John Jacob was lost at sea with the *Nancy,* a brig he had commanded for several years.

James left school and found work in a rope-walk, a long piece of ground used for twisting rope. He gave his wages of three shillings a week to his mother to help support his three brothers and a sister.

All the Heberleys had salt water in their veins. It sent James to sea when he was just 11 years old, sailing as an apprentice aboard a fishing boat for two years before breaking his indentures because of his cruel conditions. Arriving at the London docks he shipped on board the *Sarah Margaret* as cabin boy, and for the next two years sailed between London and Hamburg. When he was back in London the captain of the fishing boat found him, and forced him to return to his apprenticeship. This captain of the fishing boat flogged James with a dog fish tail, and even when his mother died he was forbidden to leave the ship to go to her funeral. His pleadings earned him a thrashing with a piece of rope.

Six months later he escaped again, and worked on several ships crossing the Atlantic to North America and the West Indies. After an argument with the ship's mate – because he'd come down from aloft due to the frozen conditions and refused to go back up – he was thrashed. At the first opportunity he left this ship, and his next voyage aboard the *Alexander Henry* in 1825 brought the 16-year-old boy to Sydney. After working on coastal boats around Australia for two years he joined up with a whaling boat, the *Caroline*, chasing the sperm whales around the Pacific and up as far as Japan, for three years.

They caught these whales mainly for the spermacetti, a high quality oil found in the cavity at the back of the head, and used for lighting purposes in the days before gas and electricity, and there was always the possibility of finding ambergris, a highly sought-after waxy substance secreted in the intestine of the sperm whale, and very valuable in the perfume industry.

When James was paid off in Sydney he shipped aboard Jackie Guard's schooner, the *Waterloo*, and arrived in New Zealand in April 1830, to work with Jackie Guard at his whaling station in Te Awaiti.

He sailed aboard the *Tory* with Colonel Wakefield to pilot the New Zealand Company's first ship on its land-buying excursion to Wanganui and New Plymouth, and later became Wellington's first harbour pilot. Some say the name 'Worser' originated from his time as harbour pilot, as when he was asked how the weather was he'd often reply, "It's getting worser and worser."

Maata Te Nahi bore James eight children. Their eldest son John, Charlie's grandfather, whaled from the rowing boats based at Te Awaiti until he set up his own whaling station in Yellaton. Three of John's sons, Charles, Harry and John Thomas, were among the group of Te Awaiti whalers who went down to Campbell Island when Gisborne man Captain W H Tucker, who leased the island, approached the men and asked if they'd work for him on Campbell Island. They were to shear his 7000 sheep and lambs in summer, and hunt whales in winter. John Thomas led the expedition. The Heberleys stayed with the group for two years.

Another of John's sons, Arthur, Charlie's father, whaled in a time-frame that crossed from the rowing boat days to the highly powered fast chasers.

There were five to seven men in a rowing boat. The only method of killing whales was with a long lance sharpened on the end, with a wooden pole on it. The men rowed up alongside the whale and when it 'rounded up' (arched its back and dived straight down, lifting its tail out of the water) they'd dart the lance in behind the ribs into the chest cavity. When the tension came on the rope, the lance swept around, cut the heart, and the whale bled to death.

These whalers took mainly the southern right whale. It was a slower-swimming whale, although renowned for its aggressive nature. The oil was used for lighting but it was the baleen that was greatly prized as it was needed for the boning in women's corsets essential in the fashions of the day. The baleen was on the top jaw, similar to a blade, and grew up to six feet in length. Where the baleen came out of the gum at the back of the jaw, they measured nine to ten inches and were spaced about four inches apart, tapering off towards the nose at the front of the mouth. Inside the blades there was a bristly substance which acted as a sieve, and when the whale took a mouthful of krill – or whale-feed – it closed its mouth, forced the water out through the baleen, wiped its tongue around its mouth, and swallowed the krill. Contrary to popular belief, the spout of a whale isn't the water taken in by the whale while feeding. It is the vapour from its breath.

When a pod of whales were feeding, Charlie said, they'd approach a big patch of krill and swim round in circles beneath them. When they released their breath the bubbles forced the krill into a concentrated heap, and, when the krill were thick enough, the whales turned around, opened their mouths and charged them.

"It's wonderful how nature provides animals with that kind of thinking," Charlie mused.

My father-in-law always believed that – to find out who you were – you had to find out from where you'd come. Charlie was a man of the sea.

Chapter Four

A WHALE IN HIS SIGHTS

Ko ia ka kite.
He who seeks will find.

CHARLIE'S LIFE revolved around the sea. The Oyster Bay farm was bounded by Cook Strait and Tory Channel. Everything was brought in by sea. He earned a living catching crayfish and wet fish. He'd worked at the whaling station beside the sea, and now he was a harpoon-gunner on the whale chaser *Awatea*, standing where Johnny Huntley had stood before his death.

Three times in Charlie's lifetime he fought and won his battle against the sea.

The first battle happened on a day when a southerly storm had kept the whalers at home. One of the chasers was moored in Whekenui Bay, quite safe unless conditions were extreme. Charlie remembers the day vividly.

"The realisation you're going to die stays with you forever."

He recalled the tremendous seas roaring in the bay that day, the wind whipping off their tops, turning the bay into a white foaming mass. Salt spray lifted over the paddocks and slammed against anything in its path. Driftwood, bottles and even pebbles tumbled along the ground until they found somewhere to escape the fury. Trevor Norton, one of the other gunners, and Charlie were crouching together on shore, out of the wind, watching the seas breaking over the bow of the chaser and wondering how long it could survive. Then Gilbert Perano appeared, and asked them if they'd row out to the boat and shift it to a mooring on the other side of the bay.

"We didn't have to, but, being young, I guess we thought we were invincible. Just as we came alongside the chaser a rogue wave swamped the dinghy and rolled us over. The seas were so turbulent you couldn't swim. I kept getting dragged down and swept along the seabed. Just when I'd think I couldn't hold my breath a moment longer I'd find myself at the surface and be able to take a gulp of air before the water closed over me again. My thigh gumboots and smockie – the waterproof coat I wore on the boat – certainly didn't help.

"We were literally dumped on the beach along with all the other rubbish being brought ashore in the storm. When I tried to stand up, I couldn't. My boots, all my clothes and pockets, were full of sand. All of that combined with the weight of water weighed me down."

Once again it seemed as if my father-in-law had the last say as, with tongue in cheek, he said, "After I'd caught my breath I told Gilly to get someone else to rescue their bloody boat."

Soon after, another chaser driven by Gilbert's brother, Joe, who lived in Jacksons Bay further down the channel, arrived on the scene. Joe managed to put a man aboard the stricken chaser, and he drove it across the bay into calmer waters.

Days like that meant the men on the whale chasers had no income. They received two pounds 17 shillings and sixpence a whale or nearly six dollars in today's currency, although of course a dollar would have bought far more then, and whoever sighted a whale that was eventually caught had an extra 11 shillings added to his pay. (Twenty shillings made up one pound.) It made the men on the lookout hill even keener to be the one who called out, "Thar she blows!"

In comparison, a man employed by the Picton Post Office in 1945 earned 11 pounds working a five-day week.

For the next 14 years, from 1943 to 1957, seven days a week from the end of April until early August, looking and hunting for whales in Cook Strait was Charlie's life. His days began before sunrise with the roar of the three whale-chasers' engines splitting the silence of Tory Channel. They cruised slowly across to West Head where the gunner nimbly hooked up the rope floating from a mooring buoy, pulled it over the bow and placed the loop over the gun post. There was always excited anticipation of what the day could bring as the men grabbed their lunch boxes from their boat before rowing to the stony beach. There they pulled the dinghy above high water mark. The narrow track took them over a bridge that joined the lower part of the lookout hill to the mainland, before winding up the side of the rock face to where the lookout was perched, 91 metres above sea level.

The definition of a peninsula is a piece of land almost surrounded by water. West Head is joined to the mainland by a rock arch, one metre wide, nine metres above sea-level, and usually referred to as 'the neck'. The hole the arch formed was referred to as 'the hole in the wall'. For the first few weeks that

Charlie was on the hill, he found that after leaving the beach they had to clamber around the rock face to the Cook Strait side and climb straight up onto the neck.

"If it was blowing we crawled along. But after a few rough days with no sightings, we changed this. Two old railway irons were brought across and we set them parallel into concrete on the rocks on either side of the neck above the high water mark. Next we brought over timber, cut the right size to fit into the grooves of the irons. That bridge made it much quicker."

The lookout 'hut' was an area dug out of the top of hill. There was no protection whatsoever and the men sat there and shivered in the rain. Each had a waterproof coat, gumboots, and a felt hat. It was nothing like the hat businessmen wore and doffed to the ladies they met in the street, but a hat that was pulled so tightly down on their heads that the crease across the top disappeared while the brim was pulled down over their ears.

During that first winter Charlie was on the hill, they put a roof over the dugout and built a stone wall on the southern side of the building to give some shelter from the stormy southerlies one could expect in the middle of winter. The rule was that anyone coming up to the lookout had to pick up a stone from the beach, carry it up the hill and put it on the wall.

"But it was still damned cold. At that time Joe Perano Senior was in Australia and when I suggested we put in a fire I was told in no uncertain terms that the old man wouldn't let us. He reckoned it would make us soft. All we had was a primus to boil up water for a cuppa."

But Charlie was determined he wasn't going to be cold. He carted a 44-gallon drum over to the lookout and made a fireplace out of it with a chimney that came out the back of the drum and straight up through the roof.

"It heated the place up lovely," Charlie said. Joe's two sons, Gilbert and Joe, both told Charlie that he'd have to get rid of it before their father arrived home and came across to the lookout.

"I told them, 'Bugger the old man. I'm not being cold again for him.' And when he came to the lookout after being in Australia, he used to sit as close to it as he could."

In later years, windows that opened out, with wooden shutters to protect them in bad weather, were put across the front of the hut, and the 44-gallon drum fireplace gave way to a Dover stove. Gradually conditions on the hill improved. A wooden floor was laid over the dirt floor, the walls were lined, lockers where the wet weather gear could hang and a shelf where lunch boxes had to be put were built, and a sink was added. And later a radio-telephone was installed in a specially built cupboard in the corner of the whalers' lookout.

Earlier in the war the navy had built a signal station on West Head. They generated electricity with a generator and built a large water storage tank, but the station was never occupied. When the war was over, and the equipment removed, the whalers drained the water from the water tank that had been left and poured a concrete pad in the bottom for an engine bed. The tank became the shed for a three-horse-powered Briggs and Stratton petrol engine with a generator drive to charge the batteries for the new radio-telephone. This allowed communication between the chasers, the lookout, the *Tuatea,* and the factory.

The one thing Charlie missed the most on the lookout hill was a toilet.

"When you get six or seven young chaps on the hill for four months, from daylight to dark unless they are off on a chase, and all needing to find a flax bush to use as a toilet two or three times a day, we created a cesspit. I put up with it for a couple of years. Then one of the other gunners, Trevor Norton, and I decided we'd do something about it."

Every morning in the weeks that followed, Charlie and Trevor brought a piece of 4x2 timber, or an old sheet of corrugated iron, with them to the lookout hill. In reply to all the questions, the two whalers grinned and told them they'd just have to wait and see.

When there were enough materials at the top of the lookout hill, Charlie brought a spade and began to dig a hole. Soon everyone guessed it was going to be a longdrop and all the men helped. When the hole was deep enough, the timber and corrugated iron that Charlie and Trevor had carried up the hill, piece by piece, became a shelter around the hole. The toilet was complete – almost.

"I'd just bought a new tractor for the farm, a Fordson Major, and the horn on that tractor is terrific. With no roads, we didn't need a horn at all, so I took it off, sneaked it over to the lookout and screwed it under the toilet seat which we'd kept loose. I found two copper tacks and drove one on the bottom and one on the top to make a contact.

"Another day I took a 12-volt battery up, and when I was asked what that was for I told them it was a spare for the radio-telephone." The memory made Charlie burst out laughing and I waited impatiently to hear what happened.

"I hid the battery outside in a bush, with a lead from it into the toilet. The idea was, when someone sat on the seat, contact was made, and the horn went off.

"I caught quite a few, but the funniest was Gordon Cuddon."

I remembered Gordon Cuddon, whose engineering company in Blenheim had played a big part in the operation of the Perano whaling station. He was a big man who probably weighed a hundred kilos or more, and he had a stutter.

Cuddon's motto, 'Peranos must come first', hung in the workshop to remind all their engineers that any engineering for the whaling station took precedence over anything else during the whaling season. Gordon Cuddon came down every year to check that everything was running smoothly, and liked to spend a day on the lookout. The whalers believed that he often knew what needed to be changed or repaired before it happened.

"This particular day, we were all waiting for Gordon to use the toilet. Sure enough, about the middle of the afternoon, he went outside, walked along the track, opened the door and went in. Binoculars were abandoned while we all went outside to wait. Next thing the horn roared, what a roar! Poor old Gordon came flying out, his trousers down around his ankles. He fell over, and all he could do was stutter for about five minutes."

Charlie reached into his pocket for a handkerchief and wiped away the tears streaming down his face. "We thought up another trick," he told me through his tears. "We were going to coat a fly swat with golden syrup or treacle and set it up with a spring. When the horn went off the spring was meant to flick the fly swat across a bared bottom. We never quite mastered that one," he sighed.

The planning of such complicated tricks often took more of their time than actually carrying them out. It became a competition to see who could dream up the most outlandish prank. For all their hilarity the seven-man crew on the lookout –

which was made up from a driver and harpoon-gunner of each whale-chaser and one permanent whale-spotter, usually an ex-whaler with sharp eyes and a good knowledge of whaling – all took their jobs seriously. They were well aware that the men across the water at the station depended on them to sight, and then catch, the whales.

Each man made himself a chair from a benzene packing box with a high supporting back which was used as an arm rest. A pair of binoculars – Charlie preferred 7x50s although many used 10x50s – was fitted on the back of the chair by a specially made swivel that had a thumb screw at its base and was used to lock onto the place where the whale was sighted. The whaler sat in a back-to-front position on his own chair and kept a tally of the whales seen and caught by cutting a notch up the back and along the arm rests. He used to rest his arms there, to keep the binoculars steady as he scanned the waters of Cook Strait. These chairs became a part of whaling history as the successful driver and harpoon-gunner of a chase, as well as the person who spotted the whale, carefully added another notch to his chair.

"The sun coming on the water at daylight was the best light to spot a spout," Charlie told me, "so it was a race to get to the hut on clear mornings and get the first sighting.

"We made rules and one was that all lunch boxes had to be put on the shelf. Trevor always raced up the hill to have the first chance to spot a whale in that first light. He'd chuck his tin lunch box on the floor and grab a pair of binoculars. To keep the place tidy, we made another rule. A lunch box on the shelf wasn't allowed to be touched – but if it was lying around," Charlie laughed, "it was fair game.

"We'd have the fire lit with the soldering iron heating up while someone else drilled a hole in the top and bottom of his tin. Then we'd solder a piece of wire right through it on the inside and join the bottom to the top. Sometimes we only had time to run the iron around the lid. If we were still on the hill it could usually be opened, but out on a chase the lunch remained where it was until he reached shore and found something to prise it open."

And there was even a rule made for those looking through the binoculars. No one was allowed to interfere with anyone while they watched but if that person went to sleep or began to relax it was their downfall. Many unsuspecting, although forewarned, visitors to the lookout found themselves flat on their face after standing up and finding bootlaces tied, shoes swapped, or just removed.

These men knew from past experience that the whales they caught migrated from the Antarctic and passed through Cook Strait from May to August. They were heading to the warmer water of the tropics for breeding. They also knew that the whales didn't come in exactly the same place. It depended on the tides – and the tides in Cook Strait can be very fickle.

Normally they ebb – go out – for six hours, then flood – come in – for six hours, but Charlie has seen the tides in Cook Strait run one way for twelve hours. He's seen the flood tide come in from due south, another from the sou'east, and yet another from the east, and blames it on the wind currents further out to sea.

From the lookout at the entrance of Tory Channel, Charlie told me, they had a vision of 27 kilometres to the horizon from Cape Campbell in the south, to Plimmerton on the Kapiti Coast in the north, an estimated area of 101 hectares. All the binoculars were set to cover a full glass from each chair. When a spout was spotted and the whale clearly identified, the Union Jack went up.

Before the days of radio-telephone this flag let the workers at the whaling station know, especially if they'd been idle, to get steam up as a whale could be coming in. It also alerted the crew of the mothership, *Tuatea*, at anchor in Okukari Bay immediately opposite the lookout, that a chase was under way. Years later the tradition was still maintained and the flag was flown until the last whale was caught in Cook Strait.

The 95-foot *Tuatea*, built especially for the Gisborne lightering trade, was used to transport passengers and freight to ships anchored off-shore. She was one of the strongest wooden ships to be built in New Zealand, able to withstand constant banging as she surged against the larger ships. She was built with three skins. One skin ran at 45 degrees diagonally from gun'wale – deck level – to keel, with a second running the opposite way. The third skin which ran in a fore to aft direction covered the first two skins. Inside, four massive stringers ran from bow to stern while the beams were six inches thick and nearly a foot wide. After whaling finished she went to Nelson where she was refitted and used as a trawler. On 23 April 1970, while fishing off the Otago coast, the *Tuatea* caught fire. No lives were lost in the blaze but the *Tuatea* was a total loss.

As the mother ship, she was usually sent out first, particularly if the whale sighted was still well south of the lookout heading north, or the visibility was bad. One of her crew would climb up into the crow's nest and guide the chasers to the whale.

Meanwhile the person on the hill who'd seen the spout locked his binoculars onto the whale and gave directions to the others. If it was on the horizon he'd guide them by cloud formations, or if it was in line with the North Island he'd describe a peak or a distinct part of the coastline. All the binoculars were then set and locked one glass vision ahead.

"That allowed us to determine the rate the whale was travelling and the length of time between each spouting. Normally a humpback stayed down about 10 minutes. He'd come up, spout three times, take a deep breath and go down again for another sounding."

"From this we worked out the direction and speed it was travelling. Its distance from the lookout hill was worked out only by experience. But once we had a fair idea, the race began."

Wet weather gear and lunchboxes were grabbed – that was another rule. If anyone left his lunch behind, no one shared their lunch with that person. They decided it was better if one man starved than if two men went hungry. The boat crews ran down the track in single file and the first person to the dinghy dragged it to the sea and took the oars. He'd row to his own boat first, then the two men would leap out, start the engine, throw off the mooring line and head out in the general direction of the last sighting.

As Charlie continued, his familiar thrust-out chin tautened the skin on his jawline. It accentuated the protruding white scar – a legacy of a whale hunt – and I felt, rather than heard, the excitement in my father-in-law's voice as he emphasised that whaling was one of the most dangerous and yet one of the most exciting jobs a young man could take on. Their lives were at risk whenever they'd go out on a chase to hunt and kill a whale. Whales weigh approximately one tonne a foot, and this equates to being ten times heavier than a whale chaser.

There was no mechanical gear to haul in the whales once they were harpooned. It was all done by man power. The arthritis in Charlie's shoulder and elbow seemed forgotten as he rubbed his callused hands over his knees. He was once again standing on the for'ard deck of a whale-chaser, knees braced against the pounding of the boat as it ploughed through the seas at 30 miles per hour.

A whale chaser was engined with a 300-400-horse-power petrol motor for speed and a very fast pick-up, although in latter years a high-revving diesel engine was used with similar capabilities. The 36-foot, V-bottom, planing hull had two watertight bulkheads which divided the hull into three compartments. This allowed flotation even if two-thirds of the boat was damaged. There was no superstructure because anything bulky on the cabin top, apart from a small windscreen to protect the driver, obstructed his vision and got in the way when he was working gear.

The whole of the cabin space was taken up with the boat's engine. When it was running it was so noisy that all communication between the driver and the gunner was by hand signals. A stop signal given by the man on the bow definitely meant stop. A forward hand movement was come ahead, while turning the hand in the opposite direction indicated to the driver to reverse, but if the agitated gunner needed more speed a few jumps on the bow of the boat soon had the boat going faster.

"We all had our own methods of communication, but the driver-gunner relationship was very important. We worked as one unit."

As the boats charged out in the direction of the whale, the man left on the lookout went outside, and watched their progress. When the boats were far enough out he'd take the dry tussock he'd gathered and brought over to the hill that morning, and set a fire. When the crews were far enough out he'd light the fire until it smoked. If they were too far north, he'd light another south of the first and they'd know to steam in a southly direction. It was the same procedure if the boats were too far south – a fire was lit to the north of the first. The fire was extinguished when they were on the spot.

"It was pretty hit and miss. But it worked. When we got the radio-telephones it made it much easier a s we could be directed straight to the whale."

The harpoon guns had no recoil system, and when the gun was fired the only thing that took the jar was the flexibility of the gunpost the gun was mounted on. This was constructed

58

from three laminations of 6x2-inch hardwood, bolted together. The actual guns were made from the cut-down barrels of Bofor anti-aircraft guns with the rifling removed, and the stock was built at the Anchor Foundry Company in Nelson. It had a similar action to a shotgun – it broke open and the two and a half inch-long brass cartridge was loaded into the breech.

The gunner was responsible for all the explosives used on the boat. These were kept in the for'ward compartment of the chaser, and accessed through a hatch in the deck in front of the engine. Five or six loaded cartridges, detonators, gelignite, time fuses, two preserving jars of blasting powder and their own 'tools' they used to reload the gun cartridges, all these were stored in a wooden chest. Normally there were three or four bombs loaded and stored on racks along with spare harpoons and heads. Most importantly, the cartridges for the guns had to be kept loaded as more than one harpoon was often shot from the gun in one chase. In the confines of his armoury the gunner first cut the cap off the end of a shotgun cartridge and poked it into the back of the brass cartridge. Then he shook a little bit of the powder on top of the cap as a primer charge before filling the rest of the cartridge with blasting powder. Down on his hands and knees, he stood the cartridge on its end, and with his 'tool', (usually a piece of dried manuka) which was the size of the inside housing, he tapped down the powder until it was firm. Grease smeared over the blasting powder sealed it before it was placed in the gun.

A wad made from newspaper was poked down the barrel and rammed in, using a one and a half inch piece of pipe.

"Five pages of *The Weekly News* was perfect," Charlie remembered. "The harpoon was pushed down the front of the barrel as far as the wad, and the gun was ready. And the reason for the paper," my father-in-law explained, "was when the gun went off the explosion forced the wad with the harpoon out of the barrel. On a rough day we'd usually only get a long range shot, so we'd hammer the wad down extra hard. It gave us more range but a lot more recoil. It kicked like a mule and hurt like hell."

At the end of the day the harpoon was taken out and a canvas gun cover tied down over the gun.

The harpoon had a diamond-shaped explosive head with a seven-second delay time-fuse which was activated by the concussion of the gun. More than once, on a rough day, Charlie accidentally set the time fuse off as he struggled to put the harpoon down the gun. The pounding of the boat could also set it off. "And once you saw smoke coming out, you pulled the trigger and fired the harpoon overboard pretty smartly."

Three toggles that acted similarly to a barb on a fish hook lay back against the shank of the harpoon. When these entered the whale and the weight came on the rope, the toggles hooked and spread out, holding the harpoon under the blubber. The explosive head of the harpoon often slowed the whale down but once the whale was harpooned it was killed as quickly as possible. Now the three chasers worked as a team. If there were two or three whales together, one had to be dealt with before catching the next, to prevent tangled ropes, rammed boats or injured men. The gunner on the chaser that was fast to the whale, (that is, that had a harpoon in it), gave directions to the other two chasers who steamed in closer. As the whale towed the boat along, the gunner on the boat which was fast to it watched the angle of the rope. If it was straight down he knew the whale was sounding but once the rope started to rise he knew by its angle how far it was from the surface. Using his hand he indicated the angle of the rope to the other crews, and as soon as it surfaced the closest boat darted the first bomb in behind the kidneys. It made the whale very sluggish and it spouted blood.

The bomb, made by the whalers, consisted of one and a half plugs of gelignite encased in a piece of one-inch pipe, with one end cut on an angle and sharpened, and the other threaded to allow a bomb pole to be screwed in. A double electric wire ran from the bomb back to the rail alongside the driver. As soon as the bomb was in place he grabbed the two ends, touched them on the terminals by the windscreen, and the bomb exploded. This was immediately followed by an air spear placed into the whale's throat or stomach to prevent its sinking. The air came from an air compressor driven off a clutch on the front end of the engine, and passed through a garden hose which had a sharpened half-inch pipe with a few holes in the end to allow the air to flow through.

A second bomb at the back of the neck, close to the vertebrae, killed the whale instantly.

"We used both hands to throw the bomb. When you're working in a 30-knot northerly with a two-to three-metre swell, it took a bit of holding on up there. I had to hook Trevor Norton up one day. A wave hit the side of the boat just as he darted in a bomb, and he followed the bomb. Fortunately he was well clear of the whale, and only his pride was hurt."

After the whale was dead the *Tuatea* took over and took it back to the factory for processing. Some days it meant a long tow for the *Tuatea,* but other days, if whales were spotted two or three miles off Tory Channel and it was flood tide, the chasers tried to herd them in through the channel and bring them closer to the whaling station.

The three chasers steamed out, and after one was fast to one of the whales the remaining boats kept either side of the pod and worked the boats in the same way as a shepherd works a heading dog to drive a mob of sheep through a gate. The same – except in this case it was whales, and they were being led to the slaughter.

After a chase, as long as there were still daylight hours left, the chasers headed back to the lookout hill where the man left behind would have the kettle boiling for a cup of tea. The successful crew added another notch on their chairs. Then once again, with eyes as sharp as the screeching seabirds that skimmed above the surface of the sea in their unceasing search for food, the men swept their binoculars over the sea from their lookout high above the waters of Cook Strait.

Chapter Five

"THAR SHE BLOWS!"

Ki a koe, e Maru. Mau e tiaki.
To you o Maru. Protect me.

"THE MOMENT a whale was spotted, our blood started to boil. You'd be all hyped up – like the All Blacks running out on a rugby field at the start of a test match. It was more like a sport than a job. We knew the dangers and were usually wet and cold from daylight to dark, no matter what clothing we wore. But it was all part of it. It'd been my ambition to be on a chaser and I know many of the young blokes at the station would have given their right arm to be in my place."

Once the driver turned that key, slipped the engine into gear and eased the throttle forward, the two men aboard were focused on one thing – the chase ahead. For the gunner it was a race against time as he hurried to ready his gear while still in the shelter of the land. At the end of the previous hunt, the first 20-25 fathoms of a two-inch nylon rope, known as the boxline and spliced on the end of the harpoon shank, had been hung over the bow rails to dry. It allowed enough slack for the expulsion of the harpoon from the gun to the whale.

Now, as the boat powered ahead, the gunner took it from the rails and coiled it on the for'ward deck in front of the gun. From there the rope ran through the fairlead, down the side deck to a six-inch diameter hardwood bollard alongside the driver. The remaining 200-300 fathoms were stowed in the back hatch until needed. The driver controlled the rope by keeping two or three running turns on the bollard, playing it out when a whale sounded. Charlie had seen smoke rising from the bollard as the rope ran out, and by the end of a season it usually needed to be replaced, because the wood was almost burnt through.

The gunner then checked his remaining gear, removed the cover from the gun and pushed the harpoon down the barrel. He was ready.

"I've been at the gun when the boat has hit a big sea that's washed me away from the gun, almost to the stern of the boat.

It certainly got the adrenalin flowing and no doubt made me hang on tighter.

"Quite often when we've been chasing a whale, they'd swim shallow and you could see their dark image under the water. You'd have to really concentrate on it because if you took your eyes off it you lost it. There was keen competition between the boats and we'd all be trying to follow the shadow, waiting for it to spout. Those times we made out we couldn't see it – while all the time we'd be giving our coded signals to our driver.

"This particular day Gilbert and I were following a pair of quite big whales north of the Brothers. It was a fine day and I'd picked up the image of the outside one but was so intent on giving secret signals to guide my driver closer to the whale I didn't see its mate which was swimming closest to us. It came up and put its nose through the bottom of the boat and when it slid back down again it'd left some skin and a couple of barnacles on the side of the engine and a hole about six feet by two feet.

"She began to go down immediately and would've sunk without those watertight bulkheads. Those whales were in luck that day as we needed the other two chasers to tow us back to the factory."

Hardly a year passed that the boats weren't involved in a collision with a whale, and now as Charlie finished one story he raced on to another.

"Gilbert and I were working a couple of whales about seven miles out. A stiff nor'wester made the sea quite choppy with a one and a half-metre swell. This whale was thrashing around and we were working in really close to it when it gave us a clout on the bow that punched a hole two or three feet in diameter just under the flare of the boat above the waterline. We had a quick check, decided we'd be OK and finished the job.

"On the way home, water started to slop in the hole. There was nothing on the boat to patch it with so I became like the little boy in Holland who put his finger in a hole in the dyke and saved a town. Except I put my backside in the hole, and saved a chaser."

What usually happened was that when the driver knew his gunner was ready he concentrated on the task ahead. Perhaps their last sighting of the whale, before they'd left the lookout hill, had been five miles out, in line with Terawhiti on the Tokori line and travelling north. In that case, once clear of the channel entrance, he headed just north of Tarawhiti and cruised out about four miles to where he could expect to see the whale if they were on the correct course, or obtain more directions from the man on the lookout.

Once it was sighted, the hunt was on. Now it was boat against boat, man against whale. To determine when and where the whale would next spout was an art. The driver would quietly idle his chaser through the water at a speed of four or five knots, keeping a similar speed to their quarry. The whale hunters knew the whale would surface within six to seven minutes, spout (take a breath), and continue swimming just below the surface, coming up to spout another two or three times before it rounded up. The whalers' aim was to get reasonably close for the first spout, and, if the gunner missed the first time, he knew he had two or three more chances before the whale rounded up and sounded again.

From the bow the gunner watched. His eyes were locked on the image of the whale swimming just beneath the surface. It had spouted twice and he knew this could be the last spout before it rounded up. Using their own code of signals, the gunner guided his driver closer. As the whale surfaced to spout, he took aim and the harpoon burst from the gun. The boxline snaked off the deck and the harpoon embedded itself in the blubber. The whale sounded, the rope screamed out the back hatch and the driver let it run, controlling it by the running turns he'd taken on the bollard beside him.

The whale could take out 60 to 80 fathoms in that first dive. The boats were accustomed to play the whale in the same way a fisherman uses a rod to land a trout. Being a mammal, the whale had to come up for air and as it came up the gunner pulled the slack in by hand, while the driver brought the boat up at the correct speed, taking care not to run over the rope.

"We'd have it almost in, and down it'd dive again. When a whale was running hard, each time it dived it'd take out 40 or 50 fathoms. The tension on the rope quite often dragged the bow down to water level, but if the driver allowed too much tension the harpoon could be pulled out. Too much slack — and the whale would get too far away and we'd lose control of it."

Charlie has never forgotten what it was like to stand on the bow in a 20- or 30-knot wind with seas breaking over him as the boat charged into a head sea.

"There were no railings for'ard of the gun post and as I hauled in the rope the only way I could keep my feet on the deck was to push back hard against the front of the gunpost."

And he has never forgotten the day of one horrific near-disaster when he stood on the rope that was fast to a running whale, and got a loop around his foot. He quickly fell on his back and grabbed the gunpost. He knew he had to go with the rope or have his leg pulled off. The question of how he'd fit through the two-inch fairlead filled his mind as he tried to free himself. Most fortunately for him, on that particular day he was wearing short gumboots and he managed to wriggle his foot out before the gumboot smacked against the fairlead and gradually disintegrated as it was dragged out through the fairlead by the whale on the other end of the rope.

As soon as the whale surfaced close enough, one of the boats landed the first bomb in behind the kidneys, making it very sick. Before it could round up, the airspear was thrown and the dying whale was pumped up with air so it wouldn't sink when the final bomb, placed in the base of its vertebrae, killed it.

The strop was then put on and the whale was taken over by the *Tuatea* to bring it back into Tory Channel to the factory at Fishing Bay.

It was this stage of a whale hunt that was the cause of Charlie's second great battle against the sea.

This particular chase had involved a pod of five whales. Gilbert and Charlie had caught the first whale and hurried to get a strop in its fluke to pass it over to the mother ship so they could continue the chase for the others. Charlie thought it was dead, and as he leaned on his stomach over the side of the boat to cut a hole in its fluke for the strop, the whale lashed out, breaking the rope holding it, and taking Charlie with it. He found himself in the water five metres away from the boat, alongside the whale. Because he was so close when the whale kicked to propel itself through the water, the blow Charlie received from its return kick wasn't so hard.

"The whale struck me across the shoulders and drove me down deep. It was a peculiar feeling with all the bubbles and froth. I couldn't see a thing, and at some stage I was hit on the jaw. I don't remember how many times I was pushed down." Charlie's main thought was, am I going to try and get to the surface and risk another smack, or dive deeper?

Fortunately, as the whale kicked it propelled itself forward, and my father-in-law was able to come to the surface. He was badly bruised around the back of his head and his jawbone remained sore for months until a piece of broken bone finally worked its way out. "By God, it was frightening down there."

My father-in-law made light of his second brush with death. But only recently I spoke with Reg Jackson, a gunner on one of the other boats and who was there that day.

"We thought Charlie was gone," he said. "It was a 50-foot bull whale, and he was so stirred up we couldn't get near him. Every time the bull threshed his tail he pushed Charlie under. Did this four or five times. The last time he went under we thought he'd had it – and when he surfaced he was lying face down in the sea, and limp. Max Kenny, a gunner off the other boat, managed to hook him in the shoulder with a boathook and pull him aboard. He was as close to death as anyone I've ever seen on the chasers. Gilbert wanted to bring him home but he refused."

Charlie declared he remembered every detail of that day. Of course he wasn't going to give up, and be taken home. There were four more whales to be caught in that pod. Bruised, wet and cold, he rummaged through a bag of engine rags Gilbert had brought to the boat. Among them was an old dress which his wife Nan no longer wore. For the rest of that day, Charlie stood at the gun, wearing Nan's discarded dress and Gilbert's jersey with his legs through its arms and the bottom rib band pulled up to his waist.

"And I added three notches to my chair."

Chapter Six

TO OKUKARI

Noku te whenua, o oku tupuna.
The land is mine, inherited from my ancestors.

EACH of those notches meant another two pounds 17 shillings and sixpence in Charlie's pay packet at the end of a season. A total of 175 whales had been caught in the first two seasons Charlie was on the gun. His chair had the most notches for the 1944 season – he could look forward to the 1945 season, "but I wanted to be able to walk on my own land."

Charlie's brother Jim had been farming Okukari since 1941. Jim's decision to sell the farm in 1945 and move to the city allowed Charlie's dream to come about.

On a fine day with no wind, Charlie and Ruby left Whekenui, the place they'd made home for the last two years, and ferried all their possessions across the bay to Okukari: furniture, the contents of a linen cupboard, blankets and mattresses, kitchen items, food, clothes, books and toys and a treadle sewing machine that had already been dropped into the sea in their first move to Te Awaiti – but it still went. Everything had to be rowed ashore, then carried to the top of the white sandy beach that curved from the rocky promontory on the eastern side, across the front of the woolshed, around a rocky point and on into Whekenui Bay.

There was no path from the beach to the house, which was built a hundred metres up from the beach – only a sheep track that wound its way through two-metre-high gorse bushes. While Charlie plied between Whekenui and Okukari, Ruby, with Donna, Jocelyn and Joe, began carting whatever they could manage up to the house.

"That night we sat in our own kitchen, eating our own food cooked on our own wood and coal range by the light of a candle. I was 27 years old and I couldn't wait for daylight, to begin work on our land."

For the next 34 years Charlie took care of his land. He discovered its past, lived in its present, and, as continuing generations remained at Okukari, he rejoiced in its future. He could recite its history as well as he could recite his whakapapa, and, just as he brought the history alive for me, I try to keep it alive for my grandchildren too.

I was always led to believe Okukari meant 'mad dog', but during my research I discovered that it also meant 'place of a young bird', the translation I naturally prefer. It is on the edge of Cook Strait at the very centre, the very place, where New Zealand's history began. It was there that, in 950 AD, Kupe, the Hawaiiki chief and navigator, made landfall.

Maori mythology tells how Kupe was fishing off Tahiti and became angry when a giant octopus known as Te Wheke o Muturangi kept stealing the bait off his line. He chased it across the Pacific into Cook Strait, eventually cornering and killing it near the entrance of Tory Channel at Whekenui. The name, Whekenui, means large octopus. Its blood stained the waters of Tory Channel so Kupe named the channel Kura-te-au (the red current). [Ref. *Kei Puta te Wairau,* W J Elvy, p 12. Whitcombe and Tombs 1957.]

Charlie believed Kupe probably saw whale-feed or krill which are actually the larvae of several species of red crustaceans. They come into the channel at times in vast shoals, turning the sea red.

There is evidence that the first inhabitants of Okukari were the Moriori people. Remains of their pit dwellings can still be sighted and stone implements, that experts have told us are pre-Maori, have been found. In the 1940s Charlie found a skeleton buried in the bank above the beach, and in 1975 our son James unearthed one when he was digging a track in the bank down to the beach. Both were sitting with their legs folded against their chests, looking out to sea. It is believed that in pre-European times when a Moriori died he was buried in a squatting position looking out to sea so he could draw the blackfish or pilot whales in to shore. The stranded fish were eaten over a long period. Other skeletons, believed to be from a race before the Maori had been discovered in the Kenepuru, were interred in the same manner. [Ref. *Old Marlborough,* T Lindsay Buick p 75. Hart and Keeling 1900.]

The whakapapa of the Moriori people on the Chatham Islands tells how their ancestors formerly lived at Arapawa but were driven from the Sounds by the invasions from the north. [Ibid p 57.] The first canoe the Moriori can trace their whakapapa back to was Kahu's. One version of the story says Kahu arrived at Kaingaroa Harbour and planted his fern-root and a kumara. The kumara didn't grow. This was the first line of his karakia (call): *Kumara no Aropawa i ko.* The translation, kumara from distant Aropawa, could mean that the kumara was brought from Aropawa, the ancient name of the north part of the Middle Island of New Zealand, or it could have been brought from Hawaiiki. [Ref. Appendices, 3. Moriori migration traditions. *Moriori,* Michael King p 205 & 213. Viking1989.]

About the year 1400, Tumata Kokiri, a Taupo chief, brought his tribe, the Waitara, across Ruakawa Moana – Cook Strait – and settled on Arapawa Island or Arapaoa – to turn towards the smoke – Island, as it was first named, because of the mist and low cloud that frequently cloaks the high hills. When the canoes left the North Island they knew they had to 'turn towards the smoke'.

Other tribes followed, and by 1769 when Captain Cook first arrived in New Zealand and named Ship Cove in Queen Charlotte Sound, there were the Rangitane, Ngatira and Ngatikuri. On his second voyage to New Zealand, Cook left his boat in Ship Cove and took his eight-oared pinnace through Tory Channel. In his journal he referred to a number of pa built on its shores.

There was a fortified pa at Okukari. When Charlie cleared the paddocks of gorse, the rectangle outline of the pa was clearly visible. Over the years, ploughing and erosion have removed all signs of it but many Maori artefacts have been found. After a heavy rain, slips come down off the bank that edges the track leading from the beach to the house, exposing patches of dark soil where the palisade posts have rotted in the ground. Along the top of the bank at the eastern end of the beach, a trench dug by the Maori is clearly visible. The years have built up the inside but the mounds of soil on each side make it three feet deep.

On 31 October 1839, Wakefield anchored his ship, *Tory,* in East Bay on the Queen Charlotte side of Arapawa Island. He rowed ashore to Wharehunga and in the company of a Waikanae chief, Wiremu Kingi Te Rangitaake, walked over the island to Okukari. Coming in sight of Okukari, the chief ordered Wakefield and his men to discharge their guns, and the natives at Okukari fired their muskets in response. When Wakefield reached the beach he found 200 men preparing for war against

Ngati Ruakawa at Waikanae. After the greetings a tangi began in honour of Te Rangitaake's arrival and their friends who had fallen in the battle of Kuititanga a fortnight earlier, on 16 October. [Ref. *Wakefield Dispatches* Supplementary Information 1839 p 137.]

The Reverend Octavius Hadfield wrote about Okukari to the Church Missionary Society on 1 February 1841. This is from his letter:

In December last I made a visit to the opposite side of the Straits which was most interesting. I crossed in my boat and reached Queen Charlotte Sound where I was well received by the natives. These people belong to the Ngatiawa tribe and are connected and related to the people among whom I live at Waikanae. There I found several well built places of worship, one especially at Okukari about sixty feet in length. At this place is a good school which I established about six months before. About eighty adults attend daily. They many times asked me whether there was no minister to live among them. I could only tell them that if they believed the gospel the Lord would provide for them.

The following July the Reverend Hadfield made the crossing again. He preached to a congregation of 900 and baptised 17. He suggested to the Church Missionary Society that Okukari would be a very good station for a missionary.

Christianity continued to expand in the Queen Charlotte Sound. In March 1842 Hadfield again rowed across Cook Strait and once more preached. This time his congregation was of 700. He also baptised 54 adults and children, and administered communion to 28. And in his report for the year ending July 1843 he gave a glowing account of the 12 days he'd spent at Okukari, preaching to 200 people daily, and more than 700 on each of the two Sundays. [These facts are taken from letters written by Hadfield from Kapiti to the Church Missionary Society,1840-1843.]

After Hadfield, the Reverend Charles Lucas Reay, an Anglican minister, visited Okukari and from September 1843 to April 1846 he baptised 76 and performed three marriages.

Today there is no sign of this church where so many gathered to worship. Yet it was a great building, and linked to the Maori church at Waikanae, and Otaki's famous Rangiatea church which was burnt to the ground on 7 October 1995. All were considered outstanding places of worship in Hadfield's extensive district. [Ref. *Rangiatea,* E Ramsden pp 292-293. Reed 1951.]

As a young man, Augustus Adolphus Alexander Hood had arrived in Wellington as a Wakefield Company immigrant aboard the *Slain's Castle* in 1841, where he was employed covering houses with zinc for 15 shillings per week. Later Captain Hood traded in the Marlborough Sounds, Nelson and Wellington with the schooner *Augusta.* In 1853 he set up a whale fishery at Okukari. [Ref. *Linkwater, A History.* Geoffrey Wilson p 68. Marlborough Express Printing Works 1962.] On one of his trips across Cook Strait he brought Archdeacon John Salisbury and his brother through Tory Channel on their way to Nelson. The brothers describe coming into a cove (Okukari) where Hood lived and being met by a native canoe. Hood spoke with the natives and arranged for them to take the brothers by canoe to Anakiwa from where they would walk to Nelson. [Ref. *After Many Days,* John Park Salisbury. Harrison and Sons 1907.]

Captain Hood married an 18-year-old English girl, Carolina Bertha Sawyer, at Nelson in 1855 and came to live in Okukari. A daughter, born in 1858, drowned at Okukari, and her grave is on a mound in a paddock, 200 metres from the beach.

The first Crown grant for land in Okukari was issued to Captain Hood on 20 May 1858, and the second in 1863. His trading business kept him away for long periods of time so he employed J A R Greensill to manage his sheep and cattle station. His house was licensed in 1864 and 1865.

Carolina was widowed in 1866 when her husband was found drowned at The Grove near Picton. Fourteen months later Goodwin George Hood, Carolina's brother-in-law, established his right to his brother's estate, leaving Carolina destitute. The unfortunate Carolina left Okukari in September 1871.

Another family lived in Okukari from 1865 until 1882. Charles Gomaz, of Portuguese descent, had been living at Te Awaiti and was a harpoonist on the *Swiftsure* (now in the Canterbury Museum) for three years. He met Mary Ann Maxted who had grown up in Blenheim, and they were married at the Picton Registry Office before coming to live at Okukari, where they had seven children.

Okukari Bay is one of the windiest in this area. To the sou'east the low neck below the lookout, combined with the low saddle to the north, funnel the wind from either direction. I have seen the northerly wind in this bay put grown men on their hands and knees, while four or five kilometres down the channel it can be calm. It is the same in a southerly or sou'east. Okukari's proximity to Cook Strait brings in heavy seas that crash up on the beach, while willy-waws pick up salt-laden spray and carry it up the 100 acres of flat land, leaving the grass as burnt as if a fire had swept through. In one such terrible storm, Charlie lost 4000 two-year-old pine trees that he'd grown for shelter belts.

And it was a southerly storm that gave Okukari its only known shipwreck when, on 4 March 1878, the *Canterbury*, a 59.2-foot schooner en route from Pelorus Sound to Wellington, dragged her anchors and was blown ashore where she broke up on a pile of rocks now called the Canterbury Rocks, in the middle of the beach. Some of the older people believe the pile of rocks is the iron ballast from the wrecked ship. The crew were forced to abandon ship and seek shelter ashore, but there was no loss of life.

In Charlie's early years at Okukari, a bad southerly storm washed most of the sand off the beach, leaving the skeleton of the *Canterbury* exposed. History – our heritage – wasn't nearly as important at that time as was a fence to keep in the first Romney sheep Charlie had bought. My father-in-law chopped bits out of the *Canterbury*, and the oak fence posts lasted for years.

Charles Godfrey seems to be the next occupier of land in Okukari. The Runholders' and Sheepowners' Directory, in *Wise's New Zealand Directory of 1880-81,* states that Charles Godfrey of Okukari owned 612 sheep which he ran on Bayonets Run, a small piece of land between Okukari and Whekenui, and leased from its Maori owners. The Government sheep returns for 1885 record Godfrey as having 660 sheep. He also had some sheep that were infected with scab, with the date of clean order listed as 20 January 1885. He was compensated two shillings and sixpence a head for any sheep that had to be destroyed, but by 1891, with the destruction of infected sheep and the containing and eradication of wild sheep, New Zealand was free of the disease.

On 14 June 1897 a lease in perpetuity from the Crown was issued to Charles Godfrey for the 126 acres of Bayonets Run. He paid two pounds four shillings and sixpence annually. In that same period, Tom Mailing and Bob Temple farmed the other two blocks of Okukari, running 515 sheep. Bob Temple's father, Captain E F Temple, was an artist of some repute. Today I have copies of some of his paintings, showing Okukari Bay more than 100 years ago. One shows the house Charlie and Ruby first lived in.

On New Year's Day 1881, the two leading-light beacons built in Whekenui Bay, that still guide ships through the entrance of Tory Channel, were lit for the first time. Charles Godfrey was appointed keeper, a position he held until one week before he died in 1907. Every evening he rowed or walked to Whekenui and lit the kerosene lights, returning in the morning to extinguish them. Charles is buried with his parents, Daniel and Emma, near the boundary of Bayonets Run, above the lagoon on the flat of Okukari. On the white marble stone, words, inlaid in lead, read:

Light in the Darkness Sailor
Brightly Gleams Our Father's Mercy
To Send A Gleam Across The Wave.

The early settlers came to a land covered mainly with beech, tree fern, manuka and vines while totara, rimu, kahikatea, miro and matai towered above the canopy. Bush fellers came in and cleared the land, leaving bridle tracks that link up many of the bays in the Sounds today. Cutting out scrub, we discovered the remains of an old fireplace built on a flat piece of land near a creek. It was easy to shut out the day's sounds of scrub cutters and motor bikes, and slip back into an earlier century when men camped out because it was too far to walk home, and felled the trees using saws and axes. But our fireplace didn't compare with the discovery by the bush fellers of an unfinished Maori canoe that had obviously had a fire lit in it to hollow out the centre. They made an effort to look after it and left the trees around it standing, but during a storm a large tree fell and smashed it.

George and Florence Kenny purchased 337 acres from Mr Temple for 1250 pounds. By 1901 they were running 796 half-breed sheep on the land. In 1905 George Kenny leased another 833 acres from the Crown for 999 years at 16 pounds 13 shillings and fourpence a year. As well as running sheep the Kennys milked 14 to 20 cows. The cream was separated and stored in cream cans in holes dug out of the creek until it was sent in to Picton on the weekly mail boat.

After Charles Godfrey died, George paid 100 pounds to Charles's widow, Emily, for the lease of Bayonets Run and an increased rent to the Crown of two pounds 10 shillings and fourpence a year. George Kenny took over the leading-light beacons and was paid 100 pounds a year. He maintained them with, in later years, his sons Oswald and Max, until 1930 when batteries were installed and the lights became automatic.

In 1908 another boat came close to joining the *Canterbury* as a wreck on the beach at Okukari. *Old Jack* was built at Kakapo Bay for Jack Guard around 1873. It was 45 feet long with a beam of 13 feet. Jack Guard later sold it to Arthur Thomas Daken who used it to carry timber from Havelock to Blenheim and manuka firewood from East Bay in the Queen Charlotte Sound to Picton. It was sold again and taken to Nelson where it was converted to steam and used for trawling. By 1908 it was owned by the Picton builders and timber merchants, C A Smith, and once again carrying timber from Havelock to Picton. While on one of these trips it came in a southerly gale, and the crew sought shelter in Okukari Bay. The anchors dragged and *Old Jack* came ashore and was holed on the Canterbury Rocks. It was retrieved and put up for tender, spending the rest of its days as a cargo boat trading between Port Underwood, Blenheim, Picton and Wellington. It was used in commercial fishing and salvage work and was involved in the attempted rescue of Charlie's brother Joe's fishing boat, *Crescent,* when this boat foundered off the Wellington coast in 1930.

In the December 1910 Public Schools List of Marlborough, Okukari is listed as having five students with a Miss C R Kirk as mistress on a salary of 30 pounds and a lodging allowance of 17 pounds. Five children attended during 1911 but in 1912 the numbers dropped to three, with a comment that there were Maori children in attendance. The school remained on the

Public Schools List until December 1913 when the roll had fallen to two and it apparently closed.

Land clearing continued and in 1919 Okukari was running 2050 sheep. Lambing was always hard with the unpredictable weather often killing many of the new-born lambs. One such time was on 16 September 1926 when a southerly storm covered Okukari with a blanket of snow.

Marlborough Express. Saturday 18 September 1926. Our Sounds correspondent writes:

'August went out with a wet and cold snap, and, although we have had several warm days, the weather has been anything but satisfactory for lambing. A heavy fall of snow on Thursday 16 September 1926 was very hard on stock. It was the heaviest fall – in fact one of the very few snowstorms the writer has ever seen in the Sounds.'

At this time the Kennys had one of the few phones on Arapawa Island. When the *Tamahine* entered Tory Channel the Kennys were responsible for ringing through to the Picton ferry wharf to let them know the ship was in Tory Channel so they could estimate her arrival time in Picton. In a photograph of the homestead taken between 1934-1941 I noticed a flagpole on the front lawn. I was told a flag was raised when the Peranos at Whekenui were wanted on the phone. When the flag was noticed, someone would come over to Okukari.

When George Kenny's two sons Max and Oswald finished their schooling they came home and worked on the farm but in the 1930s Max worked at the whaling station, and later worked alongside Charlie as a harpoon gunner. Recently Max's son, Ian, who was five when the family left Okukari, came back to the bay and reminisced. He told us how he and his father had gone down to the woolshed one morning and discovered a large hole in the roof and floor, with shattered timber strewn everywhere. Buried in the dirt was a large meteorite. "I can remember going outside, looking up in the sky and thinking what a great shot."

In 1941, when Charlie's brother Jim bought Okukari, he was the first Heberley to come back to the land that his Maori ancestors had first settled on when they arrived in the South Island.

This heritage – 2000 acres – became Charlie's in 1945. "Wherever I looked, I faced the past. The pits, the pa, stone fireplaces, greenstone and stone artifacts, the marked graves, the unmarked graves – they were all a part of Okukari."

By now much of the land was covered in secondary growth. This, and gorse with trunks like trees, covered the 100 acres of flat land from the beach to the foothills. With no electricity, no radio or television, it became the family's evening entertainment to go up the flat with a bucket of kerosene and a dried gorse stick each, to burn the gorse. The thick knobbled trunks that were left standing were Ruby's source of wood for the coal range in the first months. Up on the hills, grass fought with gorse, scrub and tawhini, and the odd Captain Cookers with their distinguishing black and tan markings and long snouts, said to be descendants of the pigs Captain Cook liberated on the island.

Susie the pig arrived home buried in Charlie's jersey. He'd disturbed a sow with her litter as he was cutting bush, and caught one of her piglets. In the warm kitchen small hands reached out to stroke the trembling body as Ruby made up some colostrum milk of cow's milk, sugar, egg and cod liver oil, the mix she gave to new-born motherless lambs. Susie progressed from using an eye dropper to a bowl, and from sleeping in a shoe box to a wooden apple box, and made herself a family member. She played tag, winning every game when a nip meant a win. As soon as she saw anyone in a bathing suit she raced them to the beach where she'd wade out into the sea. When she was too big for the apple case, a sty became Susie's new home, and she was allowed out only when someone was able to keep an eye on her.

With their first wool cheque averaging 20 pounds per bale, Charlie bought a Fordson Major, the same tractor that supplied the horn for the toilet seat on the lookout. Once the gorse was burnt, Charlie ploughed, harrowed, then seeded the flats. He made the fences stock-proof, and for shelter belts he planted the 4000 pine trees that were later wiped out in a southerly storm.

But as much as Charlie wanted to be working on his land, he knew a great deal needed to be done both inside and outside their house. There were no paths or gardens, only deep tracks that became rivers of mud whenever it rained. Ruby's wash house was in an old shed at the back of the house. The double wooden tubs were green and slimy and every time she lit the copper Ruby had to scramble down a sheep track, impossible to stand up on after rain, to the woodshed. And even if buckets had to come out again to catch the drips when it rained, the painted tin bath left its occupants with a rash unless they sat on a towel. A leg of a chair or a bed occasionally dropped through the floor, and the verandah had to be stepped on with care. No one really minded. But by the end of the first year Ruby had concrete tubs and concrete paths and steps around the house. The verandah could be played on, most of the buckets were put away, and, after a hard day's work, a soak in a new white enamelled bath was something to look forward to. The holes in the floor were mended when necessary – although there were often new ones that appeared in the shape of a .22 bullet following a sleepless night caused by squeaking penguins under the house.

They milked eight cows by hand morning and night. The milk was separated and the cream stored until the day before the mail boat, when Ruby made the butter in a wooden churn. It was patted into one-pound blocks and wrapped in butter papers printed in 100 lots at the *Marlborough Express* office, with the words *Okukari, C T Heberley,* printed inside a fancy scroll. As when they lived in Oyster Bay, Charlie's and Ruby's butter was sold by the local grocer, with the proceeds going towards their grocery bill.

"People asked for our butter," Charlie said proudly.

Donna was on the Correspondence School roll when they came to Okukari, and when Ruby wasn't busy with lessons she was either working with Charlie or busy around the house. To improve the look of the house, the front garden became a family project. After the path was laid, a stone wall about two feet high was built, the soil heaped up behind it and a lawn sown. Today, Donna, Jocelyn and Joe remember having to collect the stones and hauling them up off the beach in a trolley – they all agreed it was slave labour and the beginning of the end of Susie living at Okukari.

Susie had grown big enough to get out of her sty whenever she wanted to and the newly sown grass on the front lawn and up the flats must have been like pig's heaven. Patches of newly sown grass rooted up closed both Charlie's and Ruby's minds to the tears and pleas. With a promise it wouldn't be killed, the pig had to go, but not until a new home could be found – possibly on the lookout.

In 1946 Jocelyn came on the school roll too, so, to take pressure off Ruby, Charlie often took Joe out on the farm with him. He was rebuilding the boundary fence and every morning he'd load up the old packhorse with fencing materials, take his lunch, and head off for the day. Three-year-old Joe had pestered his father to take him out this day, but Charlie felt it would be too long a day for him. With Joe's pleas and promises that he'd be good, Charlie reluctantly lifted him on the horse and they left the house.

"About eleven o'clock he started. He wanted to go home. He was hot. He was tired. Had every damned thing wrong with him. In the end I'd had enough and I plonked him in the pack saddle. It was such a big horse and I tried not to laugh at the sight of his legs sticking straight out on either side of the saddle as I slapped the horse's rump and sent them both home."

The horse was also hot and thirsty, and as it passed through a creek it sought shelter in the low bush, and at the same time bent down for a drink. Joe has never forgotten being swept off its wide backside and landing in the creek. Free of its load the horse took off. Ruby heard Joe's outraged screams long before she found him stumbling down the track. When he finally arrived home he felt as if he couldn't straighten his legs for ages, and through the pain he was old enough to enjoy hearing his mother berate his father for sending him home on his own.

After that episode Joe was quite happy to stay home, that is, until one of the cows went missing. She was a cow that always headed off into the scrub to calve and after she'd been missing for a week Ruby decided it was time to go and look for her.

The whaling season had begun and Susie the pig was now installed on the lookout. It was a beautiful day, and as soon as the cows were milked and breakfast was over, Ruby set some lessons for the girls and headed up around the bridle track, taking Joe with her so he wouldn't disrupt school.

As they neared the back of the farm, Ruby noticed Joe was lagging behind so she sat him down on the track and told him to wait until she came back as she was certain the cow was hiding in some bush only a short distance away from them. When Ruby arrived back with the cow and calf to where she'd left Joe, he wasn't there. She yelled out but there was no answer and she presumed he'd gone home, but when she got back to the house no one had seen him. Panic-stricken, Ruby ran back up the hill and around the track, calling out and searching in the creeks. She'd taught Joe to answer her whenever he heard her calling so when there was no reply she was positive he must be in trouble or so far away he couldn't hear her shouts. Back home again she rang Nan Perano.

"A message came through to the lookout that Joe was missing at the back of the farm," Charlie said. "All I could think of were the steep bluffs, the deep pools, waterfalls and deep creeks with their vertical banks. Four of us shot over to begin a search. It was Max Kenny who finally found him. Joe had the cat slung over his shoulder, and his face was scratched, but there were no tears, or hellos. Just, 'The damned cat scratched me.' Our white cat, Wowsey, had followed Ruby and Joe and while Joe waited for his mother it had disappeared into the bush. Joe had followed it.

"Later Joe told us what he'd seen and we knew he must have been to the highest hill on the farm. And that's 1200 feet."

Joe was grounded, and it wasn't until Charlie began work on the woolshed close to home that he was able to spend the days with his father once more. He helped him repair the gratings and the inside yards, and when Charlie extended the shed he built the end wall in concrete and added a lean-to for the new tractor. Joe helped. While his father made a sledge to tow behind the tractor, Joe piled the gravel on the beach ready for Charlie to shovel into sacks which were loaded on the sledge and hauled up to the woolshed, where he mixed the cement on the floor.

"The first part was easy as I could stand and pour the cement in the boxing. When it got higher than me I built up a staging and after I mixed the cement I'd climb up, leaving Joe to fill up the buckets. He'd pass me the end of the rope tied on the handle, I'd pull them up, and tip in the cement."

Before I heard the rest of the story Charlie took me down to the woolshed and, in the shadows, pointed out the shape of a hammer in the concrete wall.

"I lost that one day," he laughed. "Blamed Joe for taking it away. It wasn't until I pulled the boxing off I found my hammer, set in the cement. It'd dropped down the side."

Joe spent even more time with his father when the polio epidemic swept through New Zealand during 1947-1948, letting Ruby concentrate on school lessons. Although the polio epidemic closed the schools throughout New Zealand, Correspondence School lessons carried on as usual and Charlie and Ruby kept their family at home as they didn't want them mixing with others – the children didn't even meet the mailboat. As Christmas approached, Charlie remembers how dreadful he'd feel some evenings after turning down phone requests from people, many of whom they didn't even know, asking them if their children could come and stay at Okukari as they wanted to get them out of town. Some of those calls were as far afield as Auckland and Christchurch. When Correspondence School lessons resumed in 1948, Joe's days of freedom were over and Ruby had three on the roll.

Charlie was emphatic they never missed not going to town, especially when a town day began at 3am when he got up to milk the cows and, by the time he had finished milking, Ruby had the coal range roaring, breakfast ready, and the children up and dressed. The two-hour boat trip into Picton, plus the 30-minute bus ride through to Blenheim, and return, meant five hours' travelling in a day. Then, when they arrived home, the groceries that were always bought in bulk, farm supplies, material and wool for sewing clothes and knitting jerseys – all had to be rowed ashore and carried up to the house. The day finished as it began with the cows being milked, the coal range lit and a meal cooked.

On 9 August 1948 a Dakota freighter belonging to New Zealand Railways crashed into the Port Underwood hills near Rununder Point, killing the two men on board. Charlie and Ruby, with Trevor and Moira Norton who lived at Te Awaiti, decided to go and have a look. They were young, they'd never seen an accident like that before, and plane crashes certainly weren't common. They steamed down Tory Channel into Maraetai Bay where they anchored the boat, rowed ashore and walked over the hills to the crash.

"It's not something you forget," Charlie said. "There'd been a fire on impact and the plane had burrowed a deep gouge in the hillside, tearing off its engines which rolled down into a gully. A policeman guarded the wreckage. There were hundreds of shoes but all one foot, bolts of material, hardware and lampshades scattered everywhere. Trevor and I each found a ballcock we took home, and the four of us each picked up a lamp-

Second generation,
John Heberley.

First Heberley generation,
James (Worser) and Te Wai.
Photo taken before 1877.

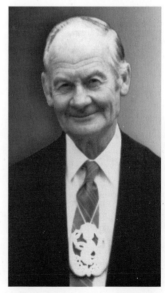

Third generation,
Arthur Heberley.

Fourth generation, Charlie
Heberley

The Heberley family about 1929. Top from left: Herbert, Joe, Jim.
Bottom; Mona, Arthur, Ada, Charlie.

Old Jack on the rocks at
Okukari, 1908.
*(Photo supplied by Paul
Kenny)*

This Okukari snowfall is the heaviest ever recorded. Florence Kenny looks towards the woolshed, with Tory Channel in the background. *(Photo supplied by Paul Kenny)*

The buildings at Okukari when Charlie and Ruby arrived; from left, the farm cottage, school house and homestead. The pole to the right is where the flag was raised to let the Peranos know there was a phone message. *(Photo supplied by Paul Kenny)*

Oyster Bay farm, Tory Channel.
(Photo supplied by Reg Jackson)

Loading wool at Oyster Bay.
(Photo supplied by Reg Jackson)

Fishing Bay whaling station in the 1930s. A whale is being hauled
up the ramp.

Charlie Heberley scans Cook Strait. His chair here is a benzine
packing box. On the chair's back he notched every whale he saw or
caught.

Charlie on *Cachelot* fast to one whale and driving the three whales into Tory Channel.

The whaling station at Whangaparapara, Great Barrier Island.

The whale oil tank with the recreation hall behind at Whangaparapara. *(New Zealand Herald)*

Ruby christens the *Surprise* in Picton, 1959.

Surprise, Kingston Whaler and *Cascade* on the lower deck of the Whangaparapara station.

Charlie and Ruby outside an accommodation block at Whangaparapara, 1959.

Splicing whaleline aboard *Colville*. From left: Ray Crawford, Jeff Morris and Joe Heberley. *(New Zealand Herald)*

Tom Norton, left, and apprentice gunner Alf Nimmo place strop around whale tail ready for the *Colville* to pick up.

Colville's crew winches whale alongside to put towing chains on tail before towing whale back to factory in Whangaparapara.

At the factory the whale is winched up the ramp to the flensing deck. *(New Zealand Herald)*

Dave Medland driving
one of the stripping
winches.
(New Zealand Herald)

Dave George sharpens
his flensing knife.
(New Zealand Herald)

Peeling blubber of the whale during the first season on Great Barrier before the station was renovated. *(New Zealand Herald)*

Surprise and *Oria* chasing whales at 30 knots off eastern coast of Great Barrier Island. *(New Zealand Herald)*

Charlie scans the horizon for a whale. *(New Zealand Herald)*

Filling in time on Cape Barrier lookout. Left: Tom Norton trims
Tom Gullery's hair. Right: Len Biddes has a shower.

Station cook Eddie Glink prepares dinner for 50 men. *(New Zealand Herald)*

Charlie, Tom Norton and Bill Gibbs in the kitchen, dishing up for dinner on Cape Barrier.

Charlie samples the end product.

Launching of the *Donna Marie*, 1970.

The two ace gunners from New Zealand's whaling history, Trevor Norton and Charlie Heberley, hold a whale's vertebra at Picton in 1982. *(Evening Post)*

shade and used them as hats on the long walk back to Maraetai Bay. It was a sombre sight."

In 1950 the family swelled to six when Florence, Ruby's younger sister, came to live with them. Since Ruby's mother had died, with her father away fishing most of the time Florence was constantly in other people's care and Ruby and Charlie wanted her to have a stable home environment. Florence came on the Correspondence School role and completed her fifth form year. She then went nursing at Nelson's Ngawhatu psychiatric hospital and then to Braemar, the hospital for intellectually disabled children.

Living and working in an isolated and harsh environment made accidents quite common but Charlie remembered only the worst. Alfie Nimmo, the young boy Arthur and Ada had brought up, came and worked for Charlie in the early stages of clearing the farm. While he was cutting out manuka the axe slipped and he cut off two fingers. Charlie and Ruby were away for the day so Alfie grabbed his chopped-off fingers, shoved them in his pocket, ran down the paddock, wrapped a tea towel around his hand and rowed across the bay to Whekenui. When he reached the Perano homestead he discovered he'd lost one finger but Gilbert said he'd take him to Picton in the chaser and perhaps one finger at least could be saved. As he rowed out to the moored chaser he found the missing finger in the bottom of the dinghy. Both fingers were stitched back but neither took and they had to be removed later by surgery.

Another man, Bill Friedrich, broke his leg on the boat while Charlie was towing the mooring into the beach to check the chain and shackles. He was standing on the side deck close to the bow when the chain slipped out the fairlead and hit his leg. Once again Gilbert Perano was called to assist and Bill was taken to Picton on the faster whale chaser.

"In those days we had nothing like the Westpac Trust Rescue Helicopter or the Marlborough Volunteer Coastguard with its medivac facilities, and we were jolly lucky to have the use of the chasers that got us to town in under an hour."

But the worst accident, Charlie recalled, happened after the family had eaten rabbit stew for dinner. Donna and Florence were chasing each other around the verandah. With a burst of laughter Donna raced inside and slammed the panelled glass door behind her. Florence put her arm out to stop the door and it went through one of the fancy glass panels. Her screams

81

brought Charlie and Ruby rushing outside. The whole muscle on Florence's upper arm was hanging down. Charlie wanted to cut it off but Ruby wouldn't let him touch it, wrapping it up in a bath towel. She was taken to Picton on a whale chaser and admitted to Wairau Hospital where she was to spend the next three months until the injury healed. In spite of the horror I felt a smile creep over my face at Charlie's next words. "I told them they'd go mad if they ate rabbit on the full moon."

The family never ate rabbit again.

As it is today, the phone was their most vital link. In 1939 when the Kennys owned Okukari, Seymour Scott and his family lived over the hill at Wharehunga Bay in the Queen Charlotte Sound. The Scott family were not on the phone so Seymour Scott, with the help of his brother-in-law, dug every pole into the ground and then ran a wire that stretched from one side of Arapawa Island to the other, linking their place to Kennys in Okukari. Whenever the Scotts needed to make an outside call they turned a handle to generate the rings and hoped someone at Okukari could take their call and switch them to the main line. Because all the calls off Arapawa Island were toll calls, every month Ruby had to fill out the oblong cards that the Post and Telegraph sent her, with the details of the calls the Scotts made. Regulations said that the Heberleys were not allowed to leave the phone switched over to the Scotts, but they did, because Charlie always worried that there could be an accident.

The telephone line draped all over the Sounds made an excellent conductor, and, during an electrical storm, not even lightning conductors ten-inches high and as round as a garden hose could stop blue sparks shooting off the phone. Batteries and fuses often blew, and twice in Charlie's time at Okukari he saw the actual phone blown off the wall. Unless Charlie could locate and fix the problem, the phone remained out until workmen from the Post and Telegraph could hire a boat and come to the island.

"We'd been visiting the Peranos one night, and rowing back across the bay we got caught in one of those storms. We couldn't see our beach through the rain and relied on the sheets of lightning to light the way. The flashes hit the water in the bottom of the dinghy and we could feel the reflected heat on our faces. The thunder rolled round the hills. Ruby was like a hedgehog with her cardigan pulled over her head. We ended up along the far end of the beach, pulled the dinghy up and walked back. When we came inside we found our phone on the floor. It was as dead as a dodo."

It wasn't only lightning that lit up the water in Tory Channel. I'd often heard about the whale that had been caught at night but I never tired of listening to Charlie and watching his face as he described the chase over and over again.

"It was a full moon and as we steamed home from Oyster Bay it was so bright the black sea and the rough outline of the hills against the sky reminded me of one of those relief maps. Everything else was blotted out and it was easy to imagine what it must have been like when Kupe and the early tribes first came to the South Island. As we passed Te Awaiti I glanced over at the *Cachalot* moored in the bay and noticed her lights had been left on. Rather than have a flat battery in the morning, I steamed over to put them out and found Gilbert on board waiting for me. Ted Huntley, who worked in the station's bone department and lived at Fishing Bay, had seen two whales spout in the channel and phoned Gilbert."

Charlie jumped aboard with Gilbert and they roared off in pursuit of the chaser driven by Joe Perano with Trevor Norton at the gun. The whales were heading towards the entrance when one spouted off Okukari. My father-in-law maintained it was the most awe-inspiring sight he'd ever seen.

"The water was lit up with phosphorescence, and, as the whale lifted, all you could see was this huge golden ball. I shot at the ball. But the sight of this damned thing coming up with all the phosphorescence streaming back on it was fantastic. Just fantastic," he repeated.

I was glad whaling had not taken away my father-in-law's ability to see beauty in nature and still remain sensitive enough to feel the primitive forces that abound in this part of New Zealand – the place where history began, when Kupe arrived here more than a thousand years ago.

Chapter Seven

INNOVATORS AND PRANKSTERS

Kei te kamakama te tikanga.
It is a proper thing to be joyful and full of high spirits.

NOW THAT CHARLIE lived at Okukari, every morning during the whaling season Gilbert Perano drove the whale chaser across the bay to pick him up. "It was great," Charlie said. "Ruby always cut my lunch at night and I had my pick-up timed to the last second. I'd lay out my clothes at night, and if I wanted to, I could lie in bed until I heard the chaser engine start. Then I'd leap out, get dressed, run my toothbrush around my teeth and a flannel over my face, grab a piece of bread and a banana or something, pick up my lunch tin and be down on the beach waiting for Gilbert to put the nose of the chaser on the beach for me to clamber up."

Their first stop was at the *Tuatea,* moored in Okukari Bay, where they'd take on fuel, explosives, or any other gear they needed. As the boat cruised on across the channel, Charlie rolled his first cigarette of the day and in a companionable silence the two men watched as the first colours of a new day lit up the sky through Cook Strait. Alongside the mooring Charlie hooked up the heavy rope loop and with excited anticipation draped it over the gunpost, hoping it wouldn't be too long before it would be flung off.

After Susie outstayed her welcome at Okukari – the children agreed she'd be happier running free on the lookout hill – Charlie brought her over in the chaser, and she'd quickly become everyone's friend. She was content to live on the West Head and never tried to escape over the metre-wide track above the rock arch that joined the lookout hill to the mainland. When the whalers left the lookout at the end of the season she became a wild pig, but on the first day of the new whaling season Susie would be waiting for them as if they'd never been away. She'd soon learnt when food was around and would stand up on her back legs with her front legs on the sill of the observation window, snuffling and dribbling, until she was given her share out of the lunch boxes. To alleviate the boredom of a day, with few sightings or bad visibility, an improvised pig hunt often took place with some of the men chasing the pig around the hut and through the bushes until they got her down and had a wrestle. Susie loved the game and would race ahead of the men to the edge of the cliffs that slid 300 feet into Cook Strait, back to the hut, through flax bushes, over the stone wall, round and round until she'd lie flat on her stomach with her front and back legs stretched out as if wanting to be caught and scratched with a rough piece of driftwood kept especially for that purpose.

Visitors to the lookout often arrived with bottles of beer, but this was never drunk on the job. "It wasn't only our gear we kept sharp. Our minds had to be just as sharp."

After a game of chase, catch and scratch, Susie was often given a bottle of beer which she drank out of her tin dish. On a day when the whales were scarce, the men were bored. Susie had been a great sport so it was suggested she probably needed more than one bottle. Then a question was raised as to how many bottles of beer a pig could drink before it got drunk.

They poured two bottles into Susie's dish, followed quickly by two more, and finally, with a total of seven bottles – way over the limit to drive – Susie began to sway, gently at first. Eyelids with curling lashes closed over her eyes. The swaying motion continued, growing wider, until her widest sway hit the ground, and after a few replete sighs and grunts she slept for a couple of hours. Later that same day she was back at the window again, letting the whalers know she was hungry, unaware that she had slept through afternoon tea.

Long before television, a radio team did a documentary on whaling. While they were speaking to the men on the lookout, someone held up a microphone to Susie. Charlie maintained her 'oink oink' probably made her the only pig in New Zealand to have had air time.

Another use for the beer on the hill was dreamt up while, day after day, the men watched a local fisherman steam out of Tory Channel and head south to pull his crayfish pots. One of the pots was immediately below the lookout in the bay behind the neck. Whenever it was pulled up, binoculars focused on the unsuspecting fisherman as the men high above counted the crays he plucked from his pot and threw in a wooden box on the boat's deck.

The thought of crayfish got too much one day. When the float of the pot broke the surface and the fisherman was nowhere to be seen, Charlie and Tom Norton, another gunner, decided they'd row out around West Head and into the bay where the pot was.

The ebb tide was running, making it an easy row out of Tory Channel and around into the bay, but, with the ebb tide running strongly, both men knew it would be a struggle to row back against it. After they'd taken out the crays they tied a bottle of beer in the pot with flax and threw it back into the water.

At the channel entrance where the ebb tide met the waters of Cook Strait, wave smashed against wave, forming peaks or leaving hollows. Tom didn't like the look of it.

"Let's go through the hole in the wall!" he shouted.

Getting a 14-foot dinghy with a beam of five feet through a hole that was barely five feet wide at low tide was an impossibility, so they tipped it up on its side and propped it up against the wall. Then, still in the dinghy, they stood on its side and tried to manoeuvre it through the gap without losing the crayfish or getting too wet. The two men spent the rest of the day in damp clothes but the crayfish soon cooked on the Dover stove made up for any discomfort.

So many of the pranks played by the whalers revolved around food. As I listened to Charlie recall some of them, and watched his face light up, I knew that what so many had told me must have been true. Charlie was usually the ringleader.

One story involved a tin of spaghetti and quite a lot of skulduggery. Roger Mirams, well known in the film industry, brought a team from the National Film Unit to the whaling station. During the filming, he stayed aboard the *Tuatea* and when he went back to Wellington he sent over a parcel of food to the *Tuatea*'s crew, in appreciation. Besides biscuits, chocolate and tinned fruit, there were some tins of spaghetti.

"We wondered where *our* parcel was, as they'd also spent days on the hill with us. We got sick of hearing about this wonderful food parcel, so thought we'd teach the boys on the *Tuatea* a lesson."

As usual on their way over to the moorings below the lookout, Gilbert and Charlie stopped alongside the *Tuatea* for fuel and explosives. But this day, while Gilbert attended to the gear, Charlie slipped down to the galley and sneaked out one of the tins of spaghetti. Back at the lookout the tin was soaked in water and the label carefully removed. They cut the tin open around the middle, and Charlie with Joe Perano Senior sat outside in the tussock and ate the cold spaghetti.

A local farmer grazed a few sheep around the lookout hill so these two men gathered a few sheep droppings that were lying around, then some kelp bubbles and kelp off the beach. They filled up the tin and soldered it together. With the label dried and glued back on it looked exactly as it had earlier in the day. That night, on the pretence of needing more gear, Charlie went on board the *Tuatea* and put the tin back in its place.

A few days later, the *Tuatea*'s crew were given a groper by one of the Italian fishermen who fished in the area, and they bragged about what they were having for dinner that night. That same day the chasers had been out cruising in the Strait looking for whales, and, when they'd finally caught one, Gilbert brought the chaser alongside to refuel while Charlie sneaked on the ship and took the groper away.

"I heard later that when the cook discovered it was missing, he blamed me. No doubt he began thinking of ways he could get one back on me, too. So the spaghetti came out. He heated up the tin in boiling water and, I was told, when he opened it up and tipped it upside down and all these droppings and kelp lay on the plate, he was speechless. He didn't know how, but he had a fair idea that I had been involved, and he told everyone that some day he'd get even with me and his revenge would be sweet."

Over the years many visitors came to the lookout. They were welcome as long as they abided by the whalers' rules, and kept out of the way once a chase began. Lena Moleta lived at Whekenui, and helped Nan Perano in the house. While staying at Whekenui her father came over to the lookout with Gilbert. Excited at his day ahead, he burst into the hut and told the men he knew all about them – how they'd try to pinch his boots or solder up his lunch tin. He certainly knew, but he forgot the rules. As he slept in the chair his boots came off and got put back on the wrong feet with the laces tied together. He slept on until someone tapped him on the shoulder and told him they were about to leave on a chase. He jumped up and immediately fell over backwards.

I could still hear indignation in my father-in-law's voice when he repeated the words that were shouted across the room to him. "Heberley! *You* did that!"

Bill Parkes from Blenheim often brought visitors out to the whaling station. When he brought five nurses from Wairau Hospital to the station and to catch the atmosphere on the lookout hill, the men, naturally, schemed. Although the girls had been warned about the men on the hill, nothing prepared them for the noise when Tom Norton and Reg Jackson, on their way to work, fired the gun, minus the harpoon, across the bow of Bill's boat. They shrieked and raced up on deck, thinking their boat had blown up. And later when everyone was off the boat the same two men rowed out to it, rifled through the girls' bags and strung up all their bras and panties on a line they'd rigged up from stem to stern.

I was delighted to hear how the girls had the last laugh when they arrived on the lookout hill with bottles of mercurichrome hidden in their pockets, and they managed to paint the mercurichrome over the men's faces, hands and hair. The men thought it would wash off so didn't put up too much of a struggle. But when they arrived home that night, seven sheepish men had to explain how they got covered in 'red stuff'.

Charlie admitted they probably did a lot of crazy things but he believed it helped lighten the fact that they were involved in an extremely dangerous game. They knew one wrong move could be their last. "I've seen a whale lift one of those 36-foot chasers clean out of the water and almost toss it over, by coming up beneath it. Working with explosives, boats getting smashed – we worked on our adrenalin every day. But it was all part of whaling." Another part was coming up with ideas and techniques that were born to the needs of the job. "We were masters of innovation."

As soon as a whale dies, because it is a warm-blooded animal the meat starts to deteriorate, and the use of explosives hastens the process. The Peranos believed that if the whales could be killed without the use of explosives, more meat could be exported to post-war Great Britain where meat rationing was still in force. The killing of whales by electrocution was introduced. It was more humane, and eliminating the explosives slowed down the deterioration of the meat.

A 230-volt, very high amperage, generator was installed in the chaser. Specially made harpoons with a bronze head instead of the regular steel head were used, with a flex that ran from the harpoon head to the generator, taped to the usual whale line. "It worked in theory," Charlie said. "We'd fire the harpoon in, apply the electricity, and kill the whale.

"But what we hadn't realised was that by using the water for a return circuit our boat became part of the circuit."

Charlie admitted to being unhappy when he thought about the system but engineer Gordon Cuddon assured him that everything had been tested in Picton Harbour and it worked splendidly. "But he didn't realise that out in Cook Strait the boats and the gunners are never dry.

"During the trial of that harpoon, we fitted the head onto the existing shaft which was made up from two half-inch steel rods. The problem was, if the harpoon was sticking out of the blubber it shorted and we couldn't get the full electric current through, so we made up shafts using Australian hardwood. There was no give in that at all, and when you fired the gun it almost knocked you over."

A deformed thumb was the result of using that hardwood shaft, although Charlie was quick to add it was his fault. "I had the habit of putting my thumb over the back of the gun. This day when I pulled the trigger to fire the harpoon with the hardwood shank the gun kicked, flew out of my hands, swung back and caught my thumb. It broke at the first joint. Gilbert taped it up with insulation tape and I stayed on whaling."

The final day the electric harpoon was used came soon after that. Charlie was fast to a whale and as he was pulling back the whale line with the electric flex taped to it, the flex broke. It wasn't until the rope was closer to the boat that he realised something was wrong.

"I could see this great blue flash snaking under the water as the flex swung from side to side. As it came over the side of the boat it hit the rail with a shower of sparks. I refused to use it again."

Another scheme was devised. If the whales were killed with carbon-dioxide, the oxygen would be driven out of the blood and thus prevent contamination from the explosives. The day it was trialed, Gilbert brought a bottle of compressed gas out on the boat with him. It had a hose connected to it which Charlie joined to the air spear. When a whale was harpooned, instead of bombs the carbon-dioxide flowing through the air-spear would kill it.

They knew Japanese whalers had tried it but they fired the actual cylinder into the whale and had some method of releasing the gas once it was in place. Charlie and Gilbert actually knew very little about this experimental method, but, undeterred, they headed the other two chasers out to the first sighting of the day.

Gilbert Perano was the senior partner of Perano Brothers. "That's one of the reasons I was able to build such a high tally," Charlie told me, "because he always had the fastest boat. But it also meant we were the mugs who got to try all these new ideas."

The lilt in his voice belied the criticism as he remembered the events of that day. "Once we were fast to the whale and were close enough, I threw in the airspear and Gilbert released the gas. We'd never thought about putting a regulator on the bottle and the gas came out with an almighty rush. We found ourselves with a whole block of ice – the cylinder just froze up. The whale took off – the airspear wouldn't pull out and we had to throw cylinder, spear, everything overboard. At the end of the day I added another notch on my chair but we went back to our old method."

In the excitement of the season Charlie soon forgot about the spaghetti episode but the crew of the *Tuatea* certainly hadn't. Memories of rotting kelp mixed with sheep droppings sliding out of the spaghetti tin on to a dinner plate were still in their minds. Ruby had bought some new chooks, and word of Charlie's egg sandwiches with their thick fillings, his pieces of rich yellow sponge cake and other culinary delights, all due to the Red Shavers' laying skills, filtered through to the *Tuatea*'s crew.

The chook house was built on the edge of the high gorse-covered bank above the beach, in full view of the *Tuatea* as she lay on her moorings. The memory of the stolen groper and the 'spaghetti' prompted skipper Charlie Perano and Billy Gillice to climb in the dinghy and row ashore in the dark, intent on raiding the chook house. If there were no eggs they planned to take a chook. It was easy to picture two grown men, no doubt full of repressed laughter, carefully digging in their oars as they sneaked ashore in the dark, pulling the dinghy just clear of the water in readiness for a quick getaway but far enough up the beach so it wouldn't drift out the bay – but they had no idea just how quick their exit was going to be.

The farm dogs realised there were strangers crawling through the gorse towards the chook house, and barked. Charlie heard them, came to the back door and roared out to the dogs, "Go and lie down!" The barking persisted.

"In the end I got out my .303 and fired it up in the air. All the dogs were gun-shy, and it shut them up fast."

Charlie had no idea that his chook house was about to be raided. He thought the dogs were just playing up and was pleased he could get back to sleep, but the would-be robbers thought Charlie was shooting at them. They forgot the chooks and took off down through the gorse and back out to the *Tuatea*. Stories of Charlie Perano and Billy Gillice digging out festered gorse prickles filtered through to Charlie in the following weeks. Now he knew why the dogs were barking, and every time he sank his teeth into another egg sandwich his mind raced as he schemed up a way to teach them a lesson.

"It was literally handed to me on a plate," he laughed.

Reg Jackson had a rooster at Te Iro. He was tired of his family complaining that it woke them every morning so he killed it and brought it to the lookout to pluck and clean before dropping it off on the *Tuatea* later in the day. The plucking was the easy bit, and when Reg admitted he wasn't sure what to remove from its innards, Charlie quickly offered to do it.

Reg used to take home whale meat which he dried over fences before feeding to his dogs. The dogs thrived on it, growing fat and glossy. The rooster also apparently thrived on it as he strutted around the paddocks where the meat hung, and it was a beautiful plump bird that was cooked in the oven on the *Tuatea* and served up to her crew. Nobody could eat it. Charlie hadn't removed its crop, and the taste of whale went right through the meat. Although they wanted to blame Charlie, no one ever knew if it was a genuine mistake or not.

Even though it seemed that Charlie had got one back on the chook robbers, when Ruby heard her precious chooks had been at the centre of the plot she made plans of her own. Whenever she fed her chooks and gathered the eggs she'd see the *Tuatea* on the mooring, unless it was out chasing or towing, and her blood boiled when she thought how close one of her Red Shavers had come to extinction. Her chance of revenge came one mail day. The *Tuatea* was out in Cook Strait, and stores for the crew had been left in the dinghy they'd left on the mooring. Ruby rowed out and opened the boxes until she found the bread. It wasn't sliced and wrapped like the bread we buy today, but it was baked as one loaf and made easy to split in half for the sale of half a loaf. She partially broke each loaf in two, poked in pieces of wood, and then closed them together again.

Over the following days Ruby waited for a reaction, but there was nothing. She wondered who'd got the blame, but gradually forgot about it. A month later she had the chance to go in to Picton for the day with some of the other wives from the factory. Knowing it was mail day, she left their mailbag in their dinghy on the moorings in the bay. She didn't cancel the meat she'd ordered to come on the mailboat as she knew it would be left with the mail.

Late in the afternoon Ruby arrived home, tired but refreshed after a day out. She planned an easy dinner with the sausages that had come in her stores, but, when she opened the parcel, twelve tarred and feathered sausages fell out – a win to the men on the *Tuatea*.

Over on the lookout hill, scraps put aside for the pig began to go missing. Uneaten sandwiches that had been left on the shelf, apples and bananas, all kept disappearing. Everyone debated what sort of animal it could be. They decided that it must be bigger than the rats and mice that invaded the hut every winter, and that it had to be caught.

Ruby's fox fur stole, made from some of the foxes Charlie had caught while in Australia, had worn out, so Charlie cut the tail off, hid it under his jacket, and took it over to the lookout. He tied a string on one end and put it under a flax bush with only the tip showing, and told Trevor Norton what he intended doing.

Charlie bailed up Max Kenny outside and asked him to come and look at the strange animal he'd found. Trevor stayed out of sight, but every time Max tried to grab it, he pulled the string.

"Trevor did a dammed good job and had Max grovelling around in the dirt for ages before he realised he'd been tricked. When we got around to setting the trap, we did in fact catch a possum."

With the possum caught they concentrated on getting rid of the mice. Every night they set traps and caught mice but they didn't seem to be getting any fewer. Their smell and the droppings had the men complaining to Joe Perano Senior, who told them to make a better trap if they weren't happy.

Between sightings and subsequent chases, Charlie and Trevor plotted. They informed everyone on the lookout that they had a superior mouse-trap, guaranteed to catch at least two if not more at one time. A cage with a ramp leading up to the door was built. Hanging above the ramp they rigged up a pulley that had a tin full of stones hanging from it for a weight. One end of the string was tied to the bottom of the ramp and the other was tied to the cheese inside the cage. In theory, the mice ran up the ramp, jumped in the cage, ate the cheese, and in doing so gnawed through the string which then sent the weight crashing to the floor. That lifted the ramp over the door and trapped the mice. Well, that was the theory. Joe Perano Senior scoffed. He told Charlie and Trevor they were crazy to think they could catch a mouse in such a trap.

That night when Charlie came home he set conventional traps and caught four mice. The next morning when he arrived at the lookout he told the others to keep Joe Perano Senior talking while he ran ahead to set up the trap. He put two mice in the trap, released the weight and positioned the other two mice under the weighted tin with just their tails showing. Then he hid outside.

Everyone stood back and let Joe go in first. As he opened the door Charlie heard him say, "Ah ha, now we'll see how your good your bloody mouse trap is." His surprise at discovering the theory had worked in practice was overwhelming, but when he saw the other two mice beneath the weighted tin he was speechless.

"You know, for years he believed we'd caught those mice in that trap."

During the season there was very little social life because everyone was always too tired. The men on the lookout worked every day. On very rough days they watched from the point at Okukari in case a whale came into Tory Channel. Some days, after a southerly had gone through, they spotted whales and knew they would be able to get out but the seas would have prevented them getting fast to the whales. Only once did they have to cut a whale loose. A southerly buster came through, and the mother ship headed in. They had caught a whale, and the three chasers started to tow it in but the seas built up quickly and it had to be cut loose, leaving it to be carried with the tide until the weather cleared enough and it could be found.

Occasionally the men played cards on the *Tuatea*. Two of those evenings were as clear in Charlie's mind as if they had happened yesterday.

"We were all down below when the whole ship shook. Everyone tore up on deck, thinking we'd been rammed. A white pointer shark, 14 or 15 feet long, was having a go at the whale that was tied alongside the *Tuatea*. It was worrying it like a dog with a bone and taking big chunks out of it. We got a bomb ready and put it in the shark. He went down."

Another night hundreds of dogfish or gummy shark swarmed round the whale that was tied alongside the *Tuatea*. These grow up to about a metre in length but because of their small flattened teeth are inoffensive to man. The frenzied fish were coming out of the water and jumping up on the whale's back. The card game was forgotten as Charlie and his brother Herbert jumped over the side and stood on the back of the whale, grabbing the tails of the small harmless sharks and throwing them up on the deck.

"We caught about 300 and were going to cut out their livers and sell them. But after cutting out a few, we decided whaling was much more fun and went back to our cards."

By August, towards the end of the season, whale sightings became fewer. The frantic pace gradually eased. They still maintained a watch, but found time to relax a little. This particular day three men were on the binoculars. It had been a perfect day, but there had been no sightings. Some were outside playing cards on top of the water tank, while others were enjoying a game of darts. Someone noticed a fire burning across the channel on the bank above the beach at Okukari. All the glasses were focused on Okukari and they could see Ruby waving frantically. She'd spotted two whales swimming in the channel right under the whalers' noses.

Charlie was very quick to tell me it was because the men were more than 90 metres above sea level. They'd actually been looking above the whales as they'd sneaked up the southern shore and come into Tory Channel on the flood tide. There was a mad scramble down the hill and out to the chasers. The whales were caught but the whalers never lived it down.

It was on another of those still, calm days when the whalers learnt that their secret cache of coal wasn't secret at all. Before the start of every season, lighters used to bring the coal to the station in 30- to 40-ton loads from Picton. As the men shovelled the coal, they'd squirrel away any big lumps and collect them when it was dark. Joe Perano Senior was sitting on one of the chairs, sweeping his binoculars across the sea, when he yelled out to his son, Gilbert, "Look at them, Gilly, burning our coal!" Charlie immediately looked towards Okukari and was thankful there was no sign of the smoke coming from their place. But in Fishing Bay all the chimneys were belching out the thick greeny-black smoke from the slag coal the station used.

"After that, I told Ruby to burn our coal only at night," Charlie said.

The most exciting part of the coal story couldn't be shared at the time but as I listened to it being told more than 50 years later I was back in a part of history that might never be repeated. "It was dark and Ruby and I were rowing home from the whaling station with our lumps of coal in the dinghy when we heard the sound of two humpback whales blowing alongside. We rowed into the kelp off Wheke Rock where we knew the whales couldn't follow, and pushed our way through it. Once we were clear, we rowed flat out across the open stretch of water between Whekenui and Okukari. It wasn't a nice feeling being so close to two whales in the dark."

Charlie always maintained that the friendships formed within the whaling community remained forever. Many of the same men returned to work at the whaling station or on the chasers every year for three months. Some brought their wives, and their children attended the school in Whekenui Bay during the season, boosting the roll to 32. Some of the boys worked alongside their fathers when they were old enough. Others took over from their fathers. Everyone worked hard for the three months, and every year at the end of the season they celebrated.

The biggest event was the rugby match on the flat at Okukari, the lookout hill versus the factory. The women baked scones, sponges and savouries. After the match there was a grand afternoon tea and get-together. Mothers caught up with mothers, children with children, and boat crews with factory workers. Day turned into night and the stories got better, the beer got better and the whales got bigger.

All the men at the factory prided themselves on their home brew, and brought bottles to sample and enjoy. The criticism was harsh, with the brewers voting only their own beer as the best. Most years Charlie, too, brewed his own beer and felt sad the year he didn't have any to enter the competition, but he wasn't deterred.

"I had a crate of DB bottled beer so I soaked them in the tub to remove the labels, replaced the DB caps with plain ones, and brought them out. The critics swirled the beer in their glasses, held it up to the light to see if it was cloudy, and sniffed it. The critics were tough. It was too rough, a bit cloudy, too much finings, rather dark.

"But before they went home they were all asking me for the recipe, and I had Ruby going through her cookbooks, looking for a recipe. I often wondered if Aunt Daisy's recipe for home brew was as good as DB's."

They made their own music, and as the evening wore on Trevor Norton would pick up his guitar and begin strumming. With Moira his wife singing, soon everyone would be joining in with the evergreens – *Don't Fence Me In, You Are My Sunshine,* and *It's A Long Way To Tipperary.* And they had their own songs they'd written and added to, while they sat in a small square hut perched on West Head during their patient vigil for whales.

The Bloody Song was sung to the same tune as the carol, *O Christmas Tree* – a German folk song.

This bloody town's a bloody cuss
No bloody trams, no bloody bus
And no one cares for bloody us
So bloody bloody bloody.
It's bloody awful when it rains
No bloody ditch no bloody drains
The council's got no bloody brains
So bloody bloody bloody.

The bloody dances make me smile
The orchestras are bloody vile
And do they cramp your bloody style
So bloody bloody bloody.

The bloody grog is bloody dear
It's 1/9 a bloody beer

And do they shout? No bloody fear
So bloody bloody bloody.

Another song, *The Whekenui Whaling Song*, was made up over a few years as they thought of new verses to fit some of the men on the lookout hill, the *Tuatea* and the chasers. You have to understand the references.

Jordy Rocks are two rocks to the south of Tory Channel entrance.

Old Sid was Sid Toms who stuttered and was lookout man and wireless operator on the lookout.

Old Joe was J A Perano Senior, founder of the station. When he retired as chaser driver he used to go to the lookout and walk up and down and growl about the way the chase was conducted.

Shucks was Trevor Norton, a gunner.

Young Joe was Joe Perano Junior, a gunner. He was not a quick rope splicer so he would sooner tie a knot if short of time.

Nicky was Alf Perano, master of the *Tuatea,* and a very excitable man.

Steve, Alf Perano's son, was stoker on the *Tuatea,* a coal-fired steamship.

Puponga Point is the point between Fishing Bay and Te Awaiti. Puponga (sperm whale) was what the Maori people called William Henry Keenan. This point was owned by the Keenan family. [From *Keenan History* by James K Keenan, verified by Mildred Connor and Lily Reeves, in the Picton Museum.] It was a good place to watch a whale chase should they come inside the channel entrance. Everyone living in the vicinity would rush up there to watch the kill.

Natives were the Maori and Pakeha locals.

This is *The Whekenui Whaling Song,* to the tune of *She'll be Coming Round the Mountain.*

They'll be coming 'round the Jordies when they come,
when they come
They'll be a pack of Jordies when they come,
when they come
Now we'll all go out to meet them and it's ten to one
we'll beat them
For they're coming 'round the Jordies when they come.

Now Old Shucks will splice an iron-on when they come,
when they come
Old Shucks will splice an iron-on when they come,
when they come
But Young Joe will do a tie on yes young Joe
will do a tie on
For they're coming 'round the Jordies when they come.

Now you'll hear Old Sid a stuttering when they come,
when they come
You'll hear Old Sid a stuttering when they come,
when they come
And Old Joe will be a muttering yes old Joe
will be a muttering
For they're coming 'round the Jordies when they come.

Now you'll hear old Nicky screaming when they come,
when they come
You'll hear Old Nicky screaming when they come,
when they come
You'll hear Old Nicky screaming, "Come on Steve and
get her steaming!"
For they're coming 'round the Jordies when they come.

There'll be Natives on Puponga when they come,
when they come
There'll be Natives on Puponga when they come,
when they come.
There to see the lucky gunner just to see
the lucky gunner
For they're coming 'round the Jordies when they come.

"They were great times," Charlie nodded. "Those parties lasted all night yet I can't remember people getting drunk. Perhaps it *was* Aunt Daisy's home brew recipe."

Chapter Eight

CHANGES

He manga wai koia kia kore e whitikia.
It is a big river indeed that cannot be crossed.

WHEN CHARLIE wasn't whaling he counted the days until he was. From late April to early August he thought of nothing else. Whaling was the topic of conversation at the evening meal. How many whales today? Did you miss any? Any accidents? Anyone hurt?

Everyone was involved and everyone wanted to know the day's events. When the flag went up and the chasers' engines revved up, the men at the station and the women and children at home all knew a chase was on. If the chaser crews herded one or more whales into Tory Channel, Nan Perano, who could see the channel entrance from her windows, would ring everyone up. Pens, paper and books were discarded and the classroom exchanged for a seat on a hill. Every move was watched, and, for the next few days, manuka sticks the boys had sharpened became harpoons which were hurled into imaginary whales they found on the hillside, on the beach or in the sea.

While the children loved the excitement, for the women there was always that element of fear. They knew that every time the boats went out the men were putting their lives at risk, especially in rough weather. "It's the same as fishing today. It's always a worry for the women. But still," Charlie shrugged, "that's part of life on the sea."

Ruby played a big part in Charlie's life on the sea. While Charlie whaled, she ran the farm. Stock had to be shifted, cows milked, and towards the end of the whaling season when the ewes were close to lambing, the flock was checked daily to make sure no sheep were cast. After heavy rain the weight of their wool and unborn lamb made it difficult for the ewes to get up and unless they were found and stood up they usually died.

As well as the farm the house had to be run – without the luxury of electricity. Ruby always kept a good supply of dry wood to help keep the coal range burning as it was used not only for cooking but also for hot water and warmth. She had sole responsibility for the children and it was always in the back of her mind how far away she was from medical help if anything went wrong. And for most of this time Ruby had little or no contact with any other women.

Before the school opened at Whekenui for the whalers' children Ruby taught hers through the Correspondence School. Having the sole responsibility for your children's education is daunting. The realisation that your children will be what you teach them lives with you always, and at times it got Ruby down. During one of these spells Charlie suggested they rent a house in Picton where Ruby and the children would live for the week while the children attended Picton Borough School.

They found a house, and a new way of life began. On Sunday afternoon or early Monday morning Charlie took his family in to Picton and repeated the trip every Friday afternoon. It lasted three months. Ruby spent her weekends bringing her house in Okukari back to the standard she set, Charlie didn't look after himself properly, and the children couldn't adapt to a small piece of land surrounded by a fence that you weren't allowed to climb.

"It wasn't good for family life," Charlie explained, "so they came home and went back on the Correspondence School roll."

To help Ruby, especially during the whaling season, Charlie hired a young woman, Ruth, to live in their home and help with lessons and around the house. Whaling was a completely different way of life for her and she enjoyed hearing the whaling stories that were told over dinner every night although she wasn't enthused when Charlie suggested he'd bring home some whale meat for her to try.

A few weeks later Charlie made a point of telling Ruby he felt like a meal of steak and suggested she order some from the butchers to come out on the next mail boat. That day, before Charlie came home, he went around to the factory and cut a nice piece of fillet steak out of a whale. He took it home and Ruby cooked it with onions. Ruth was half way through her second helping and Charlie asked her if she was enjoying it. She thought it was the most tasty and tender steak she'd ever eaten. "When I told her it was whale meat she pushed her plate away. Wouldn't eat any more," Charlie said disgustedly.

Although Charlie loved the land and looked forward to working on it again, when one whaling season closed in August he looked forward to the next. It was the sea that ruled his life, and whaling took the biggest chunk of it.

No sooner was Charlie off the lookout hill than the first sprinkling of lambs on Okukari appeared. For the first six weeks he was back on the farm lambing. That, and catching up on maintenance from the preceding months when he was whaling, took up most of his time. In October the farm was mustered and the lambs tailed. When the tailing was finished at Okukari, Charlie helped Reg Jackson at Te Iro Bay to muster and tail his lambs.

Once again he would leave the bay before it was light but this time he'd have to row out to the farm boat, the 26-foot *Wheke,* with his pack of dogs. Once alongside the boat, scrapping dogs, keen to begin mustering, leapt out of the dinghy into the cockpit of the *Wheke.* Amid the whines and snaps and the clatter of their unfamiliar neck chains, in place so Charlie could clip them to a fence if necessary, the dogs tossed their heads trying to get rid of them while he let the mooring line go. He steamed slowly out of the bay, picking up speed when he pushed the throttle down and headed to Reg's place near Dieffenbach, where the waters of Tory Channel flow into the waters of Queen Charlotte Sound.

For three days' mustering and tailing he earned five pounds five shillings, or five guineas. From that he had deducted seven shillings and 11 pence for Social Security contributions. The contribution consisted of a registration fee and a charge of one shilling in the pound. The Commissioner of Taxes was responsible for the collection of both the fee and the charge. The Social Security Act, 1938, stated:

> All persons (male and female and including natives) 16 years of age or over, who are ordinarily resident in New Zealand are required:
> *1 To register within one month after 1st April, 1939.*
> *2 Upon registration to obtain a copy book.*
> *3 To pay the Social Security charge at the rate of one shilling in the pound upon all salary and wages earned.*

*4 Unless exempted, to pay the annual or quarterly instalments
of the registration fee as these fall due.*

*5 To furnish during May of each year a declaration as to income
other than salary or wages derived during the year ended on the
previous 31 March, and to pay the Social Security charge upon
such income.*

The employer was responsible for the deductions at the time
of payment. The charge was payable by the employer in Social
Security stamps which had to be affixed in the wages book, or
upon the wages receipt, and cancelled by a signature or initials
and the date.

Charlie has never forgotten one particular day he arrived
home from Reg's. He was hot. "I was buggered." As he
headed in the bay he ran his tongue around his mouth as he
anticipated the cold beer he knew was sitting in his kerosene
fridge in the kitchen.

It had been a day Charlie would rather forget. His bitch
was coming on heat but he needed her and thought she'd be
all right for just one more day. His dogs had scrapped all the
way down the channel, his bitch had caused Reg's dogs to
fight amongst themselves, and once down in the yards where
they tailed the lambs, all the dogs had fought over her. On the
way home his bitch had backed herself up in a corner and
snarled whenever a dog came near, and the last straw was
when a huge dog fight broke out in the cockpit of the boat.

At the moorings Charlie couldn't stand any more. He flung
the lot in the dinghy, then jumped in himself. Still standing he
picked up an oar and pushed against the *Wheke*'s topsides. After clearing the dogs out of the way, he picked up the other
oar from the bottom of the dinghy, sat down on his seat and
put the oars in the rowlocks ready to row ashore.

"All hell broke loose. There was a huge donnybrook. The
dinghy overturned and the dogs – still scrapping – and I
ended up in the sea. We all seemed to surface at the same
time. Still fighting they tried to clamber up on to the hull of
the overturned boat. I was so wild I shoved them off, grabbed
the dinghy painter and swam the dinghy ashore. I let the dogs
swim to cool off." Charlie laughed.

Once ashore the dogs were tied up in their kennels and
given a good feed of goat meat and fresh water. Then Charlie

came in the back gate next to the woodshed, walked up the concrete path he'd laid in their first year on Okukari, and sank down, still dripping, on the back door-step where at last he enjoyed his beer.

Goats were introduced on to Arapawa Island by Captain Cook about 1769 and their numbers have increased over the years in spite of culls that have been carried out by the New Zealand Forest Service and more recently by the Department of Conservation. The goats destroy the native bush which contains ngaio, ake-ake, taupata and manuka on the coastal areas of Arapawa – one of the few remaining examples of Cook Strait vegetation. In earlier days the goats were controlled by the local farmers killing them for dog tucker with the added incentive of a bounty of three shillings plus three rounds of .303 ammunition paid for every tail handed in to the Department of Conservation.

Reg Jackson and Charlie hunted these goats for dog tucker. They'd head out through Tory Channel and around East Head as far as Wellington Bay on the outside coast in the *Wheke*. Any goats seen off the boat were shot and usually tumbled down the steep faces into the sea to be picked up. Sometimes Reg and Charlie became mountain goats themselves and climbed the cliffs into the bush line to shoot them. A bonus was shooting a Captain Cooker – a descendant of the pigs Captain Cook had also brought out to the island. The wild pork, coated with flour, ginger and brown sugar before it went in the oven to cook slowly, made a change from the family's usual diet of mutton.

Shearing followed tailing. By November the wound where the lambs' tails had been cut off with a searing iron was healed and all the sheep were mustered in. The lambs were crutched and the ewes, rams and wethers were shorn. Charlie believed that the weather pattern in those days was more predictable than it is today.

"When we said we'd start shearing on a certain date we usually had fine weather to start on that date. And we'd nearly always get a straight run. Not like today. You never start when you want to and very rarely do you get three or four fine days in a row in November."

I felt myself nodding my head in agreement.

Christmas was a family affair. Relatives arrived and the house bulged. Arthur and Ada always had people in their guesthouse but some time during the Christmas period they'd come to Okukari, bringing some guests with them. Many of those who came to stay at Oyster Bay with Arthur and Ada remembered Charlie and Ruby from when they'd lived in Oyster Bay, and wanted to meet up with them again.

"We had only a kerosene fridge in those days. We didn't have a generator so there was no deep freeze – our meat was stored in a safe, all the meals were cooked with the coal range, and our bread was baked in it. And I can remember the chimney on the roof of the wash house was always smoking before we'd eaten breakfast. Our table was always laden, there were always cakes and biscuits to eat at morning and afternoon tea and plenty of vegetables from Ruby's garden. But looking back, I really don't know how she managed."

As the children grew older it became a tradition on Christmas Day for Ruby and Charlie and any of the other adults staying with them to visit the locals and have a Christmas drink. They started at Te Awaiti at Trevor and Moira Norton's, and the final stop on the way home was at Nan and Gilbert Perano's at Whekenui.

The children left at home stoked the coal range to cook the chook or turkey, or sometimes a goose which had been caught on the flat in Okukari. They also made sure that the Christmas pudding, with its threepenny and sixpenny coins that they'd all had a share of stirring in while making a wish, didn't boil dry. Six weeks earlier when Ruby had made it, she had tied it up in an old cotton flour bag and pre-cooked it. To prevent mould growing on the outside of the bag she'd then hung it on the clothes-line to dry out. Now the children watched carefully as the pudding heated in the boiling water in the preserving pan on top of the coal range, adding more boiling water if it got too low. The children had been told when to put the vegetables in the oven, and by the time the grown-ups arrived home, only the vegetables on top of the stove had to be cooked.

Boxing Day and New Year's Day were holidays from cooking for Ruby. A picnic was packed and the family steamed down the channel to a different beach. Other families in the channel came and a huge crowd would congregate. While the men gathered mussels the children gathered wood and made a fire on the beach for the wives to boil the mussels in a big pot.

Later they played games and swapped yarns. It was always late when the boats headed home. The dull thump of the engine and the gentle swish the water made as it curled up the stem of the boat and fell back to the sea sent the younger children to sleep until Charlie slowed the engine down close to the beach. The loud silence woke the sleeping children. Charlie untied the dinghy from the stern and rowed everyone ashore. Joe's cries of rage from being woken up followed him all the way out to the moorings where he moored the *Wheke,* and he could still hear him as he rowed back to the beach.

Some days they'd end up at Te Iro Bay and pick wild cherries. "That wasn't so good for Ruby, though. The kids always ended up with the belly ache and when we got home Ruby lit up the coal range to bottle and make jam from the cherries."

Other times Charlie and Ruby went in to Picton for the rowing regatta on New Year's Day. The memories lit up Charlie's face as he recalled the streets closed for the day, and having to stand in a queue to buy an ice-cream. The crowds were swollen by those who paid 10 shillings to come on the special excursion from Wellington on the *Tamahine.*

One year, for a change, the family spent the day of New Year's Eve in Picton. They had brought home supplies and as the *Wheke* rounded Wirikarapa and headed up the last stretch of water Ruby began gathering the grocery boxes and children's gear together, ready for a quick exit from the boat. As they turned into their bay they noticed a large log below the lookout. It had obviously been carried into Tory Channel on the flood tide, and Charlie made a mental note to go over and bring it home for firewood in the next day or so.

The next morning as the family was sitting down to breakfast there was a knock on the back door – an unusual happening as people usually tapped and with a coo-ee came straight inside. Charlie opened the door and found a man, soaking wet, standing on the step. He told Charlie he'd paddled from Wellington in a canoe the day before and had arrived in Tory Channel late the previous afternoon. Unable to establish the entrance he'd followed the *Tamahine* in, but then the tide had carried him against Taranaki Rock, below the lookout. He'd stood in the water most of the night holding his canoe off the rocks until the tide slackened and he could climb back into it and paddle across the channel to Okukari.

Charlie soon realised this man's canoe was the 'big log' they thought they'd seen washed up on the other side of the channel, and felt bad that he hadn't taken the time to go and check the 'log'.

Everyone felt very impressed by his feat, and traipsed down to the beach to have a look at the canoe that had been paddled across Cook Strait. In Charlie's case the awe was soon replaced by anger. The canoe was made from canvas and was covered in canvas patches from where he'd holed it before he'd left Wellington Harbour. All he had in the canoe were some bottles of water.

Charlie's voice was curt, his advice sound. "Now you've had the pleasure of coming across Cook Strait, get rid of it. Go down the steps at the back of the house and pick up the axe. Put it through it and catch the *Tam* home."

The man didn't follow my father-in-law's advice. A few weeks later Charlie learnt he'd stayed in the Sounds for a week, resting. He made the return crossing from Cape Jackson at the northern entrance of Queen Charlotte Sound to Kapiti Island in 26 hours where he sheltered in the lee of the island. The next day, after concerns for his safety had been raised, he was found by a searching launch and towed to Waikanae.

I caught the anger in Charlie's voice and I thought of the many times I've watched and waited for Joe and our two sons, Joe and James, to arrive back in Okukari after they've been called out to rescue the same sort of foolhardy people.

As we live at the entrance of Cook Strait, and with Joe's experience of the sea in the area, he is always called out in an emergency. I can accept the danger if it is an unforseen event and could not have been prevented. But my blood boils when it is a situation that wouldn't have arisen if those involved had taken more care and responsibility – especially when it puts my family at risk.

Charlie's story brought back the fear I'd felt one day in particular as I'd watched my husband and two sons trying to reach a stricken boat with two men on board outside the entrance of Tory Channel. That day I'd believed I'd never see my men again. I remembered my surge of anger as I'd listened to the yachties telling Joe they weren't in any danger. I wondered why they'd sent out a Mayday. It also made me realise that as long as a Heberley lives at Okukari there will always be a willing response to any seafarer in trouble.

During January the sheep are always mustered into the home paddocks. The old ewes, the light ewe lambs and the wether lambs are culled and sent out on the barge to Picton where they are trucked either to the works or sale-yards. The re-mainder are crutched then treated for fly-strike and lice before being turned out again. Recently the plunge dip used in Char-lie's day has been filled in, and today only pour-on or spray 'dips' are used.

It was at one of these musters that some cattle had come in. One of them was a young bull that had missed out on be-ing castrated earlier, and was now too big. Charlie knew Reg Jackson was needing a bull so he rang Reg and suggested he come down and got it.

A delighted Reg with his brother Tom came a couple of days later and the rodeo began. I listened to the laughter in Charlie's voice as he described that day.

"We rounded the bull up and managed to get him in the yards on his own. Reg hung a rope over the gateway and the idea was that when he ran through the gate we'd hook up the rope and have 'im."

But it didn't work like that. The bull charged at the gate, the rope went round his neck, over his shoulder and around his front leg. Reg, Tom and Charlie were all hanging on to the rope and being dragged down to the beach towards the sea.

They let him go. Out in the bay the bull swam around and around, watching his tormentors standing on the beach. He didn't seem to notice when Reg and his brother climbed into their dinghy and rowed to their boat. Once aboard they pulled up the anchor, started the engine and steamed up close to the bull. Before he realised what was happening, Reg flung a bri-dle with a rope tied to it, over its head, down onto its neck and tied it alongside the boat.

"If the *Tuatea* could tow a whale we figured a bull would be easy," they told Charlie later.

Off Wheke Rock the leather on the bridle broke and an-other struggle ensued until they managed to get another rope around him in place of the bridle and continue their trip. When they finally reached home and set the bull free he swam ashore, charged through three fences and disappeared in the bush for two months. When he was found he was with the cows and Reg was thrilled with the calves that were born nine months later.

The last job on the farm that had to be done before whaling began was crutching the ewes before putting them out to the rams for tupping. For the next six weeks they are always rotationally grazed in paddocks on the 100 acres of flat land and the foot hills. If Charlie began on the lookout and the sheep were still being held, it was yet another job for Ruby.

The last break before the men on the hill began whaling was muttonbirding. This blackish-brown bird with bluish-grey feet, more commonly known as the sooty shearwater, is slightly bigger than a domestic pigeon. It was and still is an important item in the diet of the Maori, with some quarter of a million young birds taken annually from breeding grounds off the coast of Stewart Island. The birds are split, salted and preserved.

On a fine day with little or no swell, Charlie and some of the other whalers would head out Tory Channel, around West Head where the shutters in the hut on the lookout still remained firmly closed, and steam five miles south. They anchored in Glasgow Bay. As they rowed ashore a man kept a sharp eye on where the jagged rocks lay just below the surface, and guided the oarsman into the stony beach at the base of the lonely windswept cliffs where the men scrambled up to search for muttonbirds.

"When we found a burrow, we'd shove our hand in. If it was warm it would have a bird."

As soon as the birds were taken from the burrows they were killed and placed in a sack to be cleaned and plucked on the trip home.

The birds were then split and salted down until needed. Charlie claimed that nothing else smelt as bad as a mutton bird cooking – or tasted as good once it was cooked. To cook them, Ruby brought them to the boil four or five times, changing the water each time. Finally she put them in the oven on a meat dish to crisp up.

"The smell drove us from the house, but the end result was delicious."

In 1950 New Zealand's economy was changing, for sheep farmers in particular. On 31 May 1950 the Prime Minister, Sid

Holland, announced that petrol was no longer rationed. This was followed a few days later by butter being freed for unrestricted sale. New Zealand's wartime rationing system had ended. That same year American troops were in Korea, and American Government policy was to buy all the wool available to keep their men warm through the freezing winter conditions. This triggered the 1950s' wool price boom.

Wool that Charlie had sold for 25 pounds a bale in 1946 sold for 94 pounds a bale in 1950. The older sheep maintained their price, but the price of lambs trebled. On the sea it wasn't such a good year. The whaling season lasted only two months with 79 whales being caught.

"On the farm we were looking for any dead sheep and plucking the wool from them. We even pulled wool from the fences."

Charlie felt this was the right time to build their new house. Arthur Heberley was more cautious. He had lived through the Depression of the 1930s and remembered their financial struggles. Charlie should think carefully, he said, before building a new home. But when the minimum price scheme was set up in 1951 to ensure sound returns to wool growers, his decision was made. They would build their house.

Don Terrill, Ruby's uncle, was to build it. Charlie would work with him until the start of the whaling season. All the materials needed to build the 2000-square-foot weatherboard house were shipped in by barge and later on the *Wheke*. The old house was cut in half with a chain-saw and the front half pulled down, leaving the kitchen, scullery, pantry and bathroom. Next to the homestead there was a farm workers' cottage which had been built by the Kennys in 1934, and named Okukari-iti. Here the family slept while their house was being built.

As the old walls were torn down they discovered the walls beneath the wallpaper had been lined with old newspapers and pages from *The Weekly News* and the *New Zealand Free Lance*.

"We read some of them before they were burnt. There were articles about whaling and even stories from the rowing boat days. Old things didn't seem so important in those days. I regret not saving them now, though," Charlie admitted.

At first the house seemed to grow quickly, but as unrest on the Auckland waterfront grew, striking watersiders all over the country were beginning to close New Zealand down. "Our house virtually came to a standstill," Charlie recalled. "We couldn't get timber or roofing iron. We'd hear a little had arrived in Picton and we'd rush in and pick that up. A few days later some more would arrive but soon even this supply dried up."

With no ships being loaded or unloaded, the country was crippled. Finally the Government intervened. On 30 April 1951 headlines in the *New Zealand Herald* said:

Government Crushes Waterfront Strike.
Scenes of disorder occurred on Saturday morning outside the Auckland Town Hall, where more than 100 men, registered for wharf work, formed an Auckland Waterfront Workers Union.

As members of the new union emerged from the hall, protected by about 80 police, they had to run a gauntlet of vituperation from about 600 members of the deregistered Waterside Workers Union.

The next day the same paper wrote of an attempt by saboteurs and the use of explosives to blow up a short railway bridge near Huntly. In another incident, the president of the newly formed Auckland Waterfront Worker's Union, R S Belsham, was attacked by three men on the front doorstep of his home.

This led to Prime Minister Holland announcing that a Civil Emergency Organisation would be established, "to protect citizens from violence and intimidation".

On 4 May 1951, the Government brought in 900 men from the Army, Navy and Air Force to unload ships in an effort to get the country moving.

At night Charlie and Ruby lay in their bed, identifying the boats by their throbbing engines as they carried freight across the Strait. When they received a newspaper they knew a paper trip must have taken place recently, and, although the public wasn't meant to know, the familiar sound of one particular fishing vessel meant the local hotel bars would be patronised for the next few days. It was the waterfront strike that brought a halt to the tell-tale smoke coming from the whalers' chimneys as the Peranos found it so difficult to keep up their supply of coal that they converted the boilers at the whaling station to oil-fired boilers.

Once the watersiders' strike was over, the house building continued, with the only interruptions coming from the weather. For this reason Charlie was keen to get the roof on. Whaling had ceased mid-August and as soon as the next settled weather seemed imminent they decided to put on the roof. Charlie listened to the 5am weather forecast. It was for fine weather and light winds for the following 24 hours with the outlook similar. Don Terrill told Charlie they needed two days to finish off the large roof completely, without any of the usual Okukari gales.

"We had the building paper on and the iron being laid before mid-afternoon. Ruby and the kids painted the overlaps before they were passed up and nailed in place. Excitement grew as each room gained a roof. It disappeared at 4pm when we listened to the weather forecast and heard that a cold southerly front was moving up the country and was expected to reach Cook Strait by midnight."

I knew the shock they must have felt as I thought of some of the southerly storms I have seen at Okukari when the wind has torn huge trees out of the ground, blown in windows and brought down phone lines. More recently installed power lines have been brought down, and winds have peeled roofing iron off as effortlessly as pages turned in a book.

"We couldn't leave it half-covered and knew it wouldn't be completed before dark so we rigged up electric lights and ran the generator. We worked until we had all the iron on and nailed down. But," said Charlie, "the front went through the Strait and we missed it."

So often, in the years I have lived at Okukari, there has been the same phenomenon. The one most vivid in my mind occurred on 10 April 1968 – the day the *Wahine* was caught on the edge of a tropical cyclone that was heading south. Travelling at 10 knots and out of control in the seas generated by wind speeds averaging 75 knots, the *Wahine* was at the mercy of the storm as she headed towards Barretts Reef at the entrance to Wellington Harbour. Her starboard side hit the most southern rock of Barretts Reef, sheering off her starboard propeller and part of the shaft. Shortly after, the port engine died. The wind and sea drove the stricken ship across the reef, badly damaging the hull. Her anchors were lowered but wouldn't hold, and she was blown up Wellington Harbour.

The steady flooding of the ship ultimately caused her capsize, and 151 people lost their lives.

At Okukari, even though storm force southerly winds had been predicted, they never did eventuate. The day remained sunny with a clear blue sky and not a breath of wind. The only visible sign that made us able to comprehend the continual news broadcasts over the radio that day were the unusually high swells. They lifted out of a glassy-calm sea and crashed on our beach.

With the new house came electricity. Charlie had installed a Start-a-Matic generator before the house was begun, to enable power tools to be used in the construction. When the house was finished and Ruby needed electricity, all she had to do was turn on any switch to start the generator. The last switch to be turned off stopped it. For the first time in her married life Ruby had an electric cake mixer, an electric toaster, iron and jug, and a Bernina sewing machine. The cooking was done on a Wellstead heat-storage wood and coal range, instead of the old Shacklock 501 that had to be lit every morning.

Arthur Heberley was proud of his son's house and delighted in bringing guests with him when he came to visit. Chronic bronchitis now prevented him from mustering and working as he used to but he still enjoyed coming to Okukari whenever there was sheep work.

Ruby's memories of those days were of a rather cantankerous man, "probably because he was frustrated at not being able to get out on the hill," who stood on the front lawn and "mustered" the farm with his own commentary. Arthur would tell her to prepare morning tea, as the musterers were almost at the shed. Then he'd hurry inside to tell her they weren't stopping, they were mustering the next block and they'd be home for lunch. My mother-in-law often told me how she'd have the kitchen table set and then re-set dozens of time in a day.

Arthur's health forced him and Ada to leave Oyster Bay in 1955. They moved to Picton and lived in the house in Surrey Street which had been in the family since Worser Heberley had bought it around 1878. On 26 April 1955, Oyster Bay officially passed into the hands of Charlie's oldest brother, Herbert.

As the whaling station grew, so did the number of workers, and there were enough children for a school to be opened in Whekenui Bay. Although it was a relief to Ruby to cut her children's lunches and say goodbye to her responsibilities for six hours a day, she confessed that she sometimes wished she could be in charge of their education once more. But she had no option. The law of the country was that if there was a school within a certain distance the children had to attend.

Both Donna and Jocelyn attended a boarding school in Christchurch briefly during their secondary year schooling. Jocelyn left as soon as she was old enough but Donna came home and did her school certificate by correspondence. She has never forgotten having to stay in Blenheim and attend Marlborough College to sit her exams.

In 1956 Donna left Okukari, moved to Nelson and went nursing. I know Charlie was proud of all his family but his pride in his older daughter's achievements was evident. She became a registered nurse, and over the years studied for her diploma in health administration and her BA in social sciences, majoring in nursing studies. "And the majority of her studies were by correspondence."

In Nelson, Donna met a man whom she married. During that marriage a son was born but he died three days later. The marriage ended in divorce. Charlie never spoke a great deal about that part of his life and it wasn't until after his death and we were sifting through boxes of yellowed newspaper cuttings and old photographs that we found a framed photo of Donna taken on her wedding day. The black and white photography brought out every detail of her 'Scarlet O'Hara' gown. Row upon row of frilled lace spilled from her waist, forming a train that lay in a semi-circle on the ground, and the tight-fitting bodice accentuated Donna's tiny waist. The bouquet she carried was overshadowed as I stared at the gown. Donna's voice telling me she'd gone into a dress shop in Nelson with a picture of a gown she liked, brought me back to the present. She was measured and the details sent to Auckland. When the dress arrived in a box in the mail, it fitted her perfectly.

I felt the prick of tears as I thought what Charlie and Ruby must have gone through as they felt Donna's pain. I was glad they had kept that photo – not as a reminder of the bitterness that so often goes with divorce but a reminder of the love they shared with their first-born on her special day.

Jocelyn was married soon after Donna. She was always the tomboy, and frills and fuss weren't for her. She married Noel Davis and they lived at Okukari in the farm cottage that the family had lived in while the new house was being built.

Throughout the 1950s Charlie's income from whaling depended on the numbers caught. The payment remained at two pounds 17 shillings and sixpence per whale, and 11 shillings per sighting. In 1956 the payment for a sighting dropped one shilling to 10 shillings. Charlie questioned this as he knew the price of whale oil was rising. He was told that if he wanted to whale he must accept the terms. He stayed.

Charlie pondered his future. When the 1957 season began and there was still no increase he asked himself if it was worth it. Every season they worked mostly 12 hours a day, seven days a week. For that he took home 250 to 300 pounds. He knew he was more fortunate than most on the hill because he had a farm behind him, but with no pay rise since he'd started whaling 17 years previously, he made up his mind he was going to ask for one.

"I asked the other boys if they'd back me and they said yes. When we were paid at the end of the season I stood up and asked for a pay increase. No one else opened their mouths.

"I left for a reason – I didn't think we were getting paid enough. I left good friends. I believed I could do better concentrating on the farm. What I was making whaling wasn't enough to warrant me staying on, although I hated the idea of giving up whaling."

The winter of 1958 was the hardest Charlie ever spent. From his vantage point on the top of the hill where he was fencing he'd watch the chasers heading out in Cook Strait. He went through every manoeuvre when they were close enough for him to watch. One day he saw a whale spout and estimated it would have been about two miles out. When Charlie realised that the men on the lookout hadn't seen it he admitted that he wondered whether to light a fire or not, to attract their attention.

"No one saw my fire anyway, and I had a sort of perverse pleasure in thinking that was one whale that got away."

In December 1955 an ex-manager of Australia's Byron Bay whaling station had come to New Zealand and floated the Hauraki Whaling Company which built a whaling station at

Whangaparapara on the Great Barrier Island, 84 kilometres miles north-east of Auckland. They caught four whales in 1956 and six in 1957, and then the company was placed into receivership in August 1957. In 1958 it came up for tender. Charlie, with his brother Herbert and two other friends, put in a tender.

The tender was won by the Byron Bay Whaling Company. Later Charlie learnt that they'd got it for 10,000 pounds less than his tender had been. I heard the disgust in Charlie's voice when he told me that the managing director of the Byron Bay Whaling Company was a good friend of the manager of the Auckland bank that held the debenture on it.

Shortly after Charlie had heard they'd missed out on the tender he was working in the sheepyards when a boat came in the bay and three well-dressed men came ashore in a dinghy. They came and introduced themselves to Charlie as the managing director and two of the directors from the Byron Bay Whaling Company. The managing director told Charlie they'd made the trip to Okukari to ask him if he'd manage the factory at Whangaparapara on the Great Barrier. They'd heard he had the experience with Peranos and knew they had great success with the small boats. They wanted Charlie because they didn't know how to catch whales in small boats, as in Australia their company caught the whales using the big Norwegian-type chase boats. They told him they needed his knowledge.

"I told them my house was only six years old and a beautiful home. If they wanted me with my wife and family to go up to Whangaparapara they'd have to build me a home similar to what I had at Okukari."

All Charlie's terms were accepted and his annual income was to earn him more than he'd earned in the last 10 years as a gunner on a whale chaser.

In January 1959, as soon as the sheep work was completed, Charlie, Ruby and Joe – who was just 16 – left the farm and headed north. Jocelyn and Noel, with baby Linda, Charlie's first grandchild, remained at Okukari to manage the farm.

"It was to be the biggest river I ever had to cross, but I was determined it wasn't going to beat me," Charlie said.

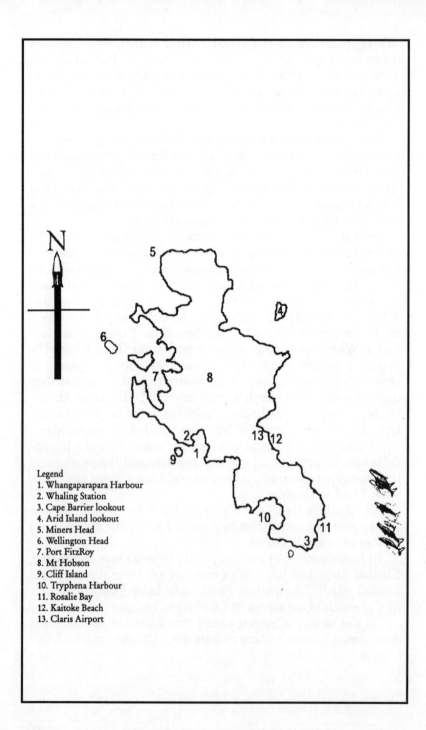

N

5

4

6

7

8

2

9

1

13 12

10

11

3

Legend
1. Whangaparapara Harbour
2. Whaling Station
3. Cape Barrier lookout
4. Arid Island lookout
5. Miners Head
6. Wellington Head
7. Port FitzRoy
8. Mt Hobson
9. Cliff Island
10. Tryphena Harbour
11. Rosalie Bay
12. Kaitoke Beach
13. Claris Airport

Chapter Nine

GREAT BARRIER ISLAND

Aotea

GREAT BARRIER ISLAND lies almost 84 kilometres north-east of Auckland. Forty kilometres long and 4-18 kilometres wide, its mostly hilly bush-clad terrain forms a barrier to Auckland's Hauraki Gulf. Today it is separated from Auckland by a 20-30-minute flight, either by private plane or with Great Barrier Airline. Its planes land on the east coast at Claris where they have a small shed which acts as a terminal for passengers to check in. All up the east coast, ocean swells, originating far out in the Pacific, thunder incessantly on the long stretches of white sandy beaches.

Alternatively, there is the two-hour trip on a fast ferry which generally calls in to the three harbours on the inner or west coast. These are Port FitzRoy at the northern end, which in early years was described as large enough to accommodate the entire British fleet, then Whangaparapara in the middle, and the southern harbour of Tryphena.

The first purchase of Maori land was made in 1838 when it was sold by the Ngatiwai tribe. After the Treaty of Waitangi this sale was disallowed, and in 1844 it was sold once again, this time to a syndicate headed by Sir Frederick Whitaker when a grant of 24,000 acres was made to the group. The population remained sparse with only a few military pensioners with 40- and 60-acre grants, and some sponsored immigrants. In 1902 there were about 500 residents on Great Barrier.

It was the discovery of silver at Okupu, and then gold quartz inland from Whangaparapara in 1892, that swelled the population. A mining settlement, Oroville, with a population of 400, sprang up around its 20-stamp battery. Whangaparapara was its port. By 1908, 23,000 pounds worth of gold had been brought out, but in 1910 the gold petered out and the operations closed.

The Kauri Timber Company's mill was built in 1909 in Whangaparapara to take advantage of free port status. Logs were towed in from Coromandel, Puketi and the Bay of Islands to be milled. That activity, combined with the mining town, made Whangaparapara the island's centre. At that time first-grade sawn kauri was worth 11 shillings per 100 feet. While in operation the company felled 79 million feet and took 55 million feet of logs off the Barrier. The system was for the men to build a huge dam in a creek. Then, using bullock teams, they dragged all the logs that hadn't already tumbled into the creek bed into the now dry creek bed below the dam. When the water was high, the sluice gates were opened. A wall of water then carried the logs before it down to the sea, where they were rafted or towed to the mill.

In 1963 I walked up to one of the remaining dams on Mount Hobson at the back of Port FitzRoy. The dam stood between the narrowed banks of the creek's headwaters. The steep grey bluffs of the summit of Mount Hobson towered above us. The silence of the thick native bush was eerie. This was where the weathered kauri timber had been pit-sawn and broad-axed. Foundations laid in the rock were built strong enough to bear the massive weight of water needed to thrust the logs downstream. Once there had been a palisade of beams which formed the main wall. These had been caulked with the decayed vegetation gathered from the foot of the kauri trees. A gate about 12 feet high – sometimes up to 20 feet wide, depending on the width of the creek – was fitted with a 'trip'.

As I gazed at the remains of the dam I counted 17 vertical logs still attached to a horizontal beam that hung drunkenly across the creek bed. Water flowed through the timber. Far down the valley I could see the blue waters of Port FitzRoy. It was good to see the distinctive green of many young kauri, or younglings, which had been planted over the years by staff from the Department of Conservation. Now they were breaking out from the canopy of bush below us. It was impossible to imagine what the noise must have been like when the gate opened, the water roared out and the logs crashed their way down the mountain on the crest of the flood.

In later years a tramline was built from Whangaparapara deep into the bush, and the remaining kauri was removed. In 1941 the Kauri Timber Company closed its mill at Whangaparapara and sold its 19,000-acre block of mostly mountainous bush to the government.

Great Barrier was the scene of one of New Zealand's worst shipwrecks. In 1894 the steamer *Wairarapa,* en route from Sydney to Auckland and travelling at full speed through heavy fog, struck the rocks at Miners Head, a cliff about 600-700 feet high on the north-western side of the island, and 121 people drowned. It was three days before the first message of the disaster reached Auckland. This wreck emphasised the need for better communication between the island and the mainland and resulted in the establishment of a 'pigeongram' service between the Barrier and Auckland. It was owned and run by a local man, Holden Howie, who had a pigeon loft attached to his house. This service had its official stamp and is said to have been the world's first airmail service. It cost one shilling to send messages from Great Barrier to Auckland.

In 1922 the steamer *Wiltshire* ran aground at Rosalie Bay, reputed to be one of the rockiest and wildest coasts of the Hauraki Gulf islands. She snapped in two. All 103 officers and crew escaped. In her cargo there was a consignment of overproof whisky which was later strewn over Kaitoke Beach. Much to the relief of the Auckland police, the Medland family who gathered it up were abstainers.

The eastern coast of Great Barrier was also the final resting place of the *Rose-Noelle*, a 12.65-metre trimaran which had left Auckland in June 1989 for a two-week voyage to Tonga. She capsized four days out from Auckland and for the next 119 days the crew survived in the up-turned hull. The Pacific swells eventually hurled the boat onto a reef 75 metres offshore from the Great Barrier. From there the crew managed to reach the beach and seek help at a near-by farmhouse.

When Charlie, Ruby and Joe arrived at Great Barrier in 1959, the population was around 200. There was no doctor. Accidents and medical complaints were in the hands of one district nurse. Six telephone exchanges with plugs and cords, each operated by a resident, maintained the link to the outside world, and the luxury of electricity on the island was for those who owned their own generator.

One luxury was the island taxi, a pre-war Chrysler Imperial once owned by the American gangster Al Capone. It was available to drive visitors on the metalled roads that linked the island's settlements. To travel from Auckland took four to five hours by boat, or 30 minutes with Captain Fred Ladd in his amphibian, flying from Mechanics Bay in downtown Auckland. Charlie with Ruby and Joe flew into Whangaparapara with Fred Ladd.

Chapter Ten

A NEW CHALLENGE

Tau mahi e te ringa whero.
Fit work for the hand of a chief.

"A SHOWER OF SPRAY and we're away!" These were the words made famous by Captain Fred Ladd as he settled back in his seat, opened the throttle in his Widgeon amphibian aircraft and sped over the sea until a loud acceleration lifted the plane above the waves and he headed towards Whangaparapara Harbour. It was 29 January 1959.

Fred Ladd began this service in 1954. In those days his company comprised one mechanic, a Widgeon plane which Fred flew, and Fred's wife Mabel who alternated between being ground staff, office administrator and ground hostess. In the beginning he advertised his business by flying from island to island in the Hauraki Gulf, and landing on any beach near where people lived. He'd then introduce himself, and tell them he was starting up a business to fly people over the Gulf.

The first year was a struggle. In 1955 they carried about 1,700 passengers but 10 years later the fleet had increased to three aircraft and they were carrying nearly 19,000 passengers.

Now, as the plane lifted, Charlie's view was blotted out by water that streamed over the windows and washed over the body of the plane. The last drops were torn from the windows as they became airborne, and he looked down on high cranes working on ships tied alongside the wharves. These soon formed the backdrop for the armada of small craft enjoying the summer's day on the sparkling Waitemata Harbour. In the distance the nearly completed Auckland harbour bridge stood out, many people still not accepting the beauty in its stark frame. Bean Rock, one of Auckland's landmarks, its round tower built like a house with windows and a decking right round, soon disappeared, and Charlie, sitting in the seat alongside Fred, with Ruby and Joe behind, settled back to enjoy the flight. Over Motutapu Island and Rakino Island, Fred ducked down, slid open his window and hurled a newspaper to each house. Charlie watched in fascination as people raced out, picked up their papers and waved. Fred wiggled the wings of his plane in reply and headed across the open expanse of the Hauraki Gulf to Whangaparapara Harbour.

The calm afternoon allowed Fred to pass close to Cliff Island at the entrance of the harbour before he touched down in the harbour, and roared up into Whangaparapara heading towards the sloping beach alongside the whaling station on the western side. He put down the fat rubber wheels, then the plane trundled up the shingle and came to a halt at the top of the beach. As their personal luggage was unloaded and dumped above the stony beach, on the sand, Charlie looked around and made up his mind. If the whales were there, he would make this station work. And he made a pact with himself to produce the best quality oil, an oil that was equal to or better than oil from anywhere else in the world.

Charlie knew the venture was precarious. No one had any idea where the whales tracked in this area. They didn't even know how many passed the Barrier. In 1890 a station had been established by the Cook family who whaled out of Whangamumu Harbour in the region of the Bay of Islands on the North Island coast. That station had taken 30 to 50 whales a year, confirming that the whales were there. From his studies Charlie knew the northern migration of whales could be expected between May through to August, and the southern migration during September and October.

"I was fortunate enough to get two ex-Perano whalers, Tom Norton and Tom Gullery, to come up with me and I was confident that with our expertise and knowledge we could at the very least break even. And even though Joe was just out of school and hadn't been whaling, I knew his capabilities."

Charlie had February, March and April to make the station operational for the start of the season at the beginning of May. The Hauraki Whaling Company had only the *Colville*, a Fairmile, 112 feet long with a triple-skinned hull that had been built for the navy during the Second World War. They had converted her to a chaser and mother-ship and she had been bought by the Barrier Whaling Company. This company wanted to use her mainly as the mother ship, and have two of the smaller chasers such as those used by Peranos to catch the whales.

"We had them built in Picton by the same builders who built the other chasers because they had the experience and knew what we required. The bottom of a chaser was constructed with an inner skin of plywood and outer skin of planked kauri. Roger Carey built one which we named *Oria,* and Jack Morgan built the other one which we called *Surprise.* Before the start of the season we flew back to Picton where Ruby christened them. Then they were shipped to Auckland where my brother Herbert, and another engineer from Picton, Clarrie Olsson, installed the American V12 Scripps petrol engines in each boat."

These engines were capable of developing 350HP at 2,600rpm and each had a total weight of 1,600 pounds. The crank case and pistons were Lyrite aluminium alloy. The cylinders and cylinder heads were cast in pairs, making maintenance easier as well as cutting down heat expansion stresses. They had dual ignition with a separate coil and distributor at the aft end of each block, and 24 spark plugs.

Because of the uncertainty of the actual passage of the whales, they built two lookout huts. "We covered all our options," Charlie explained. One was at the north-eastern end of Great Barrier on Arid Island, and the other on Cape Barrier at the southern end. All the materials to build the huts were carried on the *Colville* to the bays below the sites. From there they were rowed ashore and then hauled by ropes to the top of the hill.

Permanent moorings had to be in place at both sites to moor the chasers when the crews were on the lookouts. The concrete blocks were made at the factory in Whangaparapara and taken to each place on board the *Colville* where they were dumped overboard. The two chasers were not expected to be completed until the end of June but everything else was ready. The chasers were to be manned by Tom Norton as gunner and Charlie's brother, Herbert, as driver aboard the *Surprise,* while on the *Oria* Charlie was going to be gunning with Tom Gullery driving. Until the small boats arrived the *Colville* would be used to catch the whales.

The first year Charlie put Joe on the *Colville* as deckhand, mainly because the crew knew very little about whaling, although Jeff Morris had worked as assistant gunner on the *Colville* for the former company. Charlie put him on as head gunner and relied on Joe to give the inexperienced crew an indication of what they had to do during a hunt, and preparing a whale for towing. With everything arranged, all that remained was to find the whales.

May passed, and nothing. Then, on 3 June 1959, the first whale of the season was spotted from the hut on Cape Barrier and shot by Jeff Morris off the *Colville*, two miles east of the Cape. Jeff harpooned 36 whales before the *Oria* and *Surprise* were finally completed and arrived out at the Barrier during the last week in June.

Where possible Charlie had employed local men, and on the day the chasers arrived in the bay everyone was clamouring for a trip around the harbour on the two sleek craft. The critics criticised but others praised. A local man, Bill Frieswijk, was the boilerman. He had refused to join the union and had left other positions for that reason. When he received another letter telling him he had to join the union he refused again, so when Charlie received a similar letter, rather than lose his boilerman in the middle of a season he paid Bill's union fees.

I wondered if that had been at the back of Charlie's mind when he'd noticed Bill standing on the stern of the new chaser. Mischievously he opened the throttle. He laughed out loud at the sight of Bill's gumboot-clad legs disappearing over the stern.

On 30 June the new boats began their working life when Tom Norton on the *Surprise*, with Herbert Heberley driving, notched up their first whale of the season off Arid Island.

Tom Gullery had been the seventh foreman at the Perano whaling station when he left whaling to work in Picton. But he jumped at the opportunity to go up north to work at the Whangaparapara factory as Charlie's driver. Tom told me he felt very honoured, and added, "Charlie's a good workmate. I'd trust my life with him."

Tom never forgot his first day out with Charlie and always claimed that he was lucky it wasn't his last. "A whale spouted in front of us. Charlie fired and we were fast to it. He yelled at me to 'take a turn'. I discovered later I wasn't meant to tie the rope that was attached to the harpoon to the logger-head. I was meant to take a turn of the rope on it so I could play the whale, letting the rope run out if necessary or pulling in the slack when I could. But in the excitement of my first chase all I could think of was hanging on to this bugger. I picked up the rope and put two half-hitches around the logger-head."

I could imagine Charlie's reaction. Without the running line on the whale, the chaser could easily have been dragged under, the rope could have snapped, or the harpoon pulled out. "But we got the line off the logger-head and a 40-foot male hump-back was recorded to us."

In 1959 Joe became the first person on the station to need medical aid when he squashed his fingers on the *Colville*. The whale line was a four-inch manilla rope on a drum. They had just become fast to the whale and it took off. The line was controlled by the winch driver – when too much weight came on he released the brake, allowing rope to run out, and when the tension came off the line he winched in the slack. It was the same principle a fisherman uses as he plays a heavy trout on his line. If the brake was released quickly and not eased back, the rope occasionally flew off the pullies on the winch drum, or become crossed.

This day the rope was crossed. Joe knew if it wasn't freed smartly they'd likely lose the whale, either with a snapped line or a pulled out harpoon. When the skipper managed to get forward enough and get slack rope, Joe grabbed hold of the rope and held it over the groove, allowing it to feed back onto the drum. The winch driver was told to go in reverse to tension the rope onto the drum while Joe was holding it. Instead, he put it in forward. It pulled Joe's fingers around the drum under the rope and squashed the fingers of his right hand.

A towel was wrapped around his hand to stem the blood, and, Joe told me, to stop him fainting whenever he looked at it. Joe always went woozy at the sight of blood. After the whale was finally killed, Charlie took Joe aboard the *Oria* and steamed around to Port FitzRoy where the district nurse stitched and bandaged his fingers. She told Joe to come back in a week for them to be dressed. By the end of the week they were beginning to feel much better and he happily returned. "She cut off the bandage and tore off the dressing that had stuck to the wound and pulled the healing flesh on the tips of my fingers right off," Joe said. "I never went back. Left them for a fortnight and they came right even though they are misshapen now."

The only other accident when the district nurse needed to be called on was when a factory worker fell on a chain-saw which had jammed while cutting through the rib cage of a whale. His foot slipped from under him, he put his hand out to steady himself, and fell on the saw. He lost one finger and three-quarters of another but this time the mangled pieces couldn't be saved.

That first year 104 whales were processed in a station that wasn't really equipped to deal with that number. Most of the local men working at the station were new to whaling. In the first season, in an effort to help them learn faster, Charlie, Joe, Tom Norton and Tom Gullery, after a day out on the chasers, used to gulp a quick meal and then work in the factory, helping cut up and begin to process the whales.

"It was only because those men from Picton were so willing, and Joe was prepared to work those long hours too, that we were able to get the station up and running so quickly. And I always felt they gave me 110 percent because they knew their boss was prepared to get in and work with them."

Charlie knew they could have caught more that season. "It was hard watching whales pass by and not catch them." But his determination to produce only the best quality oil made him turn his back on them. "Whale oil is only allowed to have a certain acid content to be a first-grade oil, and to get this first-grade oil the whale oil had to be processed within 12 hours because the whales fermented and deteriorated very quickly."

My father-in-law was proud of a letter he'd received from the Amsterdam company which had bought the oil. They told him it was the best oil they'd received that year, including oil from the Antarctic.

To ensure the best possible results he learnt how to test the oil himself, and set up a laboratory in his office. Every night he made the men at the factory take a sample of each 'cook' that went through, and Charlie then tested that oil to make sure he had the acidity below the required level. Most of that oil went into margarine, soap, greases, chocolate, cosmetics and pharmaceutical products, and because it was a top grade oil they got a top grade price for it.

Tom Norton has a vivid memory of one particular morning. "We'd finished about 3am and we were all absolutely buggered. Charlie invited us into his office for a whisky. He got the bottle out, poured it neat into glasses and with 'Cheers', we all gulped it down. We knew immediately it wasn't whisky. In fact it was double-strength industrial detergent left in a whisky bottle by the previous owners. Charlie had grabbed it by mistake. We all managed to make ourselves sick but Charlie stuck to his. Reckoned he was blowing out bubbles for days."

It was during that first season that the Australian company sent over its factory manager. For the last 20 years he had been in charge of a big factory ship in the Antarctic. But Charlie had no idea of this, or of his role in Australian whaling – just that he was interested in whaling and would like to visit them for a few days. In fact he had been sent over to assess the feasibility of the factory and, with his experience, to find out exactly what they could expect it to produce. Charlie learned later that he had gone back and told the Australian company that, as it was, the Whangaparapara station would not process more than 60 whales per year.

"Our 104 was 44 more than the expert predicted," Charlie said proudly.

Seventy-one whales were caught during the northern migration which finished on 1 August 1959, while 33 were taken on the southern migration which ran from 16 September until 30 October 1959.

Forty-eight males and 56 females with an average length of 40.7 feet made up the total. The estimated oil production was 930 tonnes with the average per whale being 8.9 tonnes. Between the migrations, the tanker *Tirranna* came into Whangaparapara Harbour and shipped out 670 tonnes. The balance was stored in the tank until after the southern migration.

That season the Byron Bay Whaling Company also sent two men over from Norfolk Island to go out on the chasers with Charlie's men to learn their technique. Charlie took one of them with him and Tom Gullery on the *Oria*, while the other went with Tom Norton and Herbert Heberley on the *Surprise*.

After two or three days Tom Norton realised they were there not only to learn how to catch whales from the small boats but eventually either to take over their jobs or to cut their wages if they insisted on staying. After all, whaling was a skill, a rare skill. He discussed this possibility with Herbert. The two men decided they were no longer going to take them out. "We told them, and they were quite good about it," Tom said.

The next morning before daybreak the boats left Whangaparapara Harbour. Charlie had already left with his man when Tom and Herbert pulled away on their own.

"We shot the first whale of the day. It was travelling with a scrag – last year's calf. We left that for Charlie to shoot," Tom continued, "and, to top that off, when he looked round and saw we didn't have our man and we told him why, Charlie blew his stack. So did Herbert."

Tom's smile grew wider as he remembered the events of that day. He said he was cringing at the language because Ruby, who often came out on the boat with Charlie, was there that day, and, when Tom suggested to Herbert to cut the language down, Herbert yelled back at him, "If she likes to come out in a man's world she'll have to listen to a man's argument!"

Charlie's driver, Tom Gullery, wasn't saying a word. "He was scared stiff," Tom reckoned.

Tom and Herbert were ordered to take their man out the next day. Herbert told Charlie, "Go to hell. I'd rather go back to the station and stay there."

Both Tom and Herbert arrived back at the factory and decided that next day they'd ring Fred Ladd to fly them into Auckland and arrange tickets to fly back to Marlborough. But that night Charlie came down to their hut to talk with them.

"You pair of bastards," he told them. "You're bloody right. We came here as a gang, we'll stay here as a gang, and we'll go home as a gang. We never said we'd teach anyone."

Tom Norton believed that was the closest Charlie ever came to apologising. "He wasn't afraid to back down, but by Christ it took a lot to make him."

The last whale was caught on 30 October. Two men had lived in each of the lookout huts for the whole season so before they were closed down an inventory was taken. Charlie had asked Tom and Herbert to go out to Arid Island to help Len Biddis with the inventory, then bring him back to the factory. All Picton men, they had their plane booked to take them home the following day.

During the last few weeks of the season Tom admitted he'd been becoming concerned by the amount of water he was pumping from the *Surprise*. It had increased from a dozen or so pumps to empty her out every morning to five minutes of pumping, and now he could see little spurts of water coming in where the nails were pulling out. "I'd been plugging the holes with matches – worked pretty well," Tom told me. But when they came to leave Arid Island there was a very strong nor'easterly with a big sea running.

"We were right for the first four hundred yards. Then we started to pick the seas up from behind and away we'd go – doing about 40 miles an hour down hill, and she spun out. Herbie ripped her astern and got her head up and he let her jog home."

At the station both chasers were pulled up on the slip to dry out after the season. On the bottom of the *Surprise* the kauri planks had buckled and were hanging off in some places, pulling the nails through the plywood and causing the boat to leak. A hand could fit up where the planks had left the transom. The boat builder believed it was caused through the use of kiln-dried timber. The Auckland boatbuilders, Voss's, had to put on a complete new bottom.

Two directors of the company, Edward Coles and Trevor White, asked Tom Norton if he'd go to Norfolk Island and then on to Byron Bay to whale, as they were thinking of using the small chasers. Tom admits he was tempted and visualised himself riding around in a Mercedes Benz. But when he was offered only the same money as he was making in New Zealand, loyalty to a 'good mate' kept him where he was.

With such a good season behind him, Charlie's position as station manager seemed secure. A letter he received in early November confirmed his position, and at the same time advised him that his salary was at the rate of 2000 pounds from 1 November 1959. The letter concluded: 'I should also like to compliment you on the magnificent performance of the station under your control during the past whaling season and to express the sincere hope that your association with this company will be a long and happy one.'

It was signed E Coles, chairman of directors.

Soon after Charlie received this letter the directors came over from Australia to talk with him. Now he had proved the whales were there, and that processing them at the factory on Great Barrier was feasible, they would build the house Charlie had asked for. Up until now Charlie and Ruby had lived in one of the small accommodation houses for the workmen, and eaten meals with everyone else, meals prepared by the station cook, Eddie Glink, who lived at Glink's Gully near Ninety Mile Beach.

The factory was also to be improved. The directors wanted better whale-cooking facilities to enable the whales to be processed faster, more oil separators, and a meat meal plant put in. When Charlie asked them exactly how they wanted it built, they said they would leave it to him as they could see he knew what he was doing.

But first they wanted Charlie and Ruby to go to Norfolk Island with Edward Coles as they wanted Charlie to observe the operations of the Norfolk Island whaling station, a subsidiary of the Byron Bay Whaling Company. Like the former Hauraki Whaling Company, they used only a large chaser similar to the *Colville,* and they wanted Charlie's opinion of using the small chasers.

Their older daughter Donna had planned her holidays at that time to visit her parents at Whangaparapara so she went with them to Norfolk Island. Charlie came back saying that the small chasers would work just as well in Norfolk as they did in New Zealand, so the company had two similar chasers built in Australia, and then shipped over to Norfolk Island. They were named *Kingston Whaler* and *Cascade.*

Charlie's arrival in Auckland coincided with one of the chasers being there to have some work done on it. Donna still had some spare days, so a short time after arriving at Auckland's Whenuapai Airport she found herself with Ruby, tucked down the for'ward hatch for the two and a half-hour trip to the island, while at the wheel Charlie caught up on the news from the station as he and the two-man crew who had brought the chaser to Auckland steamed it back to Whangaparapara Harbour.

During the 1959 season, once the whales had been brought in to the factory they were hauled up the slipway onto the flensing deck where they were stripped of their blubber. From here the blubber and cut up pieces of whale and bone were winched up the ramp onto the top deck where it was cut up into pieces small enough to drop down into the cooker. There was no shelter from the weather.

A much larger building to house extra equipment was now built, and the new flensing deck, ramp and top deck were completely covered in.

Three new separators, similar to a cream separator, were installed. When they were operating, the oil passed through them with hot water to remove any remaining broken down bone and meat. Charlie installed a de-sludger which handled all the residue out of the cookers, and this ensured that every bit of oil from the whale was extracted. After the residue had been through the de-sludger it went over a vibrating screen which took any solids away from the liquids. The liquids then went through a different type of separator to extract the last of the oil.

Charlie bought a drier from a Queensland factory that had gone bankrupt. It had been used to process pineapple husks for cattlefood. It was set up in the whaling factory, and all the solids went into it so that a meat meal was produced. Charlie's idea was to sell it as a manure, but poultry farmers heard of it and trialed it. They discovered it was one of the best foods they could feed to their poultry. An interest in whale meat to use in hamburgers had come from an American company, and Charlie sent over samples. They told him they'd take all he could produce.

"I never followed that up as I preferred to concentrate on oil quality," he said.

The station renovations were complete for the start of the 1960 season. Two Blackstone generators, each with a capacity of 120KVA, were brought in to replace the smaller Leyland diesel generator which had an output of only 63KV. This was kept as a back-up while a smaller Lister with a capacity of 25KV ran for Charlie's house and the directors' cottage of 500 square feet, when the station wasn't operating.

Charlie's and Ruby's house of 1,100 square feet had been built 300 feet above the station on a site selected for the view – close to the station but far enough away from the noise and the smell. The two houses were surrounded by kowhai and puriri trees which were home for the kaka, the native parrot, while the black trunks of the tree ferns leaned drunkenly close to the house which, with its floor to ceiling windows, commanded a panoramic view of the harbour and far out into the Hauraki Gulf.

The track leading up to the house and the directors' cottage wound up through the gnarled trunks of old pohutukawa trees. In the steep clay bank, round holes which led into a tunnel a foot or more long before opening out into a spacious chamber were the homes of the kotare or kingfisher. From November through to January, when the females laid their eggs, birds flitted in and out the nest. Later, after hatching, there was a constant stream as each bird kept up the supply of grubs and insects to feed its family of five to seven chicks.

The workers, too, were comfortable. The main accommodation block of 1,391 square feet contained a mess hall, kitchen and store space, as well as four rooms each 10 feet by 10 feet. There were three detached accommodation blocks, one with four rooms, and a total floor space of 436 square feet, and three others each containing five rooms and a total floor space of 1,500 square feet. Another building, 384 square feet, housed a laundry, a shower room and toilet.

By May 1960 the factory was complete, and the boats ready. The last job was going to Auckland to pick up the explosives from the magazine at Kawakawa Bay, and any last-minute stores before the whales started to run.

Fred Ladd in his Widgeon had become well-known to the men at the Barrier whaling station. He transported them to and from the city and he also took great delight in swooping unexpectedly over the top of them while they were chasing. He'd even taken to bombing their boats with flour bombs.

On this particular day, as the chaser passed Devonport Naval Base on its way to pick up stores from Auckland, the men on board saw the Widgeon heading straight towards them. This time they were ready.

Tom Norton ran up to the gun which was always kept loaded – without a harpoon – and pulled the trigger. The paper wad shot out in a great burst of flames. Some of the burning paper went around the propellers and looked like a giant catherine wheel. Fred Ladd veered away in a hurry.

By the time they arrived back in Whangaparapara they'd forgotten about the incident. But what they'd also forgotten was that they'd fired off their gun in front of the naval base. Charlie was waiting for them at the end of the wharf.

"You'll get us hung," he hissed. "Bloody Devonport – they don't know whether to prosecute or not. Firing a gun at an aircraft!"

The culprits left Charlie to deal with it. He never mentioned the episode again and after that the only thing ever thrown out of Fred's aircraft was the *New Zealand Herald.*

Joe had served his apprenticeship. In 1960, when he was 17, Charlie had put him on as harpoon gunner on the *Surprise* while he took over the driving. "I told Joe two things. If you want to be a good gunner – shoot them before they begin to lift, or they'll kick." And memories of the day he got the rope, which was fast to a whale, around his foot made him add, "And keep your feet clear of the dammed rope.

"I'm his father and no doubt prejudiced, but looking back on those years I can say he'd be one of the best gunners New Zealand has seen. We made a good team." And when I asked him what made a 'good gunner', Charlie's reply was instant. "The ability to hit the whale at the right time."

Joe spoke of his first day on the gun and admits he was "scared as hell". But he was determined to make a success of it because at that time they believed whaling was going to go on forever, and this would be his life's work.

The first page of the Cape Barrier lookout log book for 1960 had Len Biddis of Picton, and Bill Gibbs of Great Barrier, as the two permanent lookout crew. The chaser crews were Charlie as driver and Joe Heberley as gunner on the *Surprise,* while on the *Oria* Tom Gullery was the driver and Tom Norton the gunner.

The first entry written by Bill Gibbs reads:

Sunday 8 May 1960
Wind – slight NNW
Sea – slight
Cloud – 3/10
Rain – nil
Swell – slight

Left Whangaparapara this morning with stores and equipment for Cape Barrier. Vessel used, MV *Colville.* Everything landed safely and hauled up to lookout. Basil, Charlie and Pom worked the boat while Aussie, Joe, The Plumber and yours truly flogged their guts out on the wire. Line shooting!

Found hut in reasonable condition after the summer. A few rats in residence, but we hope to make fast to those during the next few days. Have not looked for whales today as it has been a full book, stocking the hut. Looks like a hard winter.

The entries continued mostly in a similar vein – nothing to report, no sightings, always nothing.

Tuesday 24 May 1960
A day of intense marine activity although we have been silent spectators. Everyone's thoughts have been on the huge tidal waves sweeping the Pacific and how their effects have touched lookout hands. The waves have swept into New Zealand Harbours

creating untold damage and chaos. In Mercury Cove [on Great Mercury Island, south east of Great Barrier] the bay filled and emptied time after time, totally changing the shape of things. Kennedy Bay and Port Charles [on the Coromandel] were also hit, launches being wrecked and damaged. A six-foot surge rolled into Tryphena Harbour and deposited boats on roads and gardens. The lookout was unaffected. No whales were thrown up at Whangaparapara.

The following day the first whale of the season was caught.

> We are whaling. Yep, hump backing. After a short effort *Oria* made fast and duly wound him in. Nothing else of interest sighted, only an odd sie.

The long lean sie whales did not interest the whalers as they yielded very little oil.

Over the next few weeks the whales passing Great Barrier increased. The *Colville* could not keep up with the numbers that could be caught as she was also towing whales. Charlie realised he needed another boat which could be used just for towing the dead whales to the factory, so he leased the *Olympia* for a year.

The *Olympia,* a 65-foot trawler, had been bought and shipped out to New Zealand by an Auckland fisherman after the Second World War. Before she could be used to tow whales a chain plate had to be built in the deck so two bollards could be fitted, one on each side of the shoulders of the boat, to fasten the whale to when towing.

In the process of installing the chain plate a portion of deck was lifted, and another deck was discovered beneath. In it were lines of machine-gun bullets running the length of the exposed deck.

"I learnt later that during the war, when Germany occupied Norway, the *Olympia* had run from the Shetland Islands across to Norway, taking the underground movement boys across. The wheelhouse roof was concreted as well, in an effort to provide shelter from the German aircraft machine-gun fire."

A few days after the *Olympia* joined the fleet the men aboard spotted two whales and the following day three. All were caught.

The diary records beautiful days, and days with perfect light to see a spout. But far more entries describe days that were foggy, with misty rain or poor light, when it was impossible to see a thing. Heavy rain and gale-force winds often swept the Cape but the tally seemed to keep growing. These men of the sea seemed to whale in most weathers but it was Charlie who ordered the boats in if he felt the conditions were extreme.

One such day a whale had been seen heading in from Cuvier Island. It was estimated to be about four miles away when the boats set out. Tom Norton described the day as "filthy", with a strong nor'easterly blowing. They'd bashed their way out and circled a couple of times waiting for the whale to spout when Charlie told them to get in out of it. It was too rough.

"I was furious," Tom said. "Got bashed to pieces getting there and then the boss tells us to give it up."

Tom said he tied his gun down tightly and told Charlie he was finished for the day. They arrived back at the lookout, moored the boats and climbed back up to the hut. By now the whale was clearly visible as it was only one and a half miles out. Charlie suggested they have another go.

It was still very rough as the boats headed out. Tom was still furious after the last effort and refused to pick up his gun until his driver, Tom Gullery, cajoled him into it. They couldn't get near it in the big seas and realised they'd probably only have one chance.

"I had to fire a long shot. I didn't have a lot of boxline down but aimed where I thought the whale would be and gave the line another three or four feet. We got it.

"Charlie never harped on about me sulking – he could have. Questioned, he'd always say, 'You know what to do. Do it'. Now and then we'd have a bit of a flare-up, but he was a fair man," Tom added.

Tom's words brought back memories of another one of Charlie's 'flare-ups'. It was a rough day and Joe had missed the same whale twice. Just as he was trying to load the gun again Charlie yelled at him. "Come and drive the bloody boat!" He'd show him how to shoot a whale. He missed. Joe can still remember his mother, who was out with them that day, looking at him and saying, "Don't say a word." Charlie left the gun, stormed down the deck, grabbed the wheel from Joe and roared at him to get up the bow and load the gun.

Hearing Charlie's story, I found myself siding first with the whale and then with the men. I felt sorry for the hunted but also appreciated the skill of the hunter. I worried that it was all one-sided and asked myself if the whale had a chance. Then I thought of the many newspaper reports I'd read over the years of whales attacking lone yachts on the ocean, and men being lost.

"There have been many stories of this happening," Charlie told me. "But in all my years of whaling I never saw one attack unless it had been hurt. If you get close to a whale that is hurt or dying, then you can expect it to thrash out with its tail."

Charlie believed that those yachties who spoke about being attacked by a whale most probably sailed into it, gave the whale a bump, and it retaliated. "Well," he said, "you give an old milking cow a kick in the backside and you'll get one back."

An entry in the diary on 14 July 1960 read:

> Four whales were seen four to five miles out from the Cape. After a long chase these were caught. Another lone whale was seen and after a two-hour chase was shot by the *Colville* but the whale did some damage before it died. Charged the *Oria* and nearly took the rails off her then charged the *Colville* and put its head through the port bow above the waterline.

There was certainly a good reason for the whale to attack the boat that day. It was a 46- foot bull and the *Colville* was fast to it. He swum on the top of the water in a big arc, "just like he was pig-rooting". From two hundred yards away Charlie could see that the whale was heading towards the *Colville* and knew he meant business. He hit the boat just above the waterline and drove his head six feet in through the topsides.

The crew on the *Colville* didn't realise what had happened until they heard the yelling and saw the other crews pointing. They looked over the side and saw the whale backing off, his nose and a third of his body out of water, with bedding from the crew's bunks draped over his nose and splintered wood floating on the sea.

Once the whale was caught it was winched up on the starboard side of the *Colville,* thus holding her port bow high enough out of the water to stop water entering.

Fortunately the weather conditions for that day were described in the diary as being a slight sou'easterly wind with a fair to calm sea and a slight swell.

As Charlie finished one story he raced on to another, and I discovered another side of Charlie. He didn't suffer fools.

"We were north of Arid Island, following two or three whales. One of the gunners got excited and gave the wrong directions to his driver. The whale surfaced beneath the boat and the boat climbed right up on its back. It threw the gunner off his feet – there he was, down on his hands and knees, wondering what had happened.

"We laughed about it later but the whale only had to give one swipe of its tail and he'd have taken the side out of the boat."

A similar incident occurred to Joe and Charlie on the *Surprise* on a day when Ruby was aboard. This day the whale tore off some of the chaffing batten from the bottom of the keel. Bill Gibbs recorded the events in the diary:

> And still we catch whales. A pair were spotted approaching the lookout on a flood tide. All the chasers were in and both whales eventually taken. *Surprise* by name and also registered on Charlie's face as pieces of timber floated out from under his chaser. I heard the hull was inspected in record time, much to Mrs Charlie's consternation. Evidently Charlie passed a rude remark when asked if the radio worked.

During the four years Charlie whaled out of Whangaparapara there was a steady stream of reporters and photographers wanting to catch the excitement and danger of one of New Zealands oldest and most hazardous occupations. The *Auckland Star, New Zealand Herald, New Zealand Free Lance* and the *Weekly News* all ran regular features during the season, and the Australian *Pix* ran an article with graphic photos. Before the journalists came, Charlie told them they could photograph what they liked but they had to keep out of the way. They went out on the boats, and spent time at the lookout and the factory.

"In those four years, only one group stands out in my memory," Charlie told me.

Two Americans came out as an independent company and told Charlie they wanted to film an A-Z of a whale chase with the possibility of its being shown on American television. At the lookout the crews were asked to fake a whale sighting and to jump up from seats and shout "Thar she blows!" before running down the track to the boats below. Bill Gibbs, who remained on the lookout as spotter, decided he'd get onto the film somehow and came out of the hut holding a stream of toilet paper in one hand and holding the seat of his pants with the other as if he'd been caught short – a typical whaler's prank.

Later there was a genuine sighting towards Cuvier. On the way out the film makers, who were aboard the *Oria* with Tom Norton and Tom Gullery, told them they'd be watched by 30 million people if their programme went to air. Tom liked the idea and as the whale kicked, jumped, and breached he imagined how great it was going to look on film.

The next day Charlie and Joe had the film crew aboard. It was a much rougher day, and when the gun went off, the person filming found he had nothing to hold on to and jumped into the back hatch where he thought he'd be safe to continue filming.

"We were fast to a whale that had dived deep and the rope was flying out the hatch. I screamed at the stupid bugger to get out before he joined it."

A few weeks later the film arrived in the mail and the entire staff waited expectantly in the mess room to watch it. The projector whirred in the darkness.

"He'd filmed seagulls, sky, water, the other boats – everything – but somehow no whale." Charlie shook his head in disbelief. He was positive no one would ever have paid to watch that – not even with Bill Gibbs starring.

As well as the southern migration of whales taking place in September and October, so did rugby. One of the lookout points for the southern migration was up on Wellington Head, a small island off the northern entrance of Port FitzRoy. It was towards the end of the season and the whales were slow. The Saturday rugby match taking place on Auckland's Eden Park was much more exciting for Bill Gibbs on the lookout and Tom Norton, who'd left his chaser on its moorings, and brought his transistor radio ashore to listen to the match with Bill. Below them the *Colville* swung on her mooring. She had come in earlier and the skipper had called them up on his radio-telephone to report no sightings. To reply, Bill had flicked down the switch on his transmitter but in his hurry to get back to the rugby commentary he forgot to put the switch back up. That immediately cut off all incoming calls.

Both Bill and Tom remember it as being a great game but New Zealand wasn't playing at all well. They screamed encouragement, then criticised the players, and when they didn't take their advice, they swore at them. And when that didn't help they abused the management, the selectors and the referee.

When the *Colville* let go her mooring and started steaming around in circles both Bill and Tom thought they must have seen a whale so took time out of their match to look quickly through the binoculars. They couldn't see any, and the *Colville* stopped circling, so Tom and Bill settled back to enjoy their rugby.

They were so engrossed that the two men didn't think there was anything amiss with the unusually quiet radio-telephone. Well, maybe it had flat batteries, so they changed them over, thereby boosting the volume of their private rugby commentary even more. It wasn't until the match was finished that Tom Norton happened to glance up at the radio-telephone and see that the transmitter switch was down. They'd blocked channel 2168 – the channel everyone listened to in the Gulf. That's when they realised the *Colville* had been circling in an effort to attract their attention. Tom Gullery immediately called on 2168 and thanked them for their commentary. Later they learned from an extremely irate Charlie that their language was so bad that Ruby had switched off the radio-telephone she manned in the office at the whaling station.

The 1960 season had a record tally of 135 whales. One hundred and four were males, and of the 31 females, five were pregnant. Their unborn calves were measured and sexed, and in the five were four males and one female with an average length of 12 feet six inches.

"There were rules. We didn't take a cow with a calf, or whales under 35 feet. We measured this from the point of jaw to the centre of the tail, and estimated their length by comparing it with our boat which was 36 feet. In all my years at the Barrier we only caught two undersized whales. And if we saw a pair we always tried to shoot the cow first as the bull stayed with its mate – unlike the cow. It took off as soon as the bull was shot."

Charlie suggested, very tongue in cheek, that this was typical – the female leaving its mate to fend for itself. I preferred my theory that perhaps the female had more brains.

By the end of his first season Joe had caught 58 whales. Charlie's pride in his only son was evident. Joe, however, always stressed it was a two-man skill. He believed the most difficult part of whaling was the driving.

"Most of the skill was getting the boat alongside the whale close enough so the gunner could shoot it. Shooting out of range – all you'd do was pin it, stir it up, and the harpoon would pull out. The boat needed to be placed so close to the whale that it was virtually climbing on top of the whale's back before you pulled the trigger. And," Joe emphasised, "very rarely was it a beautiful calm day."

Charlie had successfully crossed his river. He had made the station work. But more important to Charlie was being able to share his success with his ailing father. It was a special time for father and son when Arthur Heberley flew to Auckland and out to the island with Fred Ladd.

On 22 November 1960 Arthur died. He had been born in 1881 a few days after the infamous bloodless affair at Parihaka in New Plymouth when the Ngatiawa chief, Te Whiti, was arrested by the Armed Constabulary for allowing his people to illegally fence the roads built through confiscated land. And Arthur was only six months old when the sailing ship *Dunedin* arrived in England with the first shipment of frozen mutton from New Zealand – that great event for farmers. But Arthur lived through so many changes and great events. In his lifetime Mount Tarawera had erupted, a horse and cart travelling at six miles an hour was deemed to be speeding, and the Brunner Mine exploded, leaving 67 men dead. A new age had begun with the first motor car and the first aircraft. There had been two World Wars, and man had explored space.

In 1957 Arthur and Ada had celebrated their golden wedding anniversary in Picton with their three remaining sons and their families. And, two months before he died, Arthur was pleased to learn that natural gas had been discovered on the Kapuni oil-field with subsequent tests showing that little refining would be required to convert the light oil condensate into high-grade petrol. He believed that New Zealand would never be short of fuel.

After his father's funeral Charlie made sure that his mother was able to cope on her own before he returned to Great Barrier.

Throughout the off-season only a skeleton staff remained at the factory, and general maintenance was carried out. Every November Charlie and Ruby, with Joe, headed back to Okukari for the mustering and shearing. Then they came back to the station where Charlie supervised the maintenance and any rebuilding until the middle of January when they headed south once again for mustering, dipping and culling, and the sheep sales.

In their spare time Charlie and Joe made a few crayfish pots which they set around the outside coast of Whangaparapara Harbour. For bait, they used fish caught in nets which they'd set the previous evening. Fred Ladd flew out regularly to Whangaparapara and on his return trips he took the excess fish, mostly snapper, and crayfish packed in sacks to Auckland where they were sold.

Ruby's life had also changed. At Christmas time, instead of cooking for the usual huge influx of visitors to Okukari, Ruby enjoyed quiet days out on the chaser with Charlie and Joe as they pulled their nets and crayfish pots. They visited little bays and enjoyed picnics on their own. They explored the bush and walked up to the kauri dams, often not heading back into Whangaparapara until late afternoon.

On the afternoon of New Year's Eve 1960, as the chaser was steaming into the harbour they passed a 28-foot yawl sailing in to Whangaparapara under full sail. They waved out to the four people they could see on deck.

"Look at the lucky old bugger," Joe pointed out to his father. "How did *he* manage to get a female crew?" The 'old bugger' was my father at the tiller of the *Mangawai*. His crew were my mother sitting alongside him in the cockpit, and my girlfriend and I. We were preparing to lower the headsails and get ready the anchor that had been lashed down. We planned to anchor in the bay with the whaling station, to have a look around.

We always cruised in company, and soon after the other four boats had arrived we all rowed ashore to be greeted on the beach by a man in white overalls who introduced himself as Gerry Morgan, the engineer. He gave us a guided tour of the modernised factory, and then invited us to the mess room to meet the rest of the men and have a drink with them. As we were leaving, Charlie invited us to come ashore later and celebrate New Year's Eve with them all.

Although I had no idea at the time, I had just met my future husband – Charlie's son Joe.

The Norfolk Island whalers didn't have the same success as the New Zealand whalers in 1960. The whales were there but the changeable weather meant that whenever bad weather was predicted the boats had to be pulled out of the water as there was no other way of sheltering them. The Norfolk Island Byron Bay Whaling Company decided to pull out of Norfolk Island and put its resources into its subsidiary, the Barrier Whaling Company. Two new chasers joined the fleet for the beginning of the 1961 season – the *Cascade* and the *Kingston Whaler*.

There was no reason to doubt that the 1961 season would differ from the previous two when the first whale of the season, a 43-foot male, was caught on 25 May from the *Cascade*. This was the same date the first whale of 1960 had been caught. By 30 May the tally of three equalled that of the previous season. Charlie was pleased they were on target, but by the end of June only 24 whales had been caught in comparison with 76 the previous year.

The men on the lookout were joined by the crews from the chasers. Everyone watched over an ocean seemingly devoid of whales. Only an occasional one came through. The month of July was worse than June.

The first whale caught was on 15 July. Five days later came what was to be the last whale of the season. It was a sie whale, not usually caught. A perfectly formed male foetus 45 inches in length was found in her. Charlie sent it to Auckland University for their marine biology studies.

"There are two things I am proud to claim," Charlie told me. "My son was the youngest harpoon gunner in the Southern Hemisphere, if not the world, and my wife is the only woman in the world to have driven a whale chaser when a whale was actually caught."

This was on a day Joe has never forgotten, either, as he was the usual gunner on the boat but that day he was left behind.

The whale had been spotted earlier in the day but had given the whalers the slip as a sie whale can stay down longer than the humpback – up to half an hour or more – and it didn't appear to be showing much of a spout which made it difficult to see. The scarcity of whales was causing tempers to become short. Frustrated at losing one of the few whales that *had* been seen, the drivers each put their gunner ashore to climb up high and have a better chance of seeing it again.

"Thar she blows!" a gunner called, pointing out to sea. There was a mad scramble down the cliff face as each gunner wanted the chance to bag this whale. Charlie saw the spout and simply couldn't wait for Joe. He started the engine and headed towards it. "Here, take the wheel," he barked at Ruby. "I'll tell you what to do."

The worst part for Ruby was the noise of the engine. She couldn't hear a thing and although she'd often seen Joe giving his father hand signals to guide him closer to the whale, she didn't know what they meant. Ruby learnt quickly. A stab of Charlie's hand to the left or right meant just that, and when he held his hand up it meant stop. He'd wind his hand forward for Ruby to go ahead or backwards if he wanted her to go in reverse and if she didn't respond quickly enough he'd bang on the deck.

Ruby admitted later she was terrified. She was terrified the whale might hit them, and she was terrified she might do something wrong and catapult Charlie overboard. But my mother-in-law placed the chaser right alongside the whale, enabling Charlie to harpoon it with his first shot. Once the air spear was in the whale, Ruby was ordered to start up the compressor motor. Finally Charlie darted in the bomb and ran down towards the stern to where the wire that ran from the bomb was tied to the rail next to the driver. This time the driver was excused from exploding the bomb, and Ruby stood back as Charlie untied the wire and touched it on the terminals on the front of the windscreen. The bomb exploded, killing the whale instantly. The *Colville* towed the whale back to the factory.

The station remained open, the lookouts were manned and the chasers ready but no more whales were caught, and when the station closed for the season the final tally was only 26. The Barrier Whaling Company announced that its activities from Great Barrier Island had ended permanently and went into receivership in July of that year. Charlie didn't believe that New Zealand whaling was finished, even with the knowledge that the Perano Whalers had also had a lean year with their catch of 55. There was a great deal of speculation that the pressure being put on the whales in the Antarctic by the Japanese, Russian and Norwegian factory ships was depleting the stocks before they even reached New Zealand.

The whales taken in New Zealand waters were migrating from the Antarctic to warmer waters to breed. They didn't come up together but in three main streams. One stream passed up the coast of South Africa, one through the New Zealand and Australia area, and one further over towards South Georgia. On their return to the Antarctic they congregated in a very small area, making them very easy to catch. "Down there it was just like putting a mob of sheep in a paddock and setting a pack of wild dogs on them," Charlie said angrily.

Through the Whaling Commission, the remaining whaling nations tried to control the slaughter and attempted to put observers on whaling vessels to set a quota, but some nations refused to take them so an accurate record couldn't be obtained.

After the station went into receivership, Charlie held a meeting with the key men who had worked with him over the past three years. It was agreed that perhaps the whales had travelled a different route north in 1961. Baleen whales feed by sifting krill. Any changes in temperature, ocean currents, and the movements of other sea dwellers all affect the krill. If the krill are affected, so are the whales.

A small group headed by Charlie approached the Barrier Whaling Company and negotiated with them to work the station on a profit-sharing basis. They would be working for themselves and would not be Barrier Whaling Company employees, while the company would still control the station but its operating activities would be under lease. The receiver was withdrawn on 31 October. Next season Charlie would still head the Whangaparapara whaling station, but it would be operating under the name of Gulf Whaling Industries Ltd.

On 19 April, one month before the start of the 1962 whaling season, Charlie's brother, Jim, died in Wellington Hospital of heart failure. He was only 49 years old. Charlie flew out with Fred Ladd and on to Wellington, to another death he felt keenly. In his absence, everything continued to be made ready for the commencement of the season. With whale oil worth 80-90 pounds a tonne, and each humpback averaging almost nine tonnes of oil as well as the profit from the by-products, everyone had a fair idea what numbers were needed to make the station viable.

On 20 May the chasers headed out into the pre-dawn darkness and cruised down to Cape Barrier where the men climbed up to the hut to begin their vigil once again. Charlie felt a deep responsibility for the men working with him this season. Whaling is always a dangerous occupation with the knowledge that one mistake can cause a man's death, but this season another hazard loomed large for Charlie. It was the unpredictable supply of whales. In the three previous seasons most of the whales that had been sighted were taken. Now he worried that they might pass only at night or on days when it was too rough to work the boats or when the visibility was bad, and he worried they might not come at all.

Joe had asked me to fly out to Whangaparapara with Fred Ladd for Queen's Birthday Weekend and stay with his parents. I found myself making excuses not to come. I'd never been up in a plane before, and didn't know if I wanted my first flight to be in a little plane that just skimmed over the sea, that might dive-bomb the men on the chasers and that would fly low over houses on isolated islands of the gulf to drop them off a newspaper. I didn't know Joe's parents well, and I had to face the fact that I didn't really know Joe well, either. But when he told me I'd be able to come out with Charlie and him on the chaser down to the lookout on Cape Barrier, with the possibility of going out on a whale chase, I put all misgivings aside.

The flight left me breathless as we flew over the same waters I'd sailed every holiday in my parents' yacht for as long as I could remember. I identified the islands by their beaches we'd lazed on or the hills we'd climbed. When I arrived at the whaling station Freddy Ladd waddled the plane up the beach to

Tory Channel from the highest point on the farm.

Okukari Bay. Charlie's and Ruby's home is in the stand of pine trees in the foreground. Whekenui Bay is to the right.
(Photo by Graeme Matthews)

Looking towards the long flat bushy peninsula which forms West Head. The Perano lookout was on the low flat peninsula. Okukari Bay is on the opposite side of the channel to the left.
(Photo by Graeme Matthews)

A page from wages book with Charlie's farm hours recorded, and showing Social Security stamps. *(Supplied by Reg Jackson)*

The Heberley Memorial Shield carved by Thomas Heberley after Charlie's brother Joe drowned on 30 September 1930.

Te Maunga o te whanau – The Mountain or head of the family was the name of Charlie's taonga.

Charlie's waka huia box and walking stick both carved by Thomas Heberley. The handle of the walking stick, replaced after the original piece was buried with Worser, is a lighter shade of wood. They sit on Ruby's Hardanger embroidery.

A harpoon strikes home. *(Photo supplied by Ian Kenny)*

The killer bomb explodes. *(Photo supplied by Ian Kenny)*

Whangaparapara station before the deck was covered in. Joe on the left and Charlie on the right beside a whale before the blubber has been flensed off.

The belly of a whale showing its corduroy.
(Photo supplied by Dave Medland)

Charlie and Ruby with, from left, Donna, Jocelyn and Joe taken on Charlie's 80th birthday and Ruby's 78th, which they celebrated on the same day.

Kaumatua Ireland Love and Kaumatua Charlie Heberley at a trust meeting on the Waikawa Marae.

The Whekenui Whalers' reunion in April 1982. Charlie is in the right front with the brown sports coat and tan trousers. This would be the last time as many whalers as this were gathered together.

Charlie in the woolshed during the merino sheep shearing.

Beside the remains of the lookout on West Head, 3 January 2000, Charlie ponders the whales – their past and their future.

where Ruby was waiting. At the house Ruby sat herself down in front of the base radio-telephone installed at the end of the bench, and called up Joe to tell him I'd arrived. It was strange hearing his voice crackling through the radio as he informed his mother they still hadn't seen a whale and they'd be leaving the Cape when the light faded.

I heard the hum of the boats' engines long before I saw their navigation lights as they rounded the point and headed up the harbour. In no time the three boats were moored, the crews ashore and I was walking back up the hill to the house with Charlie and Joe.

Early next morning I was aboard the *Surprise* as it cruised down to Cape Barrier. I realised none of these men saw the bay in daylight during the whaling season unless bad weather kept them home. It was still dark when Charlie came up to the mooring at the Cape and Joe deftly picked up the loop that was floating and flicked it over the gun-post.

"I hope you said a prayer that it's only going to be on the mooring for a short time today," Charlie laughed in the sudden silence that came when he turned off the key. I hoped today was going to be the day too and I tried to imagine the wide-eyed looks I'd receive when I told my city friends what I'd done over the weekend. No amount of scanning the sea picked up a whale spouting during the two days I spent down on Cape Barrier lookout, but two days after I'd arrived back in Auckland an excited phone call from Joe told me the whales had arrived. He'd shot the first one for the season, and Alf Nimmo who was gunning on the *Kingston Whaler* had shot the other.

By 18 June only eight whales had been caught, and with no more sightings Charlie officially closed the season on 7 July. At the bottom of the catch sheet for the season he wrote: *Owing to the absence of whales the season was terminated a month early. No sightings were made after 18 June. Only 10 humpbacks and 12 sies were sighted during the season.*

The 378 barrels of oil produced was not enough to keep the station running economically. After a meeting it was decided to wind up Gulf Whaling Industries Ltd. The Barrier Whaling Company was once more placed in receivership, with tenders closing in April 1963.

Two weeks before the station closed, one of the men who lived on Great Barrier, Ivan Miller, suggested to Charlie that he should go home but if Charlie needed him he'd come back.

The following morning on the way to the lookout Charlie dropped Ivan at Tryphena where he lived. When the final pay-out was made to the workers, Ivan was surprised and touched to find that Charlie had paid him the same amount as the men who'd stayed on.

Before Charlie left Whangaparapara he asked Bill Frieswijk to be caretaker until everything was wound up. Bill was delighted but couldn't do it until he was able to ship four bales of wool from his place in Island Bay, two miles south of Tryphena Harbour, back to the wharf at Shoal Bay in Tryphena from where it would be taken to Auckland by boat.

"No trouble," Charlie told Bill. "I'll pick it up in the chaser and drop it off on the wharf the first good day."

Years later, Charlie still speaks bitterly about the demise of whaling. "We knew what was happening, and very little was being done about it. The year we caught 135 and the Perano whalers took 226, that was only 361 whales for the whole of New Zealand. That same year the Japs, Russians and Norwegians took 42,000 blue whale units in the Antarctic."

A blue whale unit is equal to one blue whale, two fin whales, two and a half humpback whales, or six sie whales.

"We didn't believe it was a true figure we were given as many of those boats refused to take observers. You work that out," he stabbed at his figures angrily. "Presuming they caught all humpbacks, that equates to 105,000 whales."

In the 54 years of power-boat whaling in Cook Strait, less than 5,000 whales were caught, and when the whales that had been caught from Great Barrier were included, New Zealand's total catch of whales, using the power boats, was less than 6,000. "We were only catching the tip of the iceberg."

In 1962 a limit was placed on the Antarctic whale catch of 15,000 blue whale units. Charlie maintained it was "too little too late". This limit had earlier been introduced in 1946 when it was realised that the number of whales was declining rapidly in the Antarctic. It had proved impossible to agree on national shares within that limit, with the result that larger and more costly fleets were assembling in the Antarctic at the beginning of each season. They then whaled frenziedly to secure as large a share as possible, exceeding the total limit of 15,000 units. By 1948 the productive whaling season had been shortened to under 70 days, with the humpback whale quota regularly exceeded in four days of whaling. In 1959 the limitation system collapsed. The whales were taken at a more leisurely rate but their catch rose above the 15,000 unit level. Many marine biologists were of the opinion that the catch was too high for proper conservation measures.

"New Zealand's total catch in 54 years was less than the Antarctic whalers were allowed to catch in one season," Charlie summed up.

Charlie and Ruby packed up their personal belongings and returned to their farm on Arapawa Island. Joe came into Auckland where he worked with a panel-beater until Christmas, and we became engaged.

"I'd always hoped Joe would find a girl who wanted to live in the Sounds because I wanted my son working beside me," Charlie told me later. With the wedding due to take place in eight months to a girl who was looking forward to living at Okukari, Charlie found what he thought was the ideal solution.

While at Great Barrier he had enjoyed the time he'd spent crayfishing with Joe. They'd made their craypots with a wooden frame covered in wire netting, similar to what the local fishermen used, instead of the conventional supplejack pots the fishermen used in Cook Strait. Before he'd arrived home Charlie had begun to make his plans.

Situated on the edge of Cook Strait, Okukari would be the ideal place to run a commercial fishing business. This could easily be worked in conjunction with the farm. He knew in the months ahead he'd be busy on the farm because, in between sheep work, fences needed to be rebuilt and maintenance had to be carried out on various buildings. But once he'd caught up, he'd start looking around for a fishing boat and he and Joe would go crayfishing. But it had to be a boat big enough to handle the stretch of water around the rugged coastline on the Cook Strait side of Arapawa Island between Tory Channel entrance and Cape Koamaru on its northern end.

Charlie's words made me want to laugh. He was still on an island in the Hauraki Gulf and there he was, dreaming already of the next direction his life was headed, still on an island, but one where he would be able to continue to make his living from the sea while at the same time walk over the land his ancestors had walked before him.

The Whales Are Off Great Barrier

New Company's Successe[s]

Staff Reporter   **Whangaparapara** F

Whalers working from Great Barrier Island winter are confident that they can establish a profit industry in the Hauraki Gulf.

After long hours in dangerous waters they already shown that, with experience and —ning, whaling in the gulf can be —

"The whales are here," says Mr C. Heberley, a veteran Tory Channel whaler and manager of the Barrier Whaling Co., Ltd. "I think we have proved we can catch them."

Mr Heberley said that this first season is primarily one of survey and reconnaissance.

"We have to find out where the whales are, and how many there are. This season it is just as important to plot the routes the whales take as it is to catch them."

The rewards of whaling can be very considerable. Whale oil is worth about £80 a ton and eight to ten tons is won from each humpback caught in the gulf.

There is no waste. The residue after the oil is boiled off can be converted into stock food and — food companies provide a market for whale meat.

Already 45 humpback have been killed since the pany began business 36 days

The score would have nearer 100 whales if the co— plant taken over from the prev— company could have coped the whales.

Mr Heberley hopes that in a season with additional plant station will handle about whales. The Tory Channel whal— catch about this number in Co— Strait each season.

Whales travel in schools an— often whalers have seen 15 to — humpbacks together. In one da— last month 50 whales were re— ported from the watching stations.

"You have to kill them while you can," said Mr Heberley. "It's been maddening, sitting out in the gulf watching the whales

Woman Takes Helm In Whale Chase

A whale chaser with a woman at the helm harpooned a 50-foot whale off Great Barrier Island yesterday.

Mrs R. Heberley, wife of the manager of the Barrier Whaling Co., Ltd. went for a ride with her husband, who had taken over the role of gunner in the two-man chaser. The usual gunner could not go because of illness.

About four miles off the —thern head of the island —erley spotted a whale, and as her boats were nea—

WHALERS TO STAY ON

Great Barrier Island —th whalers, like their Tory Channel colleagues, are havi— up a lean time this year. B— they have no intention — to "packing it in" until — season ends on August 31.

W— — the channel twee —eat Barrier and the land have been mainly set wh— —smaller and far less valu— than humpbacks. The comp— has left them alone.

The full whaling season beg on May 1 and ends on October The northern run usually finis about the end of this month, there is a lull during August u— the whales begin moving sou again.

Whaling ends at Great Barrier

Gulf Whaling Limited has ended at Whangaparapara Great Barrier Island, taking only eight whales since the season began on May 1.

Killing season of whales on their northern migration ends on August 3. The first two whales were caught on June 9. The first whale caught in the Hauraki Gulf last year was on May 25.

Gulf Whaling Industries is the third company formed here in the last five years for whale —atching at the Great Barrier

Poor whaling season

BRISBANE.—Fishing auth— orities fear that the £100,000-a-year whaling operations from Tangalooma, on Moreton Island, may have to be abandoned soon, because of the —hortage of whales.

serio— caug— of t— w— be— has : thr— kill the bi P— And, as b C— se out there—

Share-profits scheme for whaling here

The Barrier Whaling Con— pany expects to continu— whaling next season and i— now negotiating with New Zealand operators to work —ation on a profit

CESSATION OF RECEIVER

BARRIER WHALING CO.,
A. W. Christmas ceased to act Oct. ...

is a sub— —folk Island — Whaling LTD. (Auck.) went into July. The receiver ithdrawn on October 31 by with the arrangement New Zealand Insurance Company.

Barrier Whaling's mana— ger-secretary, Captain Peter Davison, said in Auckland today that if negotiations were successful the operators —ould be working for them— —lves and would n—
—mpany a—

COOK STRAIT DRAMA

Chaser badly holed by surfacing whale

BLENHEIM, Wednesday (P.A.).—A whale chaser was ... in Cook Strait yesterday when a harpooned whale ... ow it and tossed it aside like a cork.

PAYING OFF

STRAIT WHALERS

Lean Year For Whalers

Worst ... In

Press Assn

Blenhei ... wha'

The Tory Channel seaso ... on Su

The Tory Ch ... are having a lean seaso ... with a single kill on Su ... are paying off ... the catch so far ... as they have o ... only 17. At this tir ... go to. year—also a poor s ... In a normal sea ... compa ... tions are at their pe ... at 20 ... stood at the end of ... 19 ... time with anything ... 80 ... week in June, ... men employed. This week ... .o 50 ... staff will be down to 12 or ... 14 with only one kill in the ... past week to bring the sea- ... son's tally to 24.

Antarctic Kill

The whalers are having ... their worst season in years. ... At this time last year, which ... was an extremely poor sea- ... son, the tally was 47. At the ... same time in 1960 the kill ... totalled 180.

There seemed no doubt that ... stocks of whales were being ... wiped out in the Antarctic ... where the main whaling coun- ... tries of the world were op- ... erating with fleets of chasers ... and factory ships.

No Tiddlers Even

Mr Perano said that in other ... years they saw many under- ... size whales (under 35 feet) ... passing through the strait. ... These were tagged with a ... stainless steel marker for re- ... search and were allowed to ... continue on their way to ... warmer waters.

But this year there were ... not even any small whales ... travelling from the Antarctic. ... The future seemed far from ... bright.

Whale Holes Chaser In Cook Strait

Press Assn   Blenheim

For the second time within ... a month a whalechaser be- ... longing to the Tory Channel ... Whaling fleet has been exten- ... sively damaged by a wounded ... whale.

The chaser Rorqual, driven ... by Mr Gilbert Perano, with ... Mr Trevor Norton as gunner, ... was badly holed several miles ... out in Cook Strait on Sunday ... when a 40ft humpback sud- ... denly surfaced under the ... vessel.

Towed to Safety

The chaser was towed half ... submerged to the whaling fac- ... tory inside Tory Channel. ... The Rorqual, which was ... commissioned in May, 1960, ... had a hole 18 inches wide and ... six feet long ripped in her ... hull. The engine compartment ... was flooded by the sudden ... surge of water through the ... gaping hole and the crew had ... to act smartly to close the ... hole and prevent the water ... getting into the forward and ... aft compartments.

Kill Completed

At the end of last month in ... a similar mishap the chaser ... Cachalot III was badly holed ... and headed for shore in a ... sinking condition. It was ... saved from going to the ... bottom by being lashed to ... nother chaser. ... The whale that caused the ... image yesterday did not get ... ay. The Cachalot III com- ... ...eted the kill to bring the ...

The forward bulkhead just ... in front of the engine was ... smashed and water poured ... into the engine room.

After a two-mile dash to ... land at the rocky entrance to ... Tory Channel, the chaser was ... about 100 yards offshore when ... it began to sink in about 50 ... fathoms.

Another chaser made fast ... to it and towed it, with decks ... awash, to the whaling factory ... where a crane hauled the ... damaged craft clear of the ... water.

Hectic day

It was a hectic day for the ... Tory Channel whalers. Three ... chasers had gone out into the ... Strait in pursuit of two whales ... both of which were harpooned.

It was when the chaser ... Cachalot III, manned by Mr ... Jon Perano (gunner) and Mr ... Harry Kenny (driver) went in ... to make a kill of a whale har- ... pooned by the Baleena, on ... which were Messrs Trevor ... Norton and Gilbert Perano ... that the accident occurred.

The third chaser Narwhal, ... manned by Messrs Ted Huntley ... and Joe Perano, set its whale ... adrift and saved the crippled ... craft.

Whalers being paid off

BLENHEIM,   Tuesday ... (P.A.). — The Tory Channel ... whalers are having their ... worst season in years and ... men are being paid off as ... soon as they have other jobs ... to go to.

In a normal season opera- ... ...re at their peak at this ... ...ting up to 50

Chapter Eleven

LIVING ON THE EDGE

He manako te koura I kore ai.
Wishing for the crayfish won't bring it.

"I WAS DISAPPOINTED the way things turned out. In a way I felt responsible for the money those men had lost." Even though Charlie knew no one blamed him – they'd invested their money of their own free will – no one could have predicted the outcome because of what was happening in the Antarctic. But it was in Charlie's nature to want to succeed. He was distressed.

A few weeks after they arrived back at Okukari, Ruby's father's health began to deteriorate and he was admitted to Blenheim's Wairau Hospital. Ruby stayed in Blenheim, coming home when she could. One evening she was offered a ride home with some folk who lived in Tory Channel. Many on board had been drinking and, when a child fell overboard, a man, Ray Newman, jumped in to rescue the child. He drowned.

Two days later, on 30 September, Ruby's father died. The return from Great Barrier, the workload Ruby placed on herself while trying to get everything back to the standard it was before she had left Okukari, Ray Newman's drowning followed by her own father's death – all these combined to push Ruby to the edge.

Charlie was anxious. "I knew she wasn't well. She seemed to be miles away and I couldn't reach her. Some days she'd be gone from the house for ages, and when she arrived home I could see she'd been crying. She told me she had pins and needles attacking her body. Today I would have realised she was having anxiety attacks but I didn't know about those things back then. I didn't understand."

Tailing followed lambing, and by November, when the sheep were mustered in for shearing, Ruby simply *had* to be well because someone had to prepare the meals for the men. The pride in Charlie's voice was unmistakable when he told me she just used to get on with things, but I had a sneaking suspicion that probably the quiet of Okukari and the beauty of the Marlborough Sounds had played a big part in the healing.

Whenever he could, Charlie worked on repairing the fences. Since returning from Great Barrier he'd noticed the hills seemed to be much higher and his breath much shorter, and he was smoking two packets of tailor-made cigarettes a day. At this time he was working on the fence that runs from the highest peak on the farm down to East Head.

One morning as he trudged up the hill, carrying fencing equipment, he stopped long enough to take a cigarette from its packet and light up. The sun was just lifting over the hill and for a moment, as he savoured the first puff, he watched the sunlight lay patterns on the swift moving water in Tory Channel. He saw his life set out in relief. In the distance was Oyster Bay where he was born, Te Awaiti, the first place he and Ruby had lived after they left Oyster Bay, the whaling station at Fishing Bay where he'd worked for two years, and, across the Channel, the lookout where he'd spent 14 years when he was harpoon gunner with Gilbert Perano. Closer was Whekenui, the bay where he'd nearly drowned when he and Trevor Norton had attempted to row out to the whale chaser, but, best of all, spread all around was his own land. The land where his children grew up and which they still called home, and – he hoped – the land where another Heberley generation would be born and learn to love it as he did.

"Seeing it spread out like that I suddenly realised if I kept on smoking like I was I wouldn't be around to enjoy any of it."

The half-finished smoke was thrown away but Charlie placed the opened packet of cigarettes in his shirt pocket and did up the button. He didn't touch them all day, and that evening when he got home he tore open the carton of cigarettes that was stored in the pantry and removed every packet.

"I stood them all round the house. On the mantelpiece, windowsills, shelves in the kitchen, places where I could see them and know there was a smoke there whenever I wanted one. I ate so much chewing gum my gums were sore, but I never had another smoke, and I became the world's most nagging non-smoker."

In January 1963 Joe finished working in Auckland and came back to Okukari to help his father on the farm as well as doing some work on the farm cottage we were going to live in after we were married in April. He also talked over his future with

Charlie. They decided that until they found a suitable boat it would be better financially if Joe whaled with the Peranos in the winter months while Charlie worked on the farm. Joe spoke with Gilbert Perano and he was offered the position his father had left – harpoon-gunner – with Gilbert driving. Our wedding was planned around the whaling season. We believed the day was auspicious.

It was the day the SS *Orca* set out from Tory Channel to begin its first sperm whaling season. The *Orca* was a converted German minesweeper before beginning her days as a whale chaser out of Queensland. When that station closed because of the lack of whales, the Peranos brought her out to New Zealand to use in their hunt for sperm whales. She carried a crew of 12, and in the time she operated she caught most of the sperm whales near Kaikoura and Cape Palliser.

Now it was Charlie who lay in his bed and listened to the chaser's engine start up across the bay while the next generation leapt out of bed at the sound. By the time Gilbert had idled across the bay, Joe was standing on the beach, his lunch tin tucked under his arm, waiting for the bow of the boat to nudge the beach before he climbed aboard. That season two chasers were used in the hunt for the humpback whale in Cook Strait, but only nine were caught and the lookout was closed in July. Meanwhile the *Orca*'s tally of sperm whales was 119 when they finished for the year in mid-December.

Ruby's father, Maurice Ivanhoe Guard, better known as Ivan, had been a commercial fisherman. A year after he died, his boat the *Midlothian,* (in recent years renamed *Mariner),* a 36-foot double ender built by Ernie Lane at Picton, came up for sale. Up until the Port Underwood road was built, every Saturday Ivan Guard had delivered the mail into the Port, using the *Midlothian.* Charlie knew her to be a good sea boat so he bought her. On a fine day Charlie and Ruby took the *Wheke* into Picton where Rex Guard, Ruby's brother, picked them up and drove them to Blenheim. Ivan Guard's house backed on to the Opawa River, and since his death the *Midlothian* had remained tied alongside the small jetty. They brought her down the Opawa River, over the Wairau Bar, up the coast and into Tory Channel to Okukari. Charlie's fishing venture had become a reality.

The boat was changed from a trawler to a cray-boat. She was put on the slip in Picton, and painted. Charlie and Joe made their crayfish pots. Using a style similar to what they had used up north they built the pots with a three-foot-square wooden-framed base. They drilled holes in the base and hooped supplejack frames over from each side. The pot was then covered in wire bird-netting. For weights, Charlie and Joe wired bricks into the corners.

"I had a good source until Ruby caught me digging out the bricks of a retaining wall in her garden," Charlie laughed. "After that we had to use flat stones off the beach."

Coils of rope and boxes of buoys, which all had to be painted with a distinguishing mark or colour, arrived at Oku-kari. The pots were ready. They used bait which had been supplied from the local fisheries and fish gathered from the set nets. As the *Midlothian* steamed out the bay, laden down with crayfish pots, the laughter in Charlie's and Joe's voices carried across the water. They were fishermen once more.

Local fishermen also laughed and told Charlie the only thing he could expect to catch in those pots would be chickens. But they did catch crayfish and well before the end of their first cray season Charlie was amused to see that the loudest scoffers had similar-looking newly-built pots in their boats.

Charlie and Joe set their pots north of the channel entrance up to Cape Koamaru. They fished from July, when Joe finished whaling, until late February when the females went into shallow water to shell.

The crayfish increases its growth by an extraordinary series of moults. In the process of casting its shell the whole of the cray's jointed armour-like shell comes off in one piece, and it withdraws its legs as a hand is withdrawn from a glove. Following the shelling the soft-bodied crayfish is very vulnerable to octopus, conger eels and other predators and retires to a safe hiding place until the new shell hardens.

But as much as Charlie loved fishing he was adamant. "Fishing didn't take place to the detriment of the farm." The daily catch of crays was placed in the water in wooden fish boxes which had solid tops and bottoms with slatted sides. The boxes were strung together on a continuous line which was tied to a mooring in the bay. Once a week, unless someone needed to go to Picton earlier, the crays were lifted on the deck and taken to the fish factory in Picton where they were drowned and cooked. The meat was sold on the domestic market. The system worked well until the rope tying the boxes together chafed through.

"It was one of those screamers from the north," Charlie began. "It was too rough to get out fishing so we decided to take in our crays. We rowed out to the boat – and all that was hanging off the mooring was a piece of frayed rope. A week's work was gone."

The northerly wind blows straight out of the bay, and because it had been so strong, stronger than the flow of the tide, Charlie thought the boxes might have been carried straight across the channel and washed up on the beach below the light on Scraggy. I heard the relief in Charlie's voice as he remembered the sight of the boxes spread over the beach. Two or three had broken open and some of the crayfish were crawling over the sand, but most boxes were still intact. While Charlie held the boat in on the beach, Joe clambered over the bow, gathered up their catch and passed the boxes and loose crayfish back to his father. Back on the boat, as Charlie steamed towards Picton, Joe ran the deck hose over the crays to wash off the sand before repacking them into clean boxes.

"It taught us a lesson."

That day they brought home enough timber to make a holding tank to keep the crays alive in the sea instead of keeping them in the smaller boxes. Charlie believed that by keeping the crays alive in a bigger tank where they could swim around it would be less stressful to the fish and a superior product would be presented to the market. They made a mooring for the tank from an old traction engine wheel filled with concrete which was then towed out into the bay.

The sixth generation of the Heberley line was due in June 1964. From the time I told Charlie I was pregnant he presumed I was having a boy. He always spoke about 'Little Joe' (and this was well before the age of scans). He'd see toys and typical boys' clothes and tell Ruby that 'Little Joe' would like that or 'Little Joe' would look good in those. Memories of the importance Arthur Heberley had put on Charlie's and Ruby's son Joe, made Ruby remind Charlie that, although Donna had no family at that time, Jocelyn did, and he already had five other grandchildren. But for him this was his first grandchild to carry the Heberley name. Our baby was born one month early at Picton Hospital and of course we called him Joe.

Two weeks before Joe's birth Charlie had been sawing up firewood on his sawbench when he noticed a weta sitting on the piece of wood he was about to cut. As he tried to flick it off, his finger hit the turning saw blade. Charlie had staggered up the steps from the woodshed before Ruby saw him. Our farm cottage was only across the lawn from Charlie's and Ruby's house and I was hanging out my washing when I heard Ruby yelling out to me.

At their house when I ran inside I heard sounds coming from the bathroom. There I found Ruby struggling to hold Charlie up at the basin and at the same time trying to stem the flow of blood. This great whale hunter and man of the sea, my tough father-in-law, just kept fainting. I learned later that neither Charlie nor my Joe could stand the sight of blood. When I saw the cut and all the blood I had to hold myself together as I took over his weight and let my mother-in-law attend to the wound. This was the first accident I'd been involved in since I'd lived in Okukari and I felt very inadequate as I watched my capable mother-in-law bandage Charlie's hand. A phone call to Whekenui soon had Gilbert Perano come with his whale chaser across the bay to pick up Charlie and Ruby and take them into Picton where the finger was stitched and dressed.

At this time Ruby had a dark brown mole above her ankle on the outside of her left leg. Whenever she dried it, it bled. I'd seen it bleed for no reason while she sat in the sun, and quite recently it had become raised, irregular in shape, and was growing rapidly. It was now the size of a ten-cent piece. In 1964 the importance of early detection of a melanoma was certainly not as widely known as it is today, at least not by the lay person. Donna with her nursing experience told her mother to get it seen to but for Ruby it remained a trifling thing and she didn't feel ill.

As Ruby left the surgery with Charlie she casually asked the doctor what he thought of this mole, and showed him her leg. "Come back with Charlie when he gets his hand dressed and we'll see about it," he ordered.

Ten days later Joe was born, and that same evening Ruby was admitted to Lister Hospital in Blenheim where a surgeon would operate the next day. Because of the size of the melanoma, a huge piece was cut from Ruby's leg and at the same time a 'plug' to fill the hole was taken from her thigh. During

155

the next few weeks, while it healed underneath, the dead skin from the top of the grafted flesh had to be scraped away regularly. A massive dose of antibiotics gave her severe diarrhoea. "I thought she was going to die from the surgery, and then from the effects of the drugs," Charlie admitted. "I wasn't aware of the seriousness of the melanoma until I spoke later to the surgeon."

As the years went by and all her checks were clear, Charlie believed she had been one of the very lucky ones. The doctors agreed. If it hadn't been for Charlie's accident, Ruby might have put off consulting a doctor until it was too late.

Whaling as Charlie had known it was about to end. When the Peranos began their whaling operations for the 1964 season there were no small chasers, the shutters on the lookout remained closed, and now it was only the *Orca* that hunted and killed the whales. A special summer season was allowed for the sperm whales, with the first one shot in mid-January and the last in mid-April. In October the true sperm season begun and for a short time Joe worked at the factory. Most of the men were developing infections from working with whales that had been dead for a longer period and had blasted, that is putrefaction had set in. Any small cut became infected, and itchy rashes developed over their bodies. It was the reason that Joe turned his back on whaling and went fishing again. A few weeks later, on 21 December 1964, the last whale was caught in New Zealand waters, off Kaikoura by the *Orca,* and the Perano family closed the station.

Charlie had followed the whales' demise. He now knew that in 1961, the year of the steep decline of whales at Great Barrier, there had been 268 steel-hulled chasers and 21 factory ships in the Antarctic. The bigger factory ships could process 740 whales in 24 hours. In that season two and a half million barrels of oil were taken out of the Antarctic. With those facts, his own experience and knowledge gained from newspapers, as well as material written by Bill Dawbin of the Zoology Department of the University of Sydney, and by the New Zealand Marine Department biologist, Dr David Gaskin, Charlie knew that whaling in New Zealand was almost extinct.

"The Japanese and Russians weren't satisfied with fishing in the Antarctic," Charlie said. "Now they were catching them around the New Zealand coast. And when a Japanese factory ship was seen in Cloudy Bay, and a Russian factory ship with 15 whale chasers were off the Canterbury coast actively whaling, how could the whale population be kept on a sustainable level? The majority of nations farmed them – the Russians and Japanese were butchering them."

In the years Charlie whaled in Cook Strait and Great Barrier, all whales they left because of inability to process them while they were fresh, or a cow with a calf, or an undersized whale, were tagged by firing a dart into them. This was a requirement of the Whaling Commission in an effort to study their migration patterns. In the factory whales were coming in with Russian and Japanese harpoons hanging out of them. Others had wounds where harpoons had pulled out and the whales had escaped. "But we weren't getting any they'd tagged."

For Charlie the final answer to the whales' near-extinction came when, six weeks before the whaling season started, the Japanese caught the Russians in the Antarctic with whales alongside the factory ship. "And there's only one reason why the Japs were down there early – and it wasn't to spy on the Russians."

Charlie and Joe were now full-time fishermen. The crayfish pots went out in July and they caught bucks until they began their process of shelling in August. At this time the flesh becomes quite pink and stays this way until the new shell hardens and they are able to be taken again. By then the hens are shedding their eggs. Once this is done, they are legally able be caught. The female crayfish carries her eggs attached under her tail and the number of eggs carried by one hen can vary from 3,000 to nearly 100,000. From October both sexes are caught until the hens shell. In the months between March and June, while it was relatively quiet on the farm, Charlie and Joe netted for butterfish, or greenbone as it is sometimes called because its bones and the flesh in contact with them are tinged bluish-green. It is a kelp fish found throughout New Zealand but most commonly in the South. The men set their nets from a 14-foot clinker-built dinghy, fishing north and south of the channel entrance on the outside coast. On fine days they left before daylight and arrived home after dark, always wet from hauling nets. "No different from whaling," Charlie replied when I asked if he didn't get sick of being wet and cold all day.

157

The third occasion when Charlie won his battle against the sea was on a day when they were netting for butterfish up the outside coast north of Tory Channel entrance. It was a perfect day for netting – overcast, not a breath of wind and a calm sea. As I listened to Charlie's words I vividly recalled the eeriness that particular day.

The low clouds turned the water in the bay black. Nothing moved. The silence was deafening. Even the sea birds stayed away. I couldn't shake off a feeling of apprehension that had wrapped steel bands around my forehead, bands which had tightened as the day wore on. When Ruby told me it was typical earthquake weather I was relieved as it gave me a reason for feeling the way I did.

Charlie picked up the story. "We'd listened to the weather reports all day as a sou'westerly change was predicted for later in the evening. We could see the cloud bank bulging over the hills but it was more to the south. We'd had a good day and if we could hang on for the evening set, the last one of the day which we don't usually pull until just on dark – it's always the best – we knew it would be a boomer."

With the southerly cloud bank drawing through the strait, Charlie decided they'd pull their nets slightly earlier. They left their 15 nets in the dinghy, tied the painter to the stem bollard and hauled up the anchor. Three miles north of Wellington Head (now Perano Head) the wind suddenly swung from light sou-westerly to the sou-east. Rapidly it increased to 60 knots. Conditions became worse. The *Midlothian* was taking a real hammering in the heavy seas that had so quickly built up. Off Wellington Head, Charlie went below deck to check the boat's hull.

"It was pounding badly and with every thump I saw rivets popping off the nails in the ribs. Every time she hit she'd lose a few more. When I looked closer, every seam of the boat was splitting. It was opening as I looked. I tore back on deck and yelled at Joe to turn around. We'd have to run with it and try to make the northern entrance."

Charlie's words were tumbling out as one memory brought back another and yet another of the sudden storm. "It was dark, very dark. We couldn't see a thing. The sea was massive. There were about three inches of hail on the deck and the only time we could get any indication of where we were was when there was a flash of lightning and we'd get a glimpse of the coast.

"We could hear the seas roaring up our stern. Each time they'd carry the dinghy up alongside us. Then we'd hear the loud crack as the boat surged forward and took up the slack of the painter. Without warning there was a tremendous crash when a bigger sea than usual lifted the dinghy up over the rails on to the back deck of the boat. Just as quickly it fell back into the sea. We heard a bang and all we had left was the painter. Once that was gone the boat began to yaw. She'd put her nose down, and as she ran down the sea I knew we were in danger of her broaching or rolling over.

"I yelled at Joe to make a sea anchor, using the car tyre we had as a fender on the side of the boat and two grey sharks we'd got in the net earlier in the day. He tied them all together and put them on 50 fathoms of rope out the stern to hold the boat and stop her broaching."

For Joe, the worst moment was when his father told him to go down and put on a life jacket and bring one up for him. He was glad he was with his father who knew that coast like the back of his hand. "We could hear the seas crashing against the cliffs and as I put on my life jacket I wondered what the point was. We wouldn't have survived in that sea."

When they finally reached the top end of Arapawa Island and steamed into the sheltered waters behind Cape Koamaru they were able to get to the radio telephone and call up Wellington Radio to ask them to ring Ruby and let her know they were safe.

The next morning was fine and still. Charlie thought there was a chance the dinghy might have been swept ashore. If they could locate the wreckage they might be able to salvage some nets. The tranquillity of Cook Strait belied its frenzy of less than 12 hours earlier. They found nothing. A low heavy swell that surged up the cliffs well above the high tide mark and sucked back, stretching out the long strings of bull-kelp, was the only indication that only a short time ago Cook Strait had lived up to its reputation of being one of the most dangerous strips of water in the world.

Bait, coils of rope, buoys, rolls of wire netting as well as groceries and everything needed on the farm from woolpacks to fuel, dips, drenches and chemicals, were brought in on the *Midlo-*

thian from Picton and rowed ashore. Now, with the crayfish tank, when the crayfish needed to be taken to Picton, instead of the men lifting the cases out of the water and on to the deck of the boat, the tank in the bay was towed close to the shore and pulled up the beach by the tractor. There the crayfish were packed into the wooden fish cases. These had to be stacked in the dinghy, rowed out to the boat and lifted aboard.

"I'd thought about building a wharf for years, using railway irons for piles, but the experts reckoned the constant movement of the sand, especially in a southerly storm, would cut out the irons in no time. If it wasn't going to last, the cost made it uneconomic. But with the fishing business expanding and the two of us on the farm, more and more equipment was being handled. We needed a wharf."

Dig Thacker had bought Te Iro Bay from Reg Jackson. Like Charlie, he had diversified from farming and now fished most of the time. When he wasn't fishing he was building wharves in the Sounds. He had set up the pile-driving gear on the *Oria,* the old whale chaser Arthur Heberley had owned. Because of her long narrow design she was often called the Splinter. In August 1965 Dig began driving the railway irons for the piles for our wharf.

In 1962 the introduction of the new road and rail ferry, *Aramoana,* had meant an increased volume of rail traffic in Picton. Heavier diesel locomotives were needed to haul the bigger loads. The viaduct crossing Picton's Essons Valley, which had been in use since the line opened in 1875, had to be replaced by one capable of handling the heavier engines and freight. Charlie bought some of the Australian hardwood timber beams from the original viaduct to use as stringers underneath the wharf.

The wharf wasn't quite completed when the second grandchild with the Heberley name was born on 27 October 1965. Her arrival back in the bay coincided with the arrival of a northerly gale. I watched anxiously as Helen was lowered from the boat, in her carrycot, down into the dinghy. My father-in-law rowed her ashore and came back to collect me. Up at our house, he was the first to pick her up and I watched his face as Helen opened her eyes and stared at her grandfather. The generation when so much emphasis was placed on sons had taken its first step forward. I could see Charlie loved her as much as he did our first born, who just happened to be a boy.

For the first time people arriving at Okukari for Christmas could throw their bags up on the wharf and get ashore without getting their feet wet. Worries about the iron piles rusting out in no time were soon forgotten. They lasted Charlie's time at Okukari and it was not till 1995, 30 years later, that we replaced the piles with more railway irons.

"When Joe first told me he was considering getting a boat built for himself I was disappointed." Charlie's words shocked me. I thought he'd always been keen for Joe to get ahead. "But it was only a fleeting thought," he said quickly. "We worked well together, and I could see it was the only way for us to expand."

Joe commissioned D F Robb Ltd, boatbuilders in Timaru, to build a 38-foot wooden-hulled fishing vessel. The *Heather* was launched in Timaru in March 1966, and while Ruby and I drove home Charlie came up the coast with Joe and Alf Nimmo in the new boat. In view of the new Marine Department regulations coming out the following year, she was built to the department's specifications with water-tight bulkheads throughout and a reinforced bow, an important factor, especially when Charlie thought of his brother's death when his boat was wrecked off the Wellington coast, and the night Joe and he had nearly lost their lives.

Thinking of his brother's death kindled another of Charlie's memories. He had wondered what his present was going to be when, at his brother Joe's funeral, the minister had said, "The Lord giveth and the Lord taketh away". What would the Lord be giving him? It was 36 years before he thought about those words again. His mother had not been looking after herself at her home in Picton and had been staying at Okukari for a few weeks when she became unwell and was taken to Picton and admitted to hospital. Once she was confined to bed, Ada Heberley's indomitable spirit died. Her heart stopped beating on 10 May 1967. Two months later, on 26 July, our third child, James, was born. This time Charlie knew and could take comfort from the minister's words. One Heberley had died, but another had been born.

Charlie was glad to have fishing as an income when the wool industry began to collapse. He'd enjoyed the years since 1951 when the minimum price scheme had been set up, but when the wool prices collapsed in the 1966-67 season the scheme was wrecked. The Wool Commission ended up with 40 percent of the season's clip and in a financial crisis, which forced it to drop the minimum price the following season. A supplementation introduced meant that the farmer was guaranteed a minimum price but the Commission could let auction prices fall below this level. They'd pay the shortfall to the farmer instead of buying the wool.

In the seasons Charlie had been back from Great Barrier he wasn't satisfied with the way his Romney flock was developing. The breed originated from the low marshes of south-east England where it was known as Romney Marsh. It had been in New Zealand since 1853 and, by the early 1960s, three-quarters of the country's 50 million sheep were Romney. If he could build up the Romneys' body size and produce clearer-faced sheep, Charlie felt they'd be better suited to their environment. For one season he bought Border Leicester rams instead of the usual Romneys. The first cross gave the best lambs Okukari had seen – "they looked more like donkeys" – and with the Border Leicesters' higher fertility there was a higher incidence of twins. In the following years the frame of the Romneys increased, their faces cleared, their legs were longer and their mothering qualities improved. Although Charlie remained anxious about the wool market, at least he was getting a far better return on the sale of his lambs.

It was during this period that Charlie was offered the grazing of 700 acres at Wharehunga, a property on the Queen Charlotte side of the island, and backing on to Okukari. He stocked the land from his increased lambing percentages and by buying in Romney two-tooth ewes. When he came back from Great Barrier he was running 600 ewes and 200 hoggets. Now with Wharehunga he could increase his flock by 700.

When the National Government brought in a 50 percent subsidy on spray, Charlie began a spraying programme using 245-T to get rid of the gorse which at that time covered two-thirds of the farm. The bulk of it was sprayed on by helicopter. On the lower hills and flats he sprayed it from a tank towed behind the tractor, or a knapsack sprayer. He sprayed and burnt. As the land was cleared he bought 60 Poll-Angus heifers and a Hereford-cross bull to open up the thick gullies. Every two years he sold off enough cattle to maintain the original number, as he wanted them only to help clear the land.

When the subsidy came off the spray Charlie kept on with the programme which is still in place. But today it is the income from the fishing that allows the spraying programme to continue, although no longer with the hormonal spray 245-T, but a safer chemical. "We've reached the stage where we can't afford not to spray, and," Charlie grinned, "it gave us an excuse to go fishing."

Every year the months of June and July took on an almost religious significance. They didn't need an excuse to go fishing – the fish came to them. Mackerel, a pelagic fish of coastal waters and distantly related to the tuna, came into Tory Channel to spawn. Fishermen use them for groper bait, and they are delicious smoked, but because they are very oily with dark flesh the New Zealand housewife doesn't care for them. The fishermen managed to secure a very limited market with Sealords in Nelson which canned them and paid the fishermen five cents a kilo.

From the time the mackerel were due, whenever Charlie left the house he came out the back gate by the woodshed and walked out to the edge of the bank above the beach. Here he'd stand looking out across the bay for the tell-tale bubbling greasy patches. At the first sign the net would be out and run into the dinghy, local fishermen would be alerted, coats grabbed and goodbyes said. As for Charlie and Joe, their personalities changed. They didn't need to eat or sleep, and revelled in being wet and sandy. Scales falling off the mackerel coated everything and stuck to their skin.

Fierce arguments erupted among the fishermen as they all tried to catch their winter's bait. They used a drag net and once the shoal was encircled and the fish trapped, the net was either hauled ashore or towed out to the waiting boats where the mackerel was scooped out on to the decks.

The arguing and fighting usually occurred once the net was shot around a shoal. It reminded me of rival gangs in a city street. From the bank Ruby and I would watch grown men smack their oars on the surface of the water and dart them down inside the net in an effort to scare the fish out. Like vultures, the rival fishermen drifted behind the back of the net in their dinghies, their nets ready to shoot around the shoaling fish if they pushed the back of the net flat as they tried to escape the thrashing oars. Men who last week had sat and yarned together on the fishermen's wharf in Picton now seemed sworn enemies. But when the mackerel season finished and the boats were tied up in Picton, they would all be seen catching up their yarns from where they'd left off.

In 1968 when Charlie was 50 years old, our youngest, Pauline, was born. With Jocelyn's seven children, Charlie now had 11 grandchildren. Every grandchild has special memories of a grandfather who was always working and who expected those he worked with to work just as hard. He was strict yet fair. Stern, but with a sense of humour. Quick to anger but just as quick to forget, and most of his grandchildren admitted to times when they were scared of him – even when they were older. His whakapapa was important to him and he tried to teach all his grandchildren about their ancestors so that they might grow up to live comfortably within two cultures.

Mostly remembered are his stories of a way of life gone forever. A walk with him through the remains of the whaling station brought back the sight of a whale being hauled up the ramp amidst the sound of winches clanging and banging, hissing steam and the pervading stench of cooking whales. Men, many now dead, who stare out from the interpretative panels erected by the Department of Conservation at the station, came to life as Charlie described the processing of a whale from the catch to the shipping out of the oil.

When the whaling station was operating in Tory Channel it was a highlight for visitors to Marlborough. In the few years since the Perano family had ceased whaling, time had already begun its destruction. Some of the old whalers felt that if the factory couldn't be preserved it would be a pity not to preserve some of the memories of the whaling days, so the Whekenui Whalers' Association was formed. In 1969 a committee of nine men, headed by Gilbert and Joe Perano, organised a reunion for anyone who had whaled at least one season with the Peranos out of Tory Channel. About 70 men, with their wives and families, attended the reunion in Picton. Charlie summed it up well. "I enjoyed meeting up with old friends and catching whales again. Some wanted it to be a regular event but I'm glad it wasn't. Whaling as we knew it was history. And now we knew why. It was no good mourning its demise. I'd rather see us all go forward and put our energies into the whales' conservation."

The *Heather* had proved herself to be an excellent sea boat. Charlie was also aware that a great deal of money had to be spent on the *Midlothian* to bring her up to a safe standard so he commissioned the Picton boatbuilders, Jorgensens, to build a sister ship to the *Heather.* In the winter of 1970 the 38-foot wooden vessel with a compromised stern (like a double-ender but rounded) was launched. Jocelyn smashed the bottle of champagne over her bow with the same words that have been spoken at launchings for hundreds of years. "I name this boat *Donna Marie.* May God bless her and all who sail on her."

Amidst cheering and clapping she ran down the rails towards the sea. Instead of the splash and the surge of water when her stern cut through the water for the first time, she stopped short. The tide was too low. In silence Joe ran along the wharf and climbed aboard the *Heather.* He quickly started her engine, cast off and came in close to the *Donna Marie* where he passed a towing line to his father. The new boat reached the water and floated from the cradle. The flags strung up the mast fluttered in the wind. Charlie reached over the bow and pulled aboard the New Zealand flag that had been draped over her name before the christening. As he walked across the stern deck Charlie was already calculating how many trips it would take him in the bigger boat to carry his crayfish pots to the fishing grounds at the start of the season.

Charlie employed a crewman to work with him. He never expected them to do anything he wouldn't do himself but he expected them to do as much. Many found it hard to live up to his expectations and crews came and went with great regularity. He worked his gear to suit. If he had a crew he worked more gear. On his own he worked what he could manage.

Oscar, a blackish-brown dachshund, kept Charlie company on the boat. Every day he'd be waiting to jump on the boat as soon as Charlie brought it alongside to collect his bait from the freezer in the boatshed. Oscar did his fishing from the bow, standing on the for'ward hatch. Early in his life at Okukari he'd chased Nan Perano's chooks at a time when Charlie and Ruby were away. Gilbert met Joe at the boundary fence with Oscar. Once on our property Joe had growled at the dog and chased him all the way home. It made Joe his sworn enemy. He'd know if the boat on the horizon was the *Heather* long before Charlie did, and would parade up and down the front deck, barking and snarling.

One night Oscar had jumped on the boat and found he couldn't get off so curled up in the cabin. Joe happened to go on board and when Oscar realised he was trapped in the cabin with Joe standing at the door, he disgraced himself. Dry retching from the smell, Joe quietly pulled the door ajar and climbed off the boat.

Charlie discovered Oscar the next morning when he jumped on the boat to go fishing. "I couldn't understand why he'd mucked in the cabin. He'd never done it before," Charlie told Joe later. "Poor little bugger must've had the belly-ache."

Living on the edge of Cook Strait means that life is never predictable. It changes with the seasons but is ruled by the weather. Charlie remembered the worst storms not so much by their intensity as by the damage they caused.

The aftermath of one night of northerly gales kept Charlie busy for weeks. During the day the wind had gradually freshened and by dark the rain hammering at the windows was almost blocking out the sound of the wind. The house shook with every gust. Worried about the woolshed roof, Charlie rang Joe to get him to give him a hand. Charlie put on his leggings and yellow smockie, took a torch and went outside where he met Joe. The wind had them on their knees as they crawled down to the shed. All around was the sound of the storm. At the shed they pulled open the door and swung the torch beam over the iron.

"I could see a couple of sheets starting to lift. As we watched, one peeled off. Joe climbed up on one of the pen rails and I handed him a piece of timber which he poked up through the open hole and laid flat over the flapping iron. We looped a piece of rope round the wood and tied this to a rail. Sounds pretty Heath Robinson, but it worked until we could get up on the roof to repair it properly," Charlie laughed.

That same night the fence behind the glasshouse blew down, taking a few panes of glass with it. The power lines from the generator shed to the house came down, the clothes line was flattened, the telephone lines were down, and a macrocarpa tree estimated to be at least 90 years old lay across the backyard, the garden destroyed. "It took weeks to clean up after that storm."

Strong winds also meant a new television aerial. Charlie used the battered aluminium aerials for stakes in the vegetable garden and with an average of at least one a year he had plenty to choose from. As the house was tucked in beneath a 900-foot hill, the TV reception wasn't very good so at a time when he had to buy another aerial he decided to run a line above the fenceline to the top of the hill immediately behind the house. From there the aerial was in a direct line with Mt Kaukau in Wellington. Charlie brought home a stack of 3x2 timber and cut it into two-foot lengths, and on the top of each piece he nailed a cross-tree eight inches long. On each end of the cross-tree he put an insulator. He carried these up the hill, nailing one to every third fence post. The television aerial was assembled at the house and early one morning before the wind got up anyone who glanced in the bay, and saw the stooping silhouette climbing the ridge, could have been reminded of Christ carrying his cross to Golgotha.

At the top of the hill Charlie fastened the aerial to a post he'd dug earlier into the ground. Lastly he ran two lines of copper wire from the aerial down through the insulators to the house. At first the reception was as good as it gets, but after a few gales the bars would begin to work loose or wires ping off insulators, meaning another climb up the hill if the All Blacks were playing or he wanted to watch a favourite television programme.

"Sometimes it didn't last as long as it took to fix it. But we could usually see what we wanted to through the snow on the set." And in the weeks I saw him trudging up the hill in his effort to improve his television reception I couldn't help but remember some of the comments I'd heard in town when a television set had first been bought and people moaned bitterly about the time it took for the technician to come and fit the aerial to their roof.

One of the advantages of living on the edge of Cook Strait was being close to the finish line for many of the swimmers who attempted to be the first, and later the fastest, to cross its waters. On 20 November 1963, Barrie Devenport became the first European to swim Cook Strait, in 11 hours and 13 minutes. A few months later Keith Hancox lowered this record by nearly two hours. Since then more than 100 attempts have been made. About one in 10 are successful.

Charlie went out to some of the earlier swims.

"When I saw them literally crawling through the swirling kelp and up on to the rocks, I was appalled at their condition. I admired their courage but quite frankly I thought they must have been insane."

Just as Joe follows his father's tradition of helping those in distress in Cook Strait, so Charlie followed his own father's. Time had made him forget the smaller incidents but had sharpened his memory of the more serious. Except when an accident involves death, the worst thing to watch is a boat sinking, he said. "It's like a death."

Charlie was still in bed when the phone rang on the morning of 2 May 1972. It was the Picton Police with a message to say the 49-foot fishing vessel *Takahe* had struck rocks between West Head and Jordy Rocks, and could he please go out and give assistance.

By the time Charlie arrived at the scene, skipper Bill Muir, who was the only person on board, was huddled in the wheelhouse clutching a pillowcase of valuables. The boat had slammed straight into the rock face. She was full of water and rolling from side to side on the rocks in the surge. The seas breaking over her had smashed the wheelhouse windows in. Charlie took him off the boat and brought him back to Okukari. From there they arranged for a local barge operator, Gary Kenny, to attempt a salvage. She was badly holed and all that was salvaged before she broke up in the seas was some electronic gear. A few weeks later her engine was lifted from the seabed.

"There've been others. It wasn't unusual to go to the assistance of one or two of the yachts competing in the Royal Port Nicholson Yacht Club annual Cook Strait race. It was 'the' race of the year and seemed to attract anyone and everyone. Twenty-foot boats with three or four crew raced alongside 60-footers with a crew of a dozen or more. The winner wasn't always the fastest boat but the one that handled the tides and wind best at Tory Channel entrance."

Taranaki Rock below the lookout, the sunken rocks off East Head, as well as both East and West Head, have all been the cause of call-outs for the Heberleys over the years. Skippers on racing yachts in a tacking duel as they approached the entrance, or the 'hole' as it is sometimes called, often found themselves at the whim of the current as they were swept against the rocks.

For Charlie, living on the edge and in such close proximity to one plane crash was of no help to the victims. He always believed what was needed was less 'red ribbon' to get through in some departments. This was the case when a small single-engined plane had left Nelson bound for Wellington when it ran into fog. Half way across Cook Strait they were advised Wellington Airport was closed so turned back to Nelson. The plane slammed into bush-covered cliffs 600 feet above Wellington Bay north of the channel entrance. The engine came out on impact and rolled down to the sea.

Okukari had been blanketed by fog all day. That afternoon Charlie had heard a small plane overhead and was glad he wasn't flying. Later the cloud ceiling lifted and he saw an Orion circling.

Charlie came inside and rang the Picton Police. They rang Wellington and it was confirmed that Civil Aviation had picked up a signal from an EPIRB (emergency positioning indicator radio beacon). He offered to help and was told it was on the western side of Arapawa Island in Puriri Bay. It was in the days before we had motor bikes on the farm, so Charlie and Joe ran. From the top of the hill overlooking Puriri they saw Peter Button circling in his helicopter on the Cook Strait side of Arapawa Island. Charlie and Joe quickly established there was no plane crash where they'd been sent, and came straight back to Okukari.

A short time later Peter Button landed on the flat. He'd located the wreckage, and as the terrain was too steep to land near the plane he'd landed on a ridge a short distance away to drop off the two policemen he'd flown in from Wellington. They'd scrambled down and across a steep gully to reach the crash site and confirmed there were no survivors. Peter had come to ask Charlie if he had any spare woolpacks he could use to bring the bodies back in to Okukari, before putting them on a stretcher for the flight to Wellington.

At the inquest it was learned that two died instantly while the third choked on his blood and died a short time later. "If we'd been told of the crash and given the correct directions where the damned thing was in the first place, we could have been out there by boat and up the cliff in less than 30 minutes. Times like that made me question the worth of someone sitting in an office in Wellington running a search and rescue, especially in Cook Strait," Charlie added angrily.

With increased fishing and farming returns over the past few years, Charlie and Ruby began to make plans for a world trip. Early in 1972 they visited a travel agent and came home with a pile of glossy brochures covering every country they thought they'd like to see. They planned a seven-month trip, leaving from Auckland on 24 February 1973.

It made gift buying for the family easy. Suitcases, diary, notebook, tripbook, films for the camera, toiletries – everything revolved around the trip. Whenever Ruby and Charlie went to town they came home with something new to add to their suitcases. Casual clothes, handbags to match shoes, underwear, swimming suits, nightwear. Only new things went into the new suitcases. Most exciting was the evening wear. The admiration given Charlie's tuxedo was nothing compared with the awe evoked by Ruby's evening gowns. Their lounge at Okukari had never seen the like of such shining gowns held up by Ruby as she twirled around, her Oroton evening bag slung over her wrist and bare feet slipped into elegant sling-back black suede shoes with diamante buckles.

One morning in early October, less than five months before they sailed, Ruby phoned me. "I've something I want to show you," she said. Wondering what new thing I was going to see this time, I ran down to their house. "We'll have tea outside in the sun," Ruby called out through the open kitchen window. She'd hardly sat down than she pulled her dress above her knee. "What do you make of this?"

Below Ruby's left knee was a lump. 'A lump or swelling in the breast or elsewhere.' Words I'd read after my mother-in-law's melanoma operation nine years ago clamoured in my head as I studied it. It was about one and a half inches across and as Ruby poked at it and told me it wasn't sore I could see it seemed quite spongy. She couldn't remember bumping it, "but perhaps I did," she said as I felt her trying to find an excuse for it. "I just noticed it this morning."

I was sitting on the opposite side of the sunlight from Ruby and I saw a dark shadow in the middle of the lump. Without mentioning that, I said – as she already knew – that she should go to see a doctor. He diagnosed a fatty lipoma. Donna was not satisfied and early one morning she rang the doctor, "before he was guarded by his efficient secretary", and reminded him of her mother's past history. He admitted Ruby to hospital and a second melanoma was removed.

With their trip only four months away, Charlie debated whether he should cancel it, postpone it or carry on with life and just go as arranged. The surgeon helped make the decision. He told Ruby and Charlie it could come back, or it might never come back. They could stay at home, waiting, but if they decided to go as planned he would write a letter and arrange an appointment for Ruby to have a check-up in a London hospital. "But," he warned, "make sure you have funds to fly home immediately if necessary."

On 24 February 1973 amid streamers thrown between the passengers and those on shore and to the strains of a lone piper playing *Now Is The Hour* – drowned out by people singing the words – the *Orsova* eased away from Auckland's Princes Wharf passenger ship terminal at 11pm. Joe and I with our four children had travelled to Auckland to farewell them. We stood watching the ship slide into the darkness and by the time we finally left there was no one to watch us scuffing our feet through the litter of tangled streamers along the deserted wharf.

On the voyage these two people who had spent their lives at the bottom of the world, mostly in isolation, travelled via Australia, Singapore, Ceylon or Sri Lanka as it is now known, Durban and Cape Town in South Africa, Dakar in West Africa, then Lisbon. They arrived at Southampton in the early morning of 11 April. During the next 16 weeks they travelled throughout the continent as well as through Ireland, Scotland and Wales. Between trips, Ruby kept her appointment at the hospital where she received a good report.

The final leg of their trip began when they left Southampton aboard the *Oronsay*. The first port of call was the Bahamas and on through the Panama Canal. The ship sailed up the west coast of America calling at Acapulco, San Francisco and up as far as Vancouver. Then it was across the Pacific Ocean to Hawaii and down to Fiji, arriving back in Auckland on 11 September 1973.

They'd seen the world and crossed its oceans. Of all the places, Lisbon was Charlie's favourite, and although neither Ruby nor Charlie realised at the time, it was the lacemakers Ruby had watched in the streets of Bruges who were later to lead her to take up lace making herself. And, Charlie decided, the only place comparable to the bad weather of Cook Strait was the Bay of Biscay.

"Steaming up the Sounds on the way home I asked myself why we went away. Nothing in the world matches the Sounds. But I'm glad we did it. It was all the holidays we'd never had rolled into one, and something we'd remember all our lives."

After the lambs were tailed, it was back to crayfishing which as usual was slotted around the seasonal work on the farm. Charlie remarked on the increasing number of goats coming on to the farm whenever the sheep were mustered in. Since the bounty had been taken off, "For every goat grazing on the property we could run another sheep," he muttered as he watched them coming around the heads from the outside coast. Not even culling by local farmers seemed to make any impression on their numbers.

An American family, Betty and Walter Rowe, had come to live at Aotea Bay on the opposite side of the island from us in Queen Charlotte Sound in 1972. They cleared land and ran sheep but Betty's love of animals meant she didn't want to see them sent to the works, and this made their farming enterprise uneconomic. The goats roaming Arapawa, descendants of the ones Captain Cook had brought out, captured Betty's interest. She believed the Arapawa goats to be purebred Old English milk goats now extinct in Britain, and from her side of the island she began a campaign to prevent any culling of the animals.

Charlie was adamant. "They couldn't be purebred. Many farmers brought in goats to clear the land. The Kenny family who owned Okukari before me ran Angora goats."

But it wasn't so much farmers' concern that brought in the New Zealand Forest Service to cull the goats but concern over the native bush they were destroying.

Betty organised protests on the island as well as the removal of some of the live animals off Arapawa Island by barge. Feelings ran high. The cullers were worried that someone would end up being shot, and withdrew. Meanwhile the farmers got on with farming, positive the issue would resolve itself now it was in the hands of the NZFS, while on the other side of the island Betty never stopped working on the goats' behalf.

The issue boiled up in the mid-1970s. Betty's campaign had been brought to the attention of the media. It was in the papers and on radio and television. Cullers would come in when they could, but were met with resistance from protesters. It put an island at war – neighbours against neighbours. When one of the younger protesters who had lived on Arapawa less than 10 years told Charlie he had "a lot to learn about farming in the Sounds", it nearly caused a riot.

"I think if Joe hadn't been there, I'd have killed him," Charlie said frankly. For Charlie it was the last straw. "Because we'd kept out of the issue it seemed likely that every goat on the island would be protected. We'd be over-run with goats."

It was a day when weather conditions kept Charlie and Joe in the woolshed mending nets. They'd listened to the plight of the goats on every new bulletin. Finally it became too much. They called Television New Zealand, inviting them to come and get the farmers' side of the story instead of one woman's side. This brought a helicopter across Cook Strait later that afternoon. On the television news that night the people of New Zealand were finally able to hear the farmers' views.

The goats were culled but not without bitter confrontation between cullers and supporters. The goats are still on the island but their numbers are kept down by the Department of Conservation. Betty and Walter Rowe have built a sanctuary on their own land for the feral goats. Each person maintains his or her beliefs, and once again everyone lives in harmony.

But it wasn't always harmony on the sea between Charlie and the Cook Strait ferry skippers. Two minutes from home, in sight of his house, Charlie had his first crayfish pot set. He set others around Taniwha Bay as far as East Head before heading north. Others he set in the channel entrance, always off the leads, the two white triangular structures built on the flat at Whekenui. This was much to the chagrin of some of the ferry captains who complained the yellow floats bobbing on the surface at slack water were in the shipping lane. Charlie argued that they weren't. He believed that if the ferries came in on the leads, as they were meant to, there wouldn't be a problem.

The captains on the ferries had a different view. Their ships were coming in through a very narrow gap no more than half a mile wide with a tidal flow of four or five knots. They wanted all the space. Back in Okukari it wasn't unusual to hear blasts from the ferry's horn as it sailed up Tory Channel towards the mouth of the channel, where Charlie kept working his pots off the *Donna Marie*. He'd stay put, guarding his gear if he thought the ferry was going to plough through the middle of it, gesticulating – and not always nicely – to those on the bridge as it veered away. Over the years there were times when, although he'd actually finished pulling his pots, he'd make a special trip out in the boat to stand guard over his gear if it was slack water and he knew slack rope and buoys were on the surface. "I know the bastards went out of their way to run over them," he said.

It was one of these captains who phoned up one day to tell Charlie one of his sheep appeared to be stuck down on the cliffs in Taniwha Bay. He added that he couldn't see how anyone could reach it and hoped Charlie would put it out of its misery. Joe wasn't home, and Charlie saw Helen and Pauline on the way down to his boat. "Quick!" he said. "I need a hand."

Mystified, my girls followed him and jumped aboard the boat lying alongside the wharf. "I've just had a call from one of the ferry captains," he explained as he coiled a rope around his arm. "There's a sheep stuck on the cliffs out here."

He steamed out in the bay, untied the dinghy off the mooring and looped it over the bollard before heading out to the channel. "We thought he wanted us to row him in but when we got out there he jumped in the dinghy and yelled at us to mind the boat and watch out for the rocks. We were only about seven and nine at the time, and terrified," Helen recalled. "Worst of all, between keeping an eye out for rocks, was watching Grandpa climbing up the cliff towards the sheep. We watched him as he edged his way across a sheer face until he was close enough to throw the rope and lasso it. By the time he arrived back on board Pauline and I were in tears, thinking of what might have happened. Grandpa asked us what we were howling for and we got a real dressing down. Told us he thought we were women of the sea, not blubbing kids."

In 1979 the first farm bike arrived at Okukari. As Joe learnt to ride it Charlie gave out grim warnings that "the bloody dangerous thing would be the death of someone." He'd walked the land all his life and didn't see the need to change, but Joe persevered, gathering bruises. Mustering at Okukari was changed forever.

Changes were creeping insidiously into Charlie's life. It was seven years since Ruby's second melanoma operation and she still had regular health checks but at Okukari, alone most of the time while Charlie was away fishing, her mind raced. She cleaned and polished, baked, washed and ironed, the flower garden was like a park, and the vegetable garden didn't have a weed in it. When she wasn't working she did tapestries, knitted, embroidered and sewed dresses for herself and shirts for Charlie. Both Donna and Jocelyn lived in Nelson and Charlie was always too busy to go away but Ruby had reached a stage in her life when she needed something more. She wanted to be able to see more of her daughters, and at the back of her mind there was a dream. She would like to learn lace-making but most especially she wanted to learn the art of china painting.

Charlie recognised he couldn't do what he used to do, and he knew it made him short-tempered with those he loved. Deep down he knew if he didn't move from Okukari his marriage and health could suffer and he knew it was time to make plans. They decided to go and live in Nelson, and after months of searching they found a house in Stoke. The move from one house to the other was made gradually, keeping their Okukari house furnished and wardrobes full, to enable them to step easily from town to country living.

We organised a party for them. It wasn't allowed to be called a farewell party because they weren't going for good, so in 1979 we invited the people in Tory Channel to a function to mark Charlie's and Ruby's semi-retirement. More than 20 people arrived by boat for a shared dinner. Everyone gave good wishes and their neighbour and work colleague, Gilbert Perano, summed up Charlie's and Ruby's years at Okukari best. "They were always there to help when needed."

Charlie left the land in a far better state than he'd found it. It now carried 1,450 breeding ewes, 365 ewe hoggets, 30 wethers and 35 rams. Cattle numbers had increased to 140.

"I can't say I wanted to go, but I knew it was time for me to step aside and let the next generation take over."

The large garage and workshop in the house in Nelson had been one of the main reasons Charlie had bought it. Already he knew how many lengths of the garage it would take to sling a butterfish net, the bench running along one side was a good size for making up groper and shark gear, and behind the shed was a good place to tar any ropes safely. A new way of life had begun but a big part of it still revolved around the sea.

Chapter Twelve

A DIFFERENT WORLD

Ka pu te ruha ka hao te rangatahi.
The old net is cast aside – it is time for others to step forward.

"THE HARDEST THING for me to come to terms with was pulling the blinds at night." Although their new house was built on a big corner section with a well-established garden, Charlie found it difficult to have neighbours in such close proximity. "At Okukari I could stand on the terrace and look through the binoculars. Imagine if I was spotted doing that in town – I'd be hung." But while the binoculars remained on their hook, the car keys didn't.

"I didn't mind going to the shop every day to buy a fresh loaf of bread. Never again would I eat bread that had been stored in the freezer or had gone stale, and for the first time in my life it wasn't my worry if we had no electricity or water. Linesmen didn't have to travel by boat to find a broken telephone line, so the phone never stayed out of order long. And if an appliance broke down and I couldn't repair it myself, I didn't have to wait for a fine day to cart it down to the wharf and take it into town on the boat and be without it until the next trip to Picton. What a business it used to be! Now it was so easy to call someone to come and fix it at the house. But best of all, the television aerial on our roof gave us a choice of channels and we could watch a clear picture without having to climb the hill and fiddle with the aerial whenever we wanted to watch something special."

Soon after they moved to Nelson, Ruby began making enquiries at Nelson Polytechnic about classes on china painting, and before the end of the year Charlie was dropping her off at the polytechnic for regular classes. Ruby's talent soon became evident and later she was asked if she would teach, but she felt it would put too much pressure on her. This was her relaxation, so she declined. Roses, apple-blossoms, violets, lily of the valley, fuchsias, any in-season flowers, all came to life on vases and on plates from dinner size to butter dishes. She painted a ginger jar for each of her children, and adorned it with cherries, peaches, bunches of grapes and leaves and a solid gold-painted lid. The firing of each stage was carried out at the polytechnic between classes.

The gold paint required more firing. Charlie knew if Ruby had a kiln of her own she would be able to paint whenever she wished instead of waiting for each class, so he bought a kiln and set it up in the garage with an area for her work. She experimented and one of her most unusual works was the head and shoulders of a Maori woman wearing a feather cloak and painted on a tile. Mounted on green baize and framed, it drew much praise from those who saw it on the wall of their dining room. It wasn't until after her death that a similar one was found in a cupboard, unmounted. Charlie remembered her putting it away as she didn't think it was very good but when Donna had it mounted on dark red baize and framed, they made a perfect pair.

Charlie was proud of Ruby's work, especially of a heavy square-based urn she had painted a muted pale blue with two white herons and gold painted handles. This was displayed in a lit-up glass cabinet in the foyer of Nelson's Rutherford Hotel during a conference of New Zealand china painters.

Charlie remembered that day as if it were only yesterday. "When I saw Ruby's urn displayed, I knew that, if for no other reason, our move to Nelson had been the right decision."

While Ruby painted, Charlie kept himself busy making up the groper and shark gear for the next generation of Heberleys who were carrying on the tradition of fishing in Cook Strait. Each groper drag is made up with a wire backbone. This has 35 monofiliment traces, each with a hook and joined to the backbone by a swivel. The backbone of the shark longline is 10 120-fathom coils of 7mm rope with room for 450 hooks each crimped on a nylon braid trace, which Charlie tied in bundles and then tarred. These are clipped to the line as it is being set. Practices have changed, and we now use monofiliment traces on the longline. These fish better, and don't need to be tarred. With 450 hooks on the longline, plus 35 on each groper drag and up to 10 of these set at one time, replacements are a continual need. A shark can bite through the line as it is being winched up, hooks are frequently straightened by large fish, a line can foul-hook the bottom, or be carried away and lost with the often unpredictable tides in Cook Strait.

Charlie kept up the gear replacement. Often, when we came in to unload fish in Picton, he was already sitting waiting in his car with Ruby on the end of the fishermen's wharf, sometimes with more fishing gear or else to collect drags that needed to be repaired. His chillybin always went back to Nelson loaded with groper cheeks and throats, many of which he gave away to family and friends.

The land of his ancestors kept pulling him back. In 1979 Charlie returned to Okukari to help us with our first mustering and shearing since he'd left. As Joe was bringing a mob of sheep down a steep ridge, a piece of cut scrub caught in the front wheel of his bike, causing it to lock, and he was thrown over the handlebars. He'd hurt his ankle and by the time he arrived home he was certain it was broken and needed an X-ray. Mustering still had to continue from where we'd left off before the sheep ran back, so early the next morning we set off with Charlie in charge. "Ring the float plane at first light and get it seen to," Charlie advised Joe. "We'll have to bring in that next block." Charlie's words of warning about motor bikes came back to me and I waited for him to add, "I told you so," but obvious concern for his son kept him quiet.

The next time Charlie came down to help with sheep work was at tailing time. A mob ran into a hollow in an improvised yard and more than 20 ewes and lambs smothered. That day he had plenty of advice as he dressed us down for being all "rip shit and bust", a trait I knew Joe had inherited from his father. It was a lesson well learnt and something that never happened again.

Fishing also brought Charlie back to Okukari. Organised trips, when both he and Ruby would come to the bay and Charlie was able to choose his weather to go out in the boat, often happened in their earlier retirement years although one particular visit was totally unexpected.

"Well, what else did you expect," Charlie grinned, "when Joe rang and told me they had the net around a big patch of mackerel in the bay."

Three hours later a water taxi pulled up alongside the wharf. It was Charlie, still in the suit pants, white shirt and tie that he'd been wearing when Joe had rung him.

"Didn't have time to change," he called out as he ran along the wharf to the boatshed where he found a pair of thigh gumboots. He was still pulling them up as he ran down on the beach. His gold cuff links were torn off and shoved in his pocket, and shirt sleeves pushed up.

As the afternoon wore on I could see Charlie's tie was annoying him and he'd poke it between the buttons of his shirt. Before long it would flop again out and he'd push it impatiently inside his shirt again. It finally wore him down. The knot had tightened in the water and when Charlie found he couldn't undo it he grabbed a cabbage knife used on the boat to head groper, and cut his tie off.

In those days it was a good two hours' drive from Nelson to Picton, and, taking into account parking the car and finding an available boat to bring him out to Okukari, his Austin 1100 must have broken all speed records. That day I remembered his "rip shit and bust", and I'd have loved to have had the courage to remind him, but I'd learnt over the years that sometimes silence was golden.

Charlie discovered the pleasure of trout fishing in the rivers around Motueka, a far cry from fishing off a rolling boat in the turbulent waters of Cook Strait. He enjoyed standing on the banks or in the shallow waters, casting his lure out into the deeper flowing river. From the very first day he had success. This was fishing Ruby could enjoy as a spectator without getting wet or seasick, and it was even better when they could be joined by other family members and picnic on the river bank. "You'll have to come with us and have a go at the salmon," Jocelyn told her father as she watched him reel in another trout. Jocelyn and her husband Noel had a caravan and regularly headed over to Lake Paringa between Haast and Franz Josef on the West Coast.

With salmon fishing in mind and the thought of travelling around the South Island, Charlie bought a caravan and a larger Commodore car to tow it. From the beginning Charlie could land his bag of fish as quickly as the more experienced anglers could. "I might have lacked their finesse but I got them," he said. They stayed in the caravan at Lake Paringa with Jocelyn and Noel and as they caught their quota of salmon they drove back to Franz Josef where they hooked into the power and bottled their catch. When the preserving was done, they headed back to the lake for more fishing.

They caravanned throughout the South Island and in that time came to Bluff twice, for the launching of *Te Wai* in 1994 and *Te Awa* in 1997, our two fishing boats we had built at

Gough Brothers in Invercargill. The day following the launching of *Te Wai* we steamed her out to Stewart Island for a 'shakedown' cruise with our family. Because Ruby hadn't been well, she had decided not to come and Charlie told us he'd stay behind and look after her.

"Go, Daddy," Donna then told her father. "I'll mind Mummy."

Those five words nearly had Donna on her back as Charlie pushed her aside in his excitement to board the boat. The day was windy and Foveaux Strait quite rough – unlike the day following the launching of *Te Awa* when Foveaux Strait was flat calm. That day both Charlie and Ruby had been able to enjoy the day at Stewart Island.

"I'll play when I'm old," was Charlie's reply when asked to play bowls. He preferred to spend time in a garden that wasn't subjected to the southerly and northerly batterings he'd lived with during all his years at Okukari. The creative part of his mind made a leaf sucker from an old lawn mower, the devious part of his mind devised a way of watering his garden during water restrictions, much to Ruby's embarrassment, while the cunning part built a 'dog deterrent' using high voltage fencing for one dog in particular which made a habit of crossing the street to use Charlie's flower border as a toilet. Any dog that stepped on his garden received a zap. "They never came back either," my father-in-law laughed as he visualised a culprit leaping up in the air, its legs already going through the motions of running before it landed and took off, tail between its legs.

Charlie was determined a bad hip wasn't going to stop him mowing his lawns. While he was getting rid of rubbish at the city council dump, Charlie had noticed some lawnmower wheels. He built a small platform, attached the two wheels to it, and fitted it to his lawnmower. Elderly neighbours watched in surprise and no doubt admiration at the sight of Charlie standing on the platform behind his mower and being towed around the lawn as he cut the grass.

In Nelson, Ruby learned to share Charlie. In retirement he didn't have farm produce or fish to give away, but he gave freely of his time. In the Sounds, his experience over the years of fixing things with materials on hand had made Charlie very ingenious. His years on the farm, building cement foundations or walls, and running fences, made him in demand when his new neighbours laid their concrete drives or built fences and he was often called on to help out in some way, from replacing washers to fixing windows. He liked being able to help, not only with advice but in a practical way. And when he wasn't working on our fishing gear he'd often be out in his shed, deftly slinging nets or making up lines for his friends who were amateur fishers and had asked for help.

Charlie's oldest grandchild, Linda, had married Bill Wallace who was involved in the recovery of live wild deer when this was at its height during the 1980s. For a while Charlie was kept busy making up the nets that were fired from a gun out of a helicopter, and over the deer.

But it wasn't only friends and neighbours and family with whom Ruby shared Charlie. With more free time he was becoming more interested in his whakapapa. The catalyst was a block of land in Waikawa, Picton, which had been taken by the Government in 1912 for a military rifle range. At that time the land had only been divided informally by the owners, descendants of the original Maori owners, one of whom was Charlie's grandfather, John Heberley. Over the intervening years there had been a number of attempts to have it returned to the descendants of the owners, and although Charlie was aware of the matter he had never become involved. "Suddenly I realised if I didn't stand up and be counted I wouldn't be a part of it."

In April 1990 history was made in Picton when a special sitting of the Maori Land Court returned the land to its Maori owners.

As a kaumatua of his tribe, Charlie was appointed a trustee of the land, known as the Waikawa Rifle Range, to ensure that all proven descendants received a fair and just hearing.

Becoming more familiar with his past made Charlie want to preserve its future. He had a taonga (treasured possession) designed with his whakapapa recorded on it. He commissioned a local man, Norman Clark, to carve it out of the bone of a sperm whale, and on it the Heberley family history was depicted, back to 'Worser' and Te Wai.

The name given to the taonga was Te Maunga ote whanau – The Mountain, or head of the family. The centre teko teko – figure – holds a harpoon representing Charlie – the whaler. The two shoulders on each side, shaped like a mountain peak, depict the slopes of Mt Taranaki climbed together by Worser

Heberley and the naturalist Ernst Dieffenbach, who are credited as being the first Europeans to make the ascent. Two whales curving down each side portray Te Wai and Worser, and the flukes of the whales are the moko of Te Wai. Eight spirals are engraved on the two whales, each representing Worser's and Te Wai's children. The opposite side of the taonga is identical except that the teko teko holds a mere, which depicts Charlie as the head of his whanau.

Charlie wore his taonga with pride at any important function as well as any trust meeting or hui. He also used his treasured and elaborately carved walking stick, heavily inlaid with paua, which was originally owned by Worser Heberley. It was a story I had heard so often, but one I was compelled to listen to as Charlie's face lit up when he recounted it yet again.

"I was always told that Worser's grandson, Thomas Heberley, had carved it for his grandfather. Worser drowned in Picton Harbour in 1899, after becoming trapped in the mud on an incoming tide. When found, he still gripped the walking stick in his hand. Rather than prise open his fingers to free the stick, his family chose to cut the stick off. He was buried with part of his walking stick."

As Charlie spoke he held up the walking stick to point out the newer carved piece that had been joined to the original stick. The matching of the carving was superb but, as Charlie reminded me, it was probably repaired by the original carver.

At the coroner's inquest, a local resident, Mr H Norgrove, had said he'd found the body in the water between his residence and the wharf and recognised it as that of James Heberley. He then came in to Picton and informed the police. Constables Thompson and Lloyd located the body and took it to the morgue. They listed the possessions found on him, which included a pension cheque for 12 pounds 10 shillings, six sovereigns, one pound note and two pennies. The deceased was floating in an upright position with his walking stick in his hand.

That story had hardly been told when Charlie launched into another. Apparently the name of Worser had more than one derivation. It is commonly thought to have come about when he was Wellington's harbour pilot, and he described the weather as getting "worser and worser".

"There was a much earlier source of the name," Charlie said. "When he first arrived at the Maori settlement of Te

Awaiti in 1830, before he had a house he slept in a 'whata' – foodhouse. The chief's daughter, calling him one morning, called out, "Ai tangata, whata haere mai mou te kai" – "O man of the foodhouse, come to breakfast." The whalers twisted 'whata' into Worser, and to the day he died he was called Worser."

In the 1980s, commercial fishermen were becoming aware of dwindling fish stocks. The Government planned to introduce the ITQ (Individual Transferable Quota) system in 1986. Prior to this date, current fishing permit holders received their catch histories from the Ministry of Agriculture and Fisheries, for the three years ending 1982, 1983 and 1984.

Each permit holder was asked to choose any two of the three annual catch years. This was to be averaged to represent his or her annual catch – their catch history. If fishers believed the catch history supplied to them by MAF was incorrect, they had the right to object.

A Regional Objections Committee made up of three men was set up in each region throughout New Zealand. Charlie received a letter from Colin Moyle, the Minister of Fisheries at that time, asking him to be on the Regional Objections Committee based at Nelson. Treasury approved a daily fee of 100 dollars plus travelling expenses.

For the next 10 months Charlie travelled around the top of the South Island, hearing objections against their catch history from many fishermen.

"It was a job I enjoyed. I knew where they were coming from and I felt an affinity with them," Charlie told us later. "*But* it was hard keeping friendships out of the issue – and it generated a fair bit of bitterness as fishermen realised just how much less they were going to be allowed to catch."

It was a scheme, however, that proved itself over the years. With the quota scheme firmly in place the fishing industry throughout New Zealand, run by professional fishermen, is in a healthy state.

Early in 1989 Charlie phoned us. Ruby had been admitted to Nelson Hospital in a critical condition following a massive heart attack. That day Joe and I broke Charlie's long-standing record between Nelson and Okukari, a record that had stood since the day he had arrived in the bay when we were catching mackerel.

Ruby pulled through, but she was on medication for the rest of her life. From then on, Charlie's life as well as hers changed dramatically. For the first time in his married life, Charlie ran a house. It was strange to see him washing and ironing, dusting and vacuuming, cooking and then washing the dishes. For the next two years Ruby wouldn't come back to Okukari in case she had another heart attack. Later we were to find out why. Her doctor had told her if she hadn't been near medical care when she had her heart attack she would have died. She was scared of dying.

Ruby had been raised in a strict Catholic family but left the church when she married Charlie. It appeared Ruby's early conditioning, of what might happen if she died without confession, had finally caught up with her. It wasn't until Charlie spoke to the doctor, who was also a neighbour and someone Charlie had often helped, and suggested he brought his wife and family to stay with Joe and me at Okukari, that Ruby came back to the bay. That visit gave her confidence to return, and I had a feeling that not only had she come to terms with her weakened heart, but that she had also made peace with her God.

After her heart attack, Ruby's hands shook too much to be able to paint to the high standard she had set herself, so she began working on tapestries again – large tapestries. As Charlie wandered around craft shops with Ruby, he noticed a frame which held the canvas taut, and pointed it out to Ruby. At home he drew a picture of what it was like and set about making one for Ruby. Before long Ruby had her current canvas fitted to Charlie's frame. As well as being better than the one he'd seen, it was a nice piece of furniture with its turned legs and staining to match the surrounding furniture.

Family members soon had their own tapestry frames. He made them adjustable and each one was an improvement on the last. Craft people heard of these frames and before long Charlie had a market for them throughout Nelson, Marlborough and Christchurch. I never had a need for one as I haven't as yet attempted tapestry work – but the thought of being able to use the frame I was given after my father-in-law's death might be the encouragement I need to begin.

Between tapestries Ruby did cross-stitch and taught herself the art of Hardanger, an embroidery which comes from Norway and had its origins in Italy in the 17th century. But she had never forgotten the lacemakers in Brussels. She remembered the old women all dressed in black sitting on their stools in the street, and their colourful bobbins hanging off the most exquisite lace work that was pinned out on the velvet cushions on their laps. A dream was fulfilled when Ruby saw an advertisement to learn lacemaking. Over her last years she made edgings for handkerchiefs and small cloths as well as lace placemats.

In the 1990s Charlie still had an active link to whales through the Traditional Resources Committee. He was one of the five people nominated to take the jawbones out of stranded sperm whales for use on marae for carving. When Project Jonah was formed, to enable trained groups of people to try to save stranded whales, Charlie scoffed. Amid controversy he spoke out against it. He believed it was a waste of time.

"It's nature's way of controlling the stocks. I wanted those who push these whales and dolphins out to sea to mark them in their fin, and see if they find them anywhere else."

Charlie's personal opinion was that they would go out to sea and die somewhere else. He compared them with the lemmings, the small rodents common in Norway that mass migrate, often throwing themselves off a cliff or into a river where they drown, or the crabs in the islands that go ashore and climb into trees to die when the species becomes over-populated.

"I think these people are only prolonging the whales' agony. These whales are sick and it's nature's way of elimination. When the jaw bones were taken from five whales that were stranded at Pakawau in Golden Bay, the whales were full of worms. I've seen the same thing at the factory when we were whaling. Especially sperms. They get sick the same as humans or any other living thing.

"But the biggest cause of deaths in sperms is similar to our appendicitis. Sperms live on squids that have a beak-like mouth which is like a hard plastic. When a concentration of these beaks build up in a sperm's intestines, the whale builds up a secretion around the beaks in an effort to digest them. It forms into a fatty, firm, ashy or brown-coloured ball around the beaks. This is ambergris, and was used in the making of perfumes. When I was whaling it was worth nearly two pounds an ounce, but it finally kills the whales as it irritates their intestines."

Now Charlie was in full flight as he remembered other instances. With tongue in cheek he spoke of the 'experts' who said the whales were disorientated when they beached themselves. I caught the sarcasm in his voice.

"What a lot of rot! A whale has more knowledge of navigation built in his system than a human being has. Every season the whales left the Antarctic and travelled the same path year after year. They travelled hundreds of miles to their destination and they didn't have sonar or radar. Several times we've chased whales round and round in circles, through Cook Strait, in Tory Channel and out again. They escaped us. We've taken our hats off to them and wished them good luck. And what did they do? They went straight back on their original course – I'll *never* believe that whales can become disorientated!"

Charlie took me whaling in Cook Strait and whaling at Great Barrier, all in my mind and all from my lounge at Okukari. I learnt more of my husband's and children's whakapapa whenever Charlie reminisced. History and Maori mythology intertwined. Okukari was no longer land that millions of years earlier had risen from the sea when immense tectonic forces had heaved and twisted, and pushed up and lowered the rock in the area. Okukari instead had become a part of the land that had formed when the Maori gods came down from heaven in a canoe. They had travelled too far from their souce of power and become weak. The canoe capsized. Its keel rose and formed the Southern Alps and the intricately carved prow shattered and formed the Marlborough Sounds.

In 1994, a dream I had nurtured since 1963 when I first came to live at Okukari began to take shape. I'd always wanted to write my autobiography. I had my life story, but Charlie's whakapapa gave me the beginning, his stories the substance. I began to write, and *Weather Permitting* was published in 1996. It was followed 14 months later by its sequel, *Flood Tide*. This touched on Charlie's whaling days, his family history and the history of Okukari.

After my books were published I was increasingly invited to speak at functions. I was often asked if Charlie Heberley was still alive, and whether he would speak to their group. At first he blamed me for putting him into that situation, but he soon realised that he had a story that people wanted to hear – the story of a way of life that has gone forever.

Over the next few years he spoke to many groups around Nelson. At one time he told me he had spoken to 23 different groups including Rotary, Lions and Probus Clubs, as well as Fresh Focus and the Nelson Travel Club. It was after he had spoken at the Nelson Historical Society that the society asked him if they could organise a field trip to the remains of the whaling station, and then on to Okukari, the land of Charlie's ancestors.

In 1996, we were able to tell Charlie and Ruby that Joe was being named in the Queen's Birthday Honours. He was to receive the QSM for his work in searches and rescues.

"Watching Joe standing on the dais in Government House while his medal was being pinned on his lapel was the proudest moment of my life," Charlie told me as he wiped tears of emotion from his eyes. I had felt the same pride as my father-in-law, but for me it went back further than my Joe as I remembered Charlie's brother, Joe, who had drowned in his effort to rescue his crewman, and the times Charlie himself had helped those in trouble. I know that the saving of lives at sea is a tradition that will continue as long as a Heberley lives at Okukari.

Living on the edge of Cook Strait gave us the first sight of the *Lynx* and the *Sea Shuttle*, the two fast ferries that began running from Wellington to Picton during the summer of 1994-1995. The wash they created left a path of destruction because great walls of water smashed up the beaches into the bush, destroying everything in their path. Some property owners were left with rocks, paua, crabs and kelp lying over their front lawns. The wash destroyed wharves that had been standing for years. Land slipped into the sea. Moioio Island in Tory Channel had massive slips.

The first time Charlie saw the wash and the destruction from the fast ferries he was horrified.

"I'd travelled the world and seen buildings that had stood for centuries. They are treasured in their countries. Here we have pits on Moioio Island that the Maori occupied in our earliest history. You can see them – untouched. In 1839 it was a fortified pa with 150 occupants. No one would destroy those old buildings overseas and yet a part of our history was being swept into the sea, and no one seemed to care."

But people did care. Residents of the Sounds and people like Charlie who cherished our history met, and formed a working group – Guardians of the Sounds. They took on Tranz Rail in an effort to slow the ferries down and minimise the damage. In the ensuing David and Goliath battle, David won, and a more acceptable wake comes from the reduced speed of the fast ferry.

As the new millennium approached, Charlie reflected on the past years and thought about those ahead. He was a member of the New Zealand National Party and believed the country could be run properly only by the government he believed in. He had voted against MMP, and had no sympathy with those who'd voted it in and now regretted their action. His outspoken political comments often embarrassed family members. He disapproved strongly of the fact that the harder a person chose to work the more tax he had to pay. And when he thought jealousy over possessions was the cause of one particular comment made, he silenced the offender swiftly.

"Don't forget, you were born naked the same as them. You had the same rights and the same chances. But they took them – and you chose to sit on your backside."

Charlie's family and friends knew his beliefs and admired him for them. They knew he was quick to anger but just as quick to forgive. He was a kaumatua of the Ngati Awa people and they looked up to him. He was the loved Te Ariki, the chief of his whanau, and he expected to be treated with respect.

In December 1999 Charlie and Ruby celebrated their sixtieth wedding anniversary. More than 50 members of their family gathered in Nelson for a surprise luncheon. As we teetered on the brink of the new millennium, Charlie was enthusiastic about what the year 2000 might bring. He wasn't concerned about any of the catastrophic events affecting computers that were predicted to occur on New Year's Day. The media had been full of horror stories – computers mightn't be able to cope with the change-over from 1999 to 2000. Charlie and Ruby were prepared. He advised us to be, too. They had water, candles, matches, tinned food, torches, their spare gas bottle was full and he had enough cash drawn out in case the banks closed down – Charlie had made sure he was going to be there to usher in the year 2000.

As I sat watching his enjoyment of being surrounded by his family who were listening to his advice, I could see the work of the 'old net' was complete. But Charlie was now a part of the 'new net,' and although he maintained it was time for others to step forward and go fishing, he had every intention of being there with them.

Chapter Thirteen

THE MIGHTY TOTARA

Ka hinga te totara o te wao nui a Tane.
The totara has fallen in Tane's great forest.

CHARLIE WOKE during the early hours of the dawning of the new millennium. He rolled over in bed and was pleased to see it was 3.15am. In spite of all the media warnings that computers mightn't work when 1999 ticked over to 2000, the electricity hadn't gone off. He walked down the hall to the toilet and was relieved again to find the toilet could still be flushed and water still flowed from the taps. Nothing – after all the warnings – was needed from the survival kits after all, but Charlie and Ruby kept them in case of an earthquake.

At Okukari we had woken up to thick mist covering the hills. Our anticipated trip into Cook Strait to watch the first sunrise of the new millennium from our boat was cancelled. As we sat over breakfast, feeling quite deflated after this momentous New Year had begun and nothing had happened out of the ordinary, we rang Charlie and Ruby. They were having breakfast and hadn't made plans for their day.

"Come down," Joe suggested. "I'll come into Picton and pick you up in the boat."

Less than the time Joe took to steam the *Te Awa* into Picton, Charlie and Ruby with Sam, their Alexandrine parakeet, had arrived. Charlie disputed Joe's comment that his father must have been speeding, although Ruby nodded her head in agreement, and as he carried Sam's cage down the wharf Joe grinned as he heard the bird still singing out, "Hang on Sam. Hang on Sam."

Two days later Pauline, who was down from Auckland with her special friend Michael, suggested we take Charlie to the lookout. She wanted to see it through his eyes and she also wanted Michael to hear his stories and learn more of her grandfather. Joe said he'd stay on the boat and look after it while the rest of us went up the hill. Ruby's words of warning to Charlie to take care – "you're not as young as you think you are" – fell on deaf ears as Charlie pushed his feet into his gumboots and stamped them down as he hurried along the back path.

"Just watch him. He thinks he's 18, not 82," Ruby called to me as I left the house and ran to catch them up.

Joe brought the boat close in to the shore below the lookout. As Charlie scrambled down into the dinghy followed quickly by James's wife Lisa and her two children, Haydn and Danielle, Joe yelled that there were too many for the dinghy and he'd row some ashore then come back for the rest. I watched the first load step ashore and hoped they didn't start up the hill without us. But we all headed together towards the faint outline of the narrow track leading up the hill.

The bridge straddling the gap was no longer there but it was low tide and we were able to jump across the surging water as it sucked and gurgled below. "Gordon Cuddon hated the bridge that we built there," Charlie remembered. "He'd get down on his hands and knees and crawl across. I doubt he enjoyed his time on the lookout much either, because he knew he had to get back over it again."

Once we reached the track Charlie took off with six-year-old Danielle, his youngest great-grandchild. We'd thought of letting Charlie go first to set the pace. Instead we struggled to keep up with him as we pushed through the scrub growing over the narrow clay rut that had been formed by the gumboot-clad feet of the whalers as they'd raced down after a sighting, or trudged back after a hunt or the start of a day.

Charlie's excited voice reached us before we were at the top. "There's the longdrop, my old longdrop!" Thrilled to think there was still something standing, I parted the last of the flax bushes and stared at his longdrop. All I could see was a heap of rusting corrugated iron with flax, taupata and tawhini bushes growing out of it. But Charlie saw far beyond that, into the past, and all the jokes they'd played on the unwary.

Further along he pointed to the old concrete water tank. "This had a flat roof over it. We used to sit out here in the sun. There's the old charging plant. See the remains of it over there. That's the generator still sitting on its bed, but the diesel engine's gone."

Scratching around in the debris, we found the door and chimney off the little Dover stove, a chrome rail used to hang up their tea towels, and the brass handle knob from the door of their hut. Somehow these objects made Charlie's remembered stories all the more vivid.

On the way down, the man whom we'd been asked to take care of instead took care of Danielle, leading her down the steep parts and lifting her over others. As we pulled away from the stony beach I was aware that I had just witnessed a part of our history – and most probably never again, when I heard Charlie saying he was glad he'd gone back there one last time.

Charlie didn't like to leave his garden for too long over the summer so next day he and Ruby went home to Nelson.

Charlie's next speaking engagement was on 14 February 2000. This was with the Nelson Historical Society. The field trip to Okukari tentatively arranged to take place on 5 March was also going to be finalised then. As usual, Charlie spoke on his experiences as a whaler and later answered questions. He was frequently asked how he could kill such a beautiful animal, and he'd reply with a question himself. "What did you have for your dinner?"

If they answered beef or lamb or chicken, he'd laugh and ask what they thought was more beautiful – a lamb gambolling around the paddock, a fluffy chicken pecking grain off the ground, or a calf looking at you with its brown eyes and long lashes? "It was only a job and I have no feelings of guilt for having shot over 1,000 whales. I've always believed we can take any of our natural resources and farm, chop down or fish, as long as we do it responsibly. We've proved that with the Quota system. There'd be no crayfish left in the sea if that hadn't been introduced when it was.

"In any season we sighted a little over 500 whales. When we hunted them it was winter with only about one-third of daylight hours. Whales travel 24 hours a day so it would be fair to say possibly as many as 1,500 whales were passing through Cook Strait every day. And the weather prevented us from going out every day during a season. It's only in the last few years that whales have been turned into the 'sacred cow' category by some groups of people. We weren't the ones who were decimating the whales," Charlie finished angrily.

He knew the only reason whaling finished in New Zealand was that the whale stocks were so low. They were so low they were bordering on extinction and if whaling didn't cease altogether he believed they would become extinct. In later years Charlie believed the whale numbers were building up again, and fully supported the moratorium. He enjoyed telling the groups he spoke to, that, as well as being one of the last whalers, he was now a firm conservationist. He wanted his mokopuna to be able to go out in a boat and see a whale spout. "I still feel the same thrill whenever I see one spouting. But I only imagine the chaser under my feet."

The morning after Charlie had spoken to the Historical Society he and Ruby left Nelson for Hokitika. They were towing their caravan and intended to see both their daughters, first staying with Donna before heading down to Lake Paringa to join Jocelyn and Noel who were already down there. Charlie and Ruby were still at Donna's when Jocelyn and Noel called in on their return from the lake to tell them there had been too much rain, and the water was too muddy for fishing.

Ruby hadn't been feeling well. Antibiotics had failed to clear up a persistent cough she'd had for the last few weeks. Charlie felt he should go back to Nelson and Ruby could go back to her doctor before they headed south again.

Rather than tow their caravan all the way back to Nelson, they uncoupled it from their car and parked it alongside Donna's house. Charlie told Donna they'd be back when the weather improved and Ruby was feeling better. They left Hokitika at 8.15am and stopped in Murchison for a cup of tea.

What happened next is in Charlie's own words, to the police.

> I was driving my 1989 Nissan Laurel saloon with Ruby in the front passenger seat. The weather was fine and sunny, although there had been a lot of rain in the area over the previous two days. We

were driving towards Nelson, approaching Kawatiri Junction.

I generally drive very cautiously and would only travel at 100 kilometres an hour on the longer straights. When I come to the hills I usually slow to 80 kilometres or so.

As we approached Kawatiri Junction we were behind a logging truck so I was just going along behind him. I probably could have passed a couple of times but didn't try as we weren't in any hurry.

Just before Kawatiri Junction the truck pulled over to let us pass. I gave him a toot as I passed.

A couple of area road works were being carried out with road gangs and heavy machinery. They were signposted with roadworks signs and had 'Stop' and ' Go' men working.

From about Kawatiri there had been a flooding sign on the roadside and you could see the water running off the cliffs. Water was at the side of the road and, where it couldn't take it all, it was running across the road.

There was a reasonable amount of traffic on the road but mostly going south. I am familiar with the road and drive it many times a year. I continued to drive towards Nelson.

We came to a gang clearing the road, then approached a right-hand bend which had a river on the right and a length of safety barrier at the edge of the road. I didn't see any signs at the approach to the corner or on the corner. There were no advisory speed signs or corner signs. I didn't see any roadworks signs or any warning signs. You could see the corner clearly but couldn't see if there were any cars coming the other way.

I was doing no more than 70 kilometres an hour when I saw water running across the road, and a brown mark like a pot hole on our side of the road. As I got about a car length from the water I could see that there was a large hole under the water. The hole was about three-quarters of the way across the lane, of an oblong shape.

I tried to drive around it by turning to the right but my left wheel went into it. The wheel dropped into it with a big bump, and when it came out it lifted the car up in the air. That caused the car to turn further around to the right.

At that point I was side on to the road when the other car came around the corner and hit the front passenger door of my car. I would have hit the barrier simultaneously as the other car hit me. The force of impact pushed our car into the safety barrier.

With the curvature of the bend there, the other driver wouldn't have had a chance to avoid me. There's absolutely no blame on him at all.

After the impact I checked with Ruby that she was all right but she didn't respond. She had a cut on her face from the glass, and was sore on her left side and having a bit of trouble breathing. People stopped to help us and then the emergency services arrived.

Before they could get Ruby out, she passed away.

I tried to do mouth to mouth, but it was difficult with the car seat being up. I was flown to Nelson Hospital in the helicopter.

If it hadn't been for the hole in the road we wouldn't have gone out of control and hit the other car. There should have been warning signs or cones on the road to warn drivers of the hole in the road.

When the constable arrived I told him about the hole in the road and he went to have a look at it and came back to me and told me it was in a hell of a mess.

All Charlie's life he had taken care of everything and everyone, his wife and children, and in their later years, his parents. He'd cared for his friends and his workmates, he'd treasured his past and looked forward to his future. He'd climbed his mountain and had enjoyed living at the top. After Ruby's death he turned his back on the mountain and began his journey to the valley below.

On 21 February 2000, Ruby was laid to rest in Picton's cemetery.

Back in Nelson, Charlie surrounded himself with Ruby. Her lacework, and Hardanger embroidery pieces were laid out on the dining room table. The piece of Hardanger she was working on when she died, the needle still threaded, waiting to be picked up, spoke to him of how fine the thread of life really is. Every Thursday, around the time Ruby died, Charlie relived the accident. All the Thursdays were circled on his calendar which hung in the kitchen. The merest hint of the suggestion that he might come to Okukari for a while was turned aside. He just wanted to be near Ruby.

Two weeks after Ruby's death, Bill Reid of Nelson Helicopters offered to bring Charlie and Donna, who was staying with her father, down to Okukari in a helicopter. Their company was contracted to fly passengers on a cruise ship, which was berthed in Picton for the day, on scenic tours of the Marlborough Sounds. Charlie and Donna were at Okukari for three hours. It was long enough for him to come to terms with the fact that he no longer shared this part of his life with Ruby. But it wasn't long enough for us as we watched the shell of a man – whom we recognised only by his features – taking in the places and things that he and Ruby had seen and done together.

But it was enough to make Charlie want to come back. Donna returned to Hokitika, and four days after Charlie had stepped off the helicopter at Okukari he packed his bag, put in his saw and hammer, and came over to Picton. Joe picked him up in the boat and brought him home.

At that time we were building new gratings in the woolshed. Charlie worked alongside his son and grandsons. The first Thursday he was with us we were shocked. At the exact time when Ruby had died, Charlie broke down as he remembered the events of that day. In between the bad times we were able to share happy memories, but the sadness was always there. He wept for the happiness he no longer had.

Ruby remained close to Charlie. While he stayed with us he often came out in the morning, unable to talk. He'd sit at the kitchen table, tears running down his face. My tears burnt my eyes as I watched my strong father-in-law break down.

"She came to me again. Her hand brushed my arm," he sobbed.

I saw again what love is as I wrapped my arms around the man who'd given me strength after I'd gone through this same grief after the deaths of my parents. I felt so inadequate. Nothing helped that pain. But after he'd had breakfast and time to compose himself I'd get a glimpse of the man he'd always been as he would head out the back door and down to the woolshed to begin work once more.

Charlie was at Okukari for two weeks but then he needed to go back to his home in Nelson. He wanted to sort things out, but he promised us he would be down again when he could. He had postponed the Historical Society's trip as he felt he couldn't cope with that so soon after Ruby's death. He made himself fulfil his outstanding orders for his tapestry frames. On 27 March he bought himself a new car and we heard the familiar lilt in his voice as he told us the hard bargain he had driven with the car salesman. He drove over to Picton two or three times to spend time with Ruby in the newer part of the Picton cemetery and work on the Heberley family plot in the older part of the cemetery. This was where his parents and brother Joe were buried. Another time he drove to Picton and sailed to Wellington on the Cook Strait ferry to attend a Maori trust meeting in the capital. We hoped each of these things was another step up the ladder to the place where he could begin to live again, and not just exist.

In April of that year 2000, Joe and I visited our daughter Helen and her family in Westport for Easter. There was a hunting competition, and, while the men concentrated on pigs and deer, Helen and I concentrated on trout while the children were kept busy catching eels and possums.

There had been a lot of rain and the Buller was running fast. From the river bank I sat and watched Helen as she stood out in the river, cast her line and slowly wound it back. The rhythmic pattern of casting and winding against the sounds of the fast flowing river made me close my eyes.

"Got one!" Helen yelled. I leapt up and saw her line tauten and at the same time taken out to the middle of the river where the water jostled and tumbled as it raced towards Westport Harbour.

The line was straining and the rod curved. Surely it would break, I thought, as I watched the fish leap out the water in an effort to rid itself of the hook. I held my breath as I saw Helen was slowly gaining on the fish, and then let it out with a loud sigh as the nylon screamed off the reel again. The fish never gave in.

I had my cell phone in my bag, and when Helen admitted she didn't know if she could land it we decided to phone Charlie. I dialled his number and as I stumbled over the slimy rocks to give Helen the phone I explained the situation. From his home in Nelson he gave Helen, who was standing miles away in the Buller River, instructions on the best way to land a big fish. Both Helen and her grandfather tried their hardest but on that day it was one fish that was smarter than the fisherman on the phone and the fisherman in the river. There was a loud bang, and fish and line disappeared.

For most of his life Charlie had kept good health – apart from hydatids and a gall bladder operation. In later years he had age-related chronic ill health and had been admitted to hospital for adhesions and minor surgery, but very rarely was he actually incapacitated. He regarded these occasions as simply a nuisance, as they kept him from things he'd rather be doing. But each time he was admitted to hospital he ended up with pneumonia or an infection of some sort. He knew the feeling of the onslaught of these times, and recognised the symptoms. It made him angry when he told the medical profession he was developing pneumonia and needed medication, and they told him the laboratory had to diagnose it before it could be treated. And each time, I'm positive, that – if he hadn't been so ill when medication finally arrived – Charlie would have enjoyed telling them, "I told you so."

More worrying was an abdominal aortic aneurism which was carefully monitored. Surgery was considered and, at one stage, he was all prepared and ready to go into theatre when it was called off because of the high risk. Charlie learned to live with it.

The coroner's report on Ruby had found that, although she had died as a result of the accident, she did have a small malignant growth in one of her lungs. This was undoubtably the reason for her persistent cough over the last few months. We thought Charlie might have taken comfort from the fact that, because of the accident, Ruby didn't suffer. He refused. Instead, he asked us not to mention the report again. It was as if he wanted to take all the blame and suffering on himself.

Charlie became bitter. He was short-tempered and angry towards those he loved. He became withdrawn and still he refused to leave his house. Cleaning, washing and ironing, vacuuming and dusting – he carried out all these every day. Everything was kept as if Ruby were going to walk in at any moment.

Finally Charlie made up his mind. He was going to come and stay at Okukari for a week or two. The day before he was due to come over to Picton, he went into Nelson to pick up some fishing gear Joe had ordered. In the shop he collapsed. The alarmed owner took him up to the accident and emergency clinic at Nelson Hospital. When he arrived back at the shop he phoned Joe and told him what had happened.

It was another fast trip to Nelson for Joe and me. By the time we arrived in Nelson, Charlie had been diagnosed as having a thoracic aortic aneurism – the part of the aorta where it arched behind his heart. He was in the intensive care unit and had been asked if his affairs were in order. As we sat with him, a nurse came in with papers and asked Charlie if he wanted to be resuscitated if he went into cardiac arrest. Our delight was evident when the man who had sunk so low in the past weeks answered smartly. "Too damned right I do. I have my family to live for."

It appeared that a miracle happened. The aorta sealed. Forty hours later, Charlie was transferred to the medical ward. Six days later, after he had repeatedly told the staff he was positive he was developing pneumonia, sputum samples were taken. The next day, when we came into the ward, he was being given antibiotics through an intravenous drip. With the antibiotics, Charlie improved rapidly. He asked me to bring his whaling photos to the hospital and we'd often arrive in the ward to the sound of his vivid descriptions of whales being caught, or loud laughter as he regaled the other three men in his room with the antics they got up to on the lookout hill. He wrote a letter to the *Nelson Mail,* headed 'Maori and Whaling', raising the issue of traditional 'customary' rights of the tribes to use parts of dead beached whales, such as bone, for carving. It was printed in the paper on 27 June.

Two days before Charlie was due to be discharged, Joe and I returned to Okukari because we knew Jocelyn and Noel would bring him home, and Donna was going to come and stay in the house with her father.

He was home one week – a week Donna speaks of now as being the most special in her life. "I feel I made him as happy as he would allow himself to be, and I was glad I was in the position to do so," she told us later.

During that week one of his fellow whalers, Tom Gullery, died, and on the day of his funeral Charlie wasn't well enough to travel to Picton. It lowered him further to have to admit he wasn't well enough to say goodbye to his old mate.

The next morning our phone rang at 7am. It was Donna. She told Joe she had just put Charlie in the ambulance. She suggested to Joe he shouldn't risk his neck in getting over in a hurry, as Charlie wasn't expected to live long. His aorta had split again. Less than three hours later, we were at Nelson Hospital. Then Charlie was brought from the intensive care unit into the medical ward. Donna told us this time it wasn't because he was improving – this time it was to die.

Charlie hovered between life and death for the next 30 hours. His children stayed with him constantly. Those grand-children and great-grandchildren who lived close came to say their goodbyes. At one stage I came into his room and watched four of his great-grandchildren with the man they called Hebs. The six-and eight-year-old children seemed to accept the fact that he was dying more easily than we adults could. They re-galed him with their latest fishing stories, and told him it was fun being in Nelson and going to McDonald's for lunch. When Charlie said he'd love to join them I remembered a quote I'd read recently: *A grandfather is a man grandmother. He goes for walks with boys and they talk about fishing and stuff like that.* Since Ruby had died, Charlie had been these children's man-grandmother.

For us the hours flashed by as we realised how short our time would be with the man who had moulded our lives. For him, as we watched the pain on his face as he waited for the increasing doses of pethidine to take effect, the hours dragged. But when he was awake there was more laughter around his bed than we'd heard since Ruby had died. He discussed fishing, and types of fishing gear.

As the afternoon passed, Charlie drifted in and out of con-sciousness. When James walked in, wearing a Bledisloe Cup rugby shirt with the bright green, gold, black and white colours of the Wallabies and All Blacks, Charlie opened his eyes and discussed the rugby match he had watched on television the previous weekend.

Tom Norton, who'd whaled with Charlie and gone up to the Barrier with him, came over from Picton to say goodbye.

At this time Charlie was drifting in and out of consciousness and hardly spoke. When Tom stood up to leave, Joe bent over his father and told him he was just going to the carpark to see Tom off. Charlie must have remembered Joe was giving up smoking at that time. "You're just going outside to have a bloody smoke – aren't you, son!"

Those words remain in Joe's memory. Today he says he's sure that if he ever starts smoking again he'll feel a tap on his shoulder.

Charlie died at 6.30pm on 30 June 2000. His last two hours were the worst as he struggled for breath. In the sudden silence in the room where Charlie had fought and lost his last battle, Joe's words reverberated around the room. "Thank Christ for that."

The mighty totara had fallen. Even the birds stopped singing in Tane's great forest.

The funeral was arranged. Joe and I came home with all our family to Okukari until we had to return to Picton for Charlie's service. With us were Pauline and Michael who had flown from Auckland, Helen and Peter with three of Charlie's great-grandchildren, Amanda, Carl and Glen, who had driven up from Westport, and Charlie's niece, Lois, and her son Johnny who had driven from Tauranga.

On the way home the constant chatter in the cabin drove me outside. We had just rounded Dieffenbach and turned into Tory Channel. As we steamed past bays that all held stories of Charlie, I tried to focus my thoughts on other things, but no matter where I started my thoughts came back to the source of my pain.

Charlie had lived in the Sounds for 61 years. I multiplied that by 52 and tried to work out how many times he might have passed Dieffenbach in those 3,172 weeks. Not many times in his early childhood, but when he was going to school in Wellington with three terms, Easter and the long weekends it would have to be at least 10 times a year. As a young man going in to play sport, shearing around Blenheim or just going out, probably at least twice a month. After he married I knew there weren't too many trips to Picton as there wasn't any spare money, but, as times improved, I allowed for one trip a fortnight.

There were the 46 weeks Charlie was in Australia after he'd had hydatids. I counted up the months he'd whaled in the 17 seasons he'd worked for Peranos, and the number of months in the four years he'd been at Great Barrier. I converted these to weeks. He certainly didn't pass Dieffenbach in the seven months they were overseas. I subtracted these tallies from my grand total. The ache remained.

A sudden 'whoosh' right beside me made me forget my inane calculations. One dolphin had separated from the pod that was frolicking closer to shore. It lifted clear of the sea's surface in a gesture of complete freedom. Tears washed my face and they became part of my pain. I felt the wonder of creation and the finality of death. What right did God have to cause so much anguish in such a beautiful universe?

The day of Charlie's funeral was cold, a wet southerly. Just before the coffin was carried in I played *Sailing* on the organ, as a tribute to the man of the sea whom I'd met as the manager of a whaling station, who later became my father-in-law, but was my friend and father at the end.

Then, in a noble tribute, Rita Powick of Picton led in the coffin with a karanga, which was followed by the extended family.

The spirit of one of the last of the whalers was captured in his eulogies. First there was the little boy who poked dough between his brothers' toes and let his pet penguins into the schoolroom to peck it out. We saw once again the young man and fellow whaler, Reg Jackson, who now sat in the church, catching a pig while out mustering and killing it with nails, and glass from a Vicks bottle. Then we were transported to the Barrier. Tom Norton recounted the time they were racing out to the chasers in the dinghy after a whale sighting. Twenty feet off the beach, Alf Nimmo stepped on the gun'wale and over went the dinghy. Everyone tipped out.

"I had a change of clothes on the chaser. In fact all of us had a change – but Charlie didn't. He was roaring his head off. We got out to the chaser and I guess he remembered wearing women's clothes once before after he'd fallen in Cook Strait, because the next thing we saw him ratting around in the rag-bag. But this wasn't the dress belonging to someone he knew. These rags had come out from Auckland. He found a dress and put it on. I still see him, the wind streaming through his hair, his flowery dress flapping against his legs as he stood on the bow, hanging on to the gunpost, while the boat sped through the waves. He shot the whale – which cheered him up no end."

At the cemetery he was laid to rest with Ruby. Joe, now kaumatua, and Haydn, the youngest male Heberley, walked up to the coffin. Haydn placed on it a piece of turf from Okukari, and Joe placed on it a sperm whale tooth.

George Martin of Picton joined with Rita in one last karanga, before we left the grave.

> Haere atu ra e te papa, e te matua
> E te koroua, e te rangatira
> Haere atu ki to hoa rangatira
> Ki o tupuna
> Kua wehe atu ki te po

> Farewell father, parent,
> Respected elder, chief,
> Go to your chiefly friend – your wife –
> To your ancestors
> Who have gone before you – lost to the night.

Epilogue

SIX WEEKS after Charlie died, the inquest on Ruby's death was held in Murchison, on 10 August 2000.

Transit New Zealand contractor Glen Linton said he had been aware for about three months of the unstable nature of the section of road south of the Lamb Valley intersection with SHW6. He was aware of the pothole and over that period it had been filled with OGEM (cold mix) on about three occasions before the accident.

His company did not permanently repair the hole because there was a holding strategy in place on that stretch of road, and Transit New Zealand would not approve permanent repairs prior to the full rehabilitation. They could, however, carry out any emergency work with temporary repairs.

The history of this pothole prior to the accident was that, after the heavy rain which had fallen 24 hours previously, it had been seen by one of Transit New Zealand's crew. This was on the night before the accident, when he was returning from other road works. He immediately put out 'workman' signs at each end of the highway to warn motorists.

The worker noted that the hole was 600 x 600mm and 30mm deep, and as he didn't have a shovel with him he pushed the dislodged gravel back into the hole with his boot.

The following morning, the day of the accident, an inspection showed the hole was now one metre x 700mm and 60-70mm deep. The contractors discussed the pothole and agreed that they would wait for the water level to go down, but monitor the hole every couple of hours. Then they would proceed to install subsoil drainage and a stabilising patch.

At no time were steps taken to reduce traffic speed at the site because that section of road had a permanent 55 kilometres per hour restriction in place. We were informed that the contract that Works Infrastructure had with Transit New Zealand did not allow them to lower speeds below 50 kilometres, except in emergencies.

A short time before Charlie and Ruby arrived at the scene, a passing motorist had tried to call the police to warn them of the hole after her car wheel had dropped in it. She believed an older person might not have had the strength to correct the steering. Her cell phone was in a 'no service' area. The pothole remained unreported.

The coroner found that Ruby's death was caused by a poorly-repaired pothole after the car which Charlie was driving had hit it causing the car's tie-rod on the front steering to sheer off. It then spun out of control into an oncoming vehicle. Tests performed by the Department of Scientific and Industrial Research proved the tie-rod broke from the impact of the car hitting the pothole. He said no one was directly to blame for the accident but a poorly repaired pothole and inadequate signposting contributed to it.

The coroner pointed out that the accident highlighted deficiencies in Transit New Zealand's roading regulations. They needed to be sorted out, to give contractors greater autonomy at hazard sites.

Although our family did not blame anyone for Ruby's death, we believed she would not have died if the road had been in a better condition.

The Nelson Historical Society's first field trip to the whaling station and Okukari took place in the following November, with a second trip in February the next year, 2001. Nearly 200 members made the trip in the two days combined. They retraced Charlie's steps as his son Joe retold the stories and history he had learnt from his father. At the whaling station I listened to Charlie's words through Joe as he carried on preserving the culture, the history and the traditions of which Charlie had been so proud. While such rich stories of whaling, history and Maori mythology are being told, and so many people still want to hear them, Charles Thomas Heberley, one of the last of the whalers, rests in peace.

On the bank above the beach at Okukari, a memorial seat in stone has been built. Its plaque says:

In memory of
Charles Thomas Heberley
11.12.1918 – 30.6.2000
and
Ruby Elna Heberley
11.12.1920 – 17.2.2000
They lived at Okukari 1945 – 1979
They gave us all their love
Donna Jocelyn Joe and families

Appendix

HUMAN BEINGS have used whales ever since a prehistoric race found a whale stranded and discovered it was a wonderful source of meat, with the bone useful for making weapons and implements.

Before the advent of shore-based stations, whaling operations were carried out at sea. Once a whale was spotted and its course determined, the rowing boats were lowered and the chase was on. The boats were clinker-built, and sharp at both ends. They varied in size from 20 to 30 feet long, were higher in the bow and stern than amidships, and capable of great speed. The mast carried a large sail. On the boat was a selection of lances and harpoons, the harpoon line which was stowed in two tubes, a small anchor, a water cask, some biscuits and a bottle of the infamous arrack rum the whalers brewed.

The headsman stood in the stern, steering with a large oar which was as long as the boat. An uneven number of rowers, usually five or seven, ensured an even number when the steersman, who rowed from the bow, stood up to throw the harpoon.

Back at the ship, the whale was stripped of its blubber which the men then cut into thin pieces and put in the trypot – the smaller the pieces and faster the boiling, the higher the quality of oil. The trypots were set on the deck which had been especially strengthened to support the weight of the brick furnaces. These were fired with pieces of blubber from which the oil had been extracted. The pieces were called scrag. The oil was baled into copper tanks and then, while it was still warm, decanted into casks.

As well as the expected dangers of the sea, whaling brought its own special hazards. There was the risk of a ship being destroyed by fire, rowing boats being smashed by infuriated whales, or lost when caught in darkness or fog. The occurrence of scurvy, the sickness so common among the early sailors because of lack of vitamin C contained in fresh vegetables and fruit, also took its toll.

The earliest whalers came to New Zealand's shores as fleeting visitors while they hunted the cachalot or sperm whale in the open sea. By the early 1800s, these whaling ships catching large numbers of sperm whales had discovered the sheltered harbour of the Bay of Islands. Soon they were using the area as a base to obtain fresh supplies. Pigs and potatoes were traded, prostitution grew steadily, and many Maori men took the places of whalers who had deserted or died due to accidents.

The burning of the *Boyd* in 1809, with the massacre of her crew and most of the passengers, was due to the ill treatment of a young Maori chief who was working as a member of the crew. This caused boats to stay away from the Bay of Islands for several years.

When the Reverend Samuel Marsden arrived in the Bay of Islands in 1814, his mission helped end the bitterness and suspicion that the *Boyd* incident had begun. By 1827 it was not uncommon to see up to 14 whaling ships anchored in the Bay of Islands during the months of December and January, but, as shore-based whaling was established around New Zealand's coast, the sperm whalers moved away.

Shore whaling was based on the regular migrations of the right whales from the beginning of May. It ended in late September as they came into sheltered waters to calve. These stocks were soon depleted as the whalers killed the calves first, knowing that the cows would stay close to their dead babies. This made the whales an easy target.

Humpback whaling followed. These whalers were important to the nation as many came as residents, unlike the sperm whalers.

The first shore-based whaling station in New Zealand is believed to have been at Te Awaiti in Tory Channel, when Captain John Guard came out to New Zealand in the *Waterloo* in 1827. It was here that Worser Heberley arrived, to begin whaling with John Guard on 1 April 1830.

A station owned by Bunn and Company and run by Peter Williams was also operating in Preservation Inlet by 1830.

During the 1830s and 1840s there was a rapid growth in the number of shore stations in New Zealand, from Preservation Inlet up the East Coast of the South Island to Cape Runaway in the North Island. Cook Strait was the most important centre, with stations at Port Underwood and Tory Channel, while across Cook Strait there were stations on Kapiti Island, Mana Island and the adjacent mainland.

The whalers built their own houses. Most were built of wattled supplejack filled with yellow clay, with slit windows and a thatched roof. The houses were of two or more rooms, and the dirt floors were beaten hard. A huge chimney stood at one end, and usually bunks with curtains ran the full length of the room. A large table and two long benches stood in the middle of the room while up in the rafters the whalers kept spare coils of rope, oars, lances, spades to cut off the blubber, and harpoons.

On the beach were the trypots, with furnaces beneath fed by pieces of blubber from which the oil had been extracted. The procedure for extracting the oil was the same as on board the ships. Both ground and beach were saturated with oil, and the smell of carcasses and lumps of rotting whale meat permeated the bay.

Most of the smaller whaling stations had closed down by the 1860s.

In 1890 a shore station was established by the Cook family in Northland's Whangamumu Harbour. They caught their whales by running a steel wire net between Cape Brett and a large rock. The net was made in sections, tied together with rope. When a humpback whale struck the net, the rope broke and the whale became entangled in the wire net. The whalers then moved in and killed their quarry.

In 1911 the Cooks bought a steam whale-chaser and increased their usual annual catch from 11 to 16 whales to more than 50 whales annually. This station closed in 1933.

Te Awaiti in Tory Channel remained operational until 1916. At the turn of the century, Worser Heberley's oldest son, John, who for most of his life had whaled alongside the Jacksons, Nortons and Thoms, out of Te Awaiti, had left to set up his own factory at the head of Yellaton in Tory Channel. There were many small stations around the New Zealand coast and John wanted to own his factory. The outdated equipment, as well as the problem of five miles in rowing boats to the entrance of Cook Strait, made John Heberley give up the idea of his own factory.

John Heberley died in 1909, and in 1911 Joe Perano Senior, the founder of the Perano whaling, bought the remains of John Heberley's station. After one season he learnt why John Heberley had given up whaling out of Yellaton. He closed that station and began whaling from Tipi Bay, closer to the channel entrance, where they began motorised whaling from the small chasers. Whaling was carried out from here until 1924 when the Peranos began operating out of Fishing Bay on the opposite side of the channel.

The last Maori shore-based station in the Bay of Plenty closed down in 1926. After the Whangamumu station closed in 1933, the Perano whaling station was the only one remaining in New Zealand until 1955. Then a whaling station was opened at Whangaparapara on Great Barrier Island. Lack of skills caused the first company's collapse, and dwindling whale stocks over the last three years saw whaling at Great Barrier Island cease in 1962.

The lack of whales over the last years saw Peranos' last whale caught on 21 December 1964. Shore-based whaling, which had been a part of New Zealand history for 137 years, had come to an end.

Humpbacks were taken almost to extinction by intensive whaling during the 20th century. In 1946 the International Whaling Commission (IWC) was set up to provide for the proper conservation of whale stocks and allow the controlled growth of the whaling industry. Membership of the IWC is open to any country that adheres to the 1946 Convention. The whales were given total protection from commercial whaling by the IWC in 1966, and presently have an International Union for Conservation of Nature status of Vulnerable. In spite of this protection, subsistence hunting of humpbacks continued in Tonga until 1979 when whaling was prohibited by Royal Decree. In Antarctica, illegal Russian whaling of an estimated 47,000 humpbacks continued until the 1980s.

The IWC brought in a moratorium on commercial whaling on all whale stocks from 1985-86. The moratorium does not affect aboriginal subsistence whaling which is permitted by Denmark for fin and minke whales, the Russian Federation for grey whales, St Vincent and The Grenadines for humpback, and the USA for bowhead and occasionally grey whales. Under the IWC's whaling regulations, native communities are allowed to catch their quota for subsistence and cultural purposes. It prohibits the sale of any edible whale products from aboriginal subsistence hunts.

In 1993, after a five-year break, Norway resumed ordinary commercial whaling for minke whales. Their quota has gradually been increased and in 2000 their quota was set at 655 minke whales. On board each vessel is a government-appointed veterinary-trained officer, and an international observer.

Japan is an island. Outside its cities the land consists of mountains and forests. The Japanese have always relied on ocean resources for food. This includes whales.

In western countries whales have traditionally been killed for their oil but for the Japanese the whale is a food source. It is used in banquets on special occasions. The Japanese believe the ban on commercial whaling is stripping Japan of an important part of its culture and tradition. They continue to whale under the guise of a whale research programme.

In a media release on 3 August 2000 by Japan's Fisheries Agency, Masayuki Komatsu, Counsellor for Fisheries Policy of the Fisheries Agency, said, "It is unfortunate that the politicians in the United States, the United Kingdom and New Zealand have criticised Japan's whale research programme." He believed they were ignoring science and international law as a result of pressure from certain radical environmental organisations. The convention requires that by-products be processed. Mr Komatsu denied that whale meat ending up on the market is commercial whaling in disguise, as anti-whaling groups suggest. Japan conducted a research programme in the western North Pacific from 1994 to 1999 under Special Permit as provided for by the IWC to study the population and feeding of the minke whales.

In the years 2000 and 2001 a maximum of 100 minke whales, 50 Bryde's whales and 10 sperm whales, were to be sampled in each of these years. Still in dispute is Japan's quota of 500 minke whales, a quota which they still maintain is for scientific purposes only.

Five Japanese whalers left the port of Shimonoseki during November 2001, expecting to catch about 440 minke whales during the summer. Some gourmets consider the meat from minke whales to be the tastiest, and New Zealand scientists have found that whale meat is being sold in Japanese supermarkets and restaurants. This is commercial whaling, not scientific research.

In New Zealand a report on a survey carried out by the Science and Research Unit of the Department of Conservation in Wellington, and published in 2000, says that the number of sightings of humpback whales during 1990-2000 suggests a slow increase, particularly in the previous four years. The report shows little evidence of a change in the migration patterns along the New Zealand coast.

The large numbers of humpbacks which were killed in commercial whaling around New Zealand, particularly around Cook Strait and along the north-east coast of the North Island, show that New Zealand has an important role in the whales' migratory patterns.

For its information, New Zealand's Department of Conservation relies on reports from relevant DOC field centres and Ministry of Fisheries scientific observers. Fishermen, whale-watching tour operators, whale researchers, media reports as well as the public, all play an important role by reporting whale sightings. Whale stranding numbers from records kept at Te Papa, the Museum of New Zealand, are also documented. DOC has distributed sighting forms to information centres, ferry operators and commercial pilots so future sightings can be recorded.

Japan and other nations still apply increasing pressure to resume commercial whaling. Accurate information is essential to prove that whale stocks are too low for such a move to be contemplated.

New Zealand stands firm among the ranks of those intent on keeping the present moratorium on commercial whaling, and maintaining the Southern Ocean Whale Sanctuary.

Bibliography

Maori Proverbs, Reed Books 1992.

The Perano Whalers, Don Grady. Reed 1982.

Kei Puta te Wairau, W J Elvy. Whitcombe and Tombs 1957.

Old Marlborough, T Lindsay Buick. Hart and Keeling 1900.

Moriori, Michael King. Appendices, 3. Moriori Migration Traditions. Viking 1989

Letters written by Hadfield to the Church Missionary Society 1840-1843.

Rangiatea, E Ramsden. Reed 1951.

Linkwater, A History, Geoffrey Wilson. Marlborough Express Printing Works 1962.

After Many Days, John Park Salisbury. Harrison and Sons 1907.

Wise's New Zealand Directory 1880-81.

Keenan History. James K Keenan – Picton Museum.

Proceedings of the First International Conference on the Southern Ocean Whale Sanctuary – October 1994. M F Donoghue 1994.

Validity of Whaling Data. A V Yablokov 1994.

Humpback Whales Around New Zealand, Conservation Advisory Science Notes: 287. Department of Conservation Head Office Wellington 2000.

Sealers and Whalers in New Zealand Waters, Don Grady. Reed Methuen 1986.

The Whaling Trade In Old New Zealand, L S Rickard. Minerva 1965.

New Zealand's Heritage, the Making of a Nation. Paul Hamlyn 1971.